good news of the day

Dedication

DEDICATED to the amazing God who reveals Himself in so
many ordinary, everyday ways. Thanks for keeping me
on my toes.

good news of the DAY

by Johann Snyder

BRIDGE
LOGOS

Alachua, Florida 32615

Bridge-Logos

Alachua, Florida 32615 USA

Good News Of The Day

Johann Snyder

Printed in the United States of America.

Library of Congress Catalog Card Number: 201393374
International Standard Book Number 978-1-61036-106-4

Unless otherwise noted, all Scripture is from the New International Version of the Bible.

CH 04-26-13

Contents

January

The lazy man will not plow
because of winter;
He will beg during harvest
and have nothing.

Proverbs 20:3-5

January 1
To Resolve or Not to Resolve

"Forget the former things; do not dwell on the past.
See, I am doing a new thing!"
(Isaiah 43:18-19).

AH, NEW YEAR'S RESOLUTIONS. Do you make them every year? Do you keep them? People are funny about New Year's Resolutions. There are some who say as Christians we should be resolving something new every day, not just once a year, so they don't make resolutions. There are others who say God is God of fresh starts, so why not start the year with a fresh set of resolutions? Then there are those who feel they're perfect and the rest of the world needs to change, so their resolution is to point that fact out to everyone else. Here's my take on the whole New Year's Resolution thing: I know I'm not perfect, I know God wants to change me, so every New Year I set some goals for the year and then I renew my commitment to keep those goals every day. Of course, my goals aren't always the same as God's, so I try to make sure I'm sensitive to His direction for my new year instead of just doing what I want. One thing I know for sure: God doesn't want us to dwell on the mistakes of the past. Whatever we screwed up this past year, God has forgiven and wiped clean to give us a new start. The great thing about God is that He's always doing something new. He's doing something new in my work, He's doing something new in my family, He's

2

doing something new in my day-to-day life, and He wants to do something new in your life. As we get ready for another New Year, I think that's really good news.

January 2
Broken Xboxes and a Healing God

"Come to me, all you who are wearied and burdened, and I will give you rest"
(Matthew 11:28).

FOR A TIME, it was a common occurrence . . . the red ring of death. Three little lights on your Xbox 360 that announced it was now a brick. I remember those days. I remember that happening to me . . . a few times. That might not seem to have anything to do with deep, insightful, or spiritual subjects, but stay with me. You see, when my 360 broke I had to send it back to the manufacturer in order to get it fixed. They sent me another one . . . and that one broke too. That's pretty much how my life feels at times—lots of inconvenience, a little bit of pain, and plenty of brokenness. However, that usually means I need to spend time going back to my manufacturer to get fixed, and the good news is, once He fixes something, it stays fixed (unless I decide to break it again, which I usually try to avoid doing). It's easy to look back on a year and praise God when everything's gone well, but it's more of a challenge to do that when just about everything was broken. Yet, I have to say even when it seemed everything went wrong, those are the most blessed years I've experienced. That's when God has shown just how faithful and comforting He is, when life is full of trials. So that broken Xbox 360 represented my life in a small, unreliable, technical microcosm, and the strange thing is I can honestly say it was good news.

January 3
Combating "Next Year Syndrome"

"In the time of my favor I heard you, and in the day of salvation I helped you. I tell you, now is the time of God's favor, and now is the day of salvation"
(2 Corinthians 6:2).

LET'S TALK ABOUT NEW YEAR'S RESOLUTIONS again for a moment. The problem with New Year's Resolutions is they can lead to "next year syndrome." This is what happens when we mess up or break our resolutions and then simply shrug our shoulders and decide to wait until next year to start anew. "Next year syndrome" can lead to a dangerous increase in apathy, especially in our Christian life. While it's nice to have a fresh new start—a clean slate, as it were, each and every New Year—the good news is through the grace of Jesus Christ we can enjoy a fresh new start and a clean slate every day, even every hour if necessary. (Hopefully it won't come to that.) We don't have to wait for a New Year to start over; the grace and forgiveness of Jesus Christ can do that for us right now. So if you are going to make a resolution for this New Year, make it to avoid "next year syndrome" by embracing the "... *now is the day of salvation*" syndrome made available through Christ. When you do, you'll find this New Year will be full of good news.

January 4
No PhD Required

"Whenever you are arrested and brought to trial, do not worry beforehand about what to say. Just say whatever is given you at the time, for it is not you speaking, but the Holy Spirit"
(Mark 13:11).

NOT LONG AGO, the nation's top scientists declared the evidence for evolution was overwhelming and compelling. It was just another indicator that the assault on what we believe as Christians was going to continue to be direct and intense. While it's certainly intimidating to have scientists and intellectuals attack our beliefs as Christians, it really shouldn't surprise us when it happens. In fact, Jesus warned us this would happen, and He even warned us of far worse things to come. I know this sounds pretty discouraging, but Jesus did give us some good news as well. Although we may not have PhDs and doctorates on our resumes to match up with the experts who are denouncing Christianity, we do have something far more valuable: the Holy Spirit. Don't worry if you don't know quantum mechanics or molecular biology, you know the truth of God's Word which can stand against even the most intellectual of intellectuals. So let's not be afraid of speaking out when we hear things like the "overwhelming evidence" for evolution. Those claims don't change the truth of God's Word, and if we're willing to speak out, the Holy Spirit will help us speak boldly, intelligently, and lovingly.

January 5

Making Some Noise During Playoffs and Worship

After this I looked and there before me was a great multitude that no one could count, from every nation, tribe, people and language, standing before the throne and in front of the Lamb. They were holding palm branches in their hands. And they cried out in a loud voice: "Salvation belongs to our God, who sits on the throne, and to the Lamb."
(Revelation 7:9-10)

AH, THE NFL PLAYOFFS. It's one of my favorite seasons of the year. The air is electric with excitement as fans all over the nation watch and cheer their teams on to the Super Bowl, or jeer to make sure the enemy team doesn't get there. One Sunday at church the sermon was about worship and as the pastor preached, I couldn't help thinking about the NFL Playoffs. No, I was not zoning out and not paying attention, which I admit I do from time to time . . . and I'm not proud of it. But at that moment I was, in fact, thinking of the similarities between the ways fans watch the playoffs and the way we as Christians should worship. Football fans are always excited to see their teams play, but that excitement increases ten-fold during the playoffs because there's so much more at stake. Here's my question: How do you feel about God? Are you excited about Him? Does He really mean anything to you? If so, how do you express it? My point is if we can get excited and emotional during the NFL Playoffs for a team we've never even met, we certainly can get excited and emotional for a personal God we know and who loves us. You see the good news is worship doesn't have to be quiet and reserved. If anything, worship should sound like the NFL Playoffs—noisy!

January 6
Missing Snowboarders and Searching for the Lost

What do you think? If a man owns a hundred sheep, and one of them wanders away, will he not leave the ninety-nine on the hills and go to look for the one that wandered off?
And if he finds it, I tell you the truth, he is happier about that one sheep than about the ninety-nine that did not wander off. In the same way your Father in heaven is not willing that any of these little ones should be lost.
(Matthew 18:12-14)

A FEW YEARS BACK, two snowboarders from Albuquerque, New Mexico, the city where I live, went missing in Wolf Creek, Colorado. As the search for them dragged on and on, it reminded me of something very important: God is constantly searching for missing people and He needs our help to find them. A lot of people were praying the snowboarders would be found, just as we need to continually pray for the missing people who are all around us. They're not missing in the sense that we don't know where they are; they're missing in the sense that they're separated from God. When someone goes missing in the mountains, we hear all about it because it's such a tragedy.

People volunteer their time and give up their comfort to assist in search and rescue efforts to bring those people home. It's a vivid illustration of what those of us who know Christ should be doing every day—sacrificing time and comfort in search and rescue operations to bring home God's missing children. It's always good news when the missing are found, whether it's in the mountains of Wolf Creek, Colorado, or in the neighborhoods where we live out our daily routine.

January 7
News, Politics, and Hanging Out With Loved Ones

"Call to me and I will answer you and tell you great and unsearchable things you do not know"
(Jeremiah 33:3).

ONE TIME, when my daughter was about five, we spent part of an evening curled up on the couch under a cozy blanket watching the news about the 2008 New Hampshire caucuses. Now keep in mind she probably wasn't all that interested in politics (and still isn't), but that's what she said she wanted to do. In a strange way, that touched me. To think my daughter wanted to be with me so much she was willing to watch the news with me, even political news, was special. It got me thinking about the people I like to spend time with—my wife, my family, my friends—and how I'll make time and sacrifice my wants just to be with them. It also got me thinking about whether or not I included God on that list of people I desire to be with. When you love someone, you're willing to do just about anything to be with that person. My daughter reminded me of that one cold night while watching the news, and sadly it also reminded me that more often than not I don't feel the same way about God. Why is that? I know *He* desires to spend time with *me*. Well, the good news is I can change things, and better yet, when I do spend time with God it will be a lot more precious and even more informative than hanging out watching the news. How much do you love God? How much do you desire to spend time with Him? Being married and having kids has taught me the two really do go hand in hand. If you love someone, you'll naturally want to spend time with that person.

January 8
Peace Among Siblings: Is That Even Possible?

"Make every effort to keep the unity of the Spirit through the bond of peace"
(Ephesians 4:3).

I DON'T KNOW ABOUT YOU, but I didn't always get along with my siblings. There were times when I thought they were annoying, times when I felt they were aggravating, and that meant my parents didn't always have a peaceful home . . . and we'll just leave it at that. Now that my siblings and I are older, we have an entirely different relationship. I have learned just how precious my family is and how precious my brothers and sister are. They are a source of encouragement and strength. They are a joy and a blessing to be around. And we also have a lot of fun together. I'm not sure at what point my attitude toward my siblings changed, but I'm so grateful it has. Now, here's my question: How are you treating your spiritual brothers and sisters? Do you squabble and fight with them because you find them annoying or immature or unable to live up to your standards? Or do you find them to be people of comfort and encouragement? Do you like being around them? If you're experiencing division among your fellow Christians, if you're having trouble getting along with them, the good news is the Prince of Peace can help you be a peacemaker in those situations. Siblings won't always get along, (even my sibs and I still don't always get along), but it's a beautiful blessing when we do, and that's especially true of our brothers and sisters in Christ.

January 9
The Transformers and Choosing Sides
"He who is not with me is against me, and he who does not gather with me scatters"
(Matthew 12:30).

INVADERS of vastly superior power and intellect have brought their endless war of good versus evil to our planet. Not only is that the plot for the first Transformers movie by Michael Bay, it's the plot of reality. There are forces of unimaginable power waging war in this world. The difference between the fiction of the movie and the reality we find ourselves in is while, in the movie, people are most often innocent bystanders caught in the crossfire, in reality there is no neutral ground; we have all chosen sides. Now you may think you haven't made a choice; that you don't want to make a choice. However, the fact of the matter is your non-choice is, in fact, a choice. There are only two sides in this war, and if you don't choose to side with Christ, then by default, you choose the other side. The good news is the Bible tells us exactly who will win this war, so that fact should make choosing a side fairly easy . . . if you want to be on the winning one. Transformers may be an eye-popping, action-packed, special-effects extravaganza, but it doesn't even begin to compare with the reality of the war between Heaven and hell. It's their war, it's our world, and it's your choice. Choose wisely.

January 10
The Price of Freedom
"Now the Lord is the Spirit, and where the Spirit of the Lord is, there is freedom"
(2 Corinthians 3:17).

REGARDLESS OF YOUR FEELINGS about the recent wars in Iraq and Afghanistan, I've found the struggle for freedom and independence there to be a poignant reminder of just how costly freedom can be. In fact, if you look throughout history, freedom has always been costly and it's often been secured through a violent struggle of some sort. From the Revolutionary War to the battlefields of World War II to the fight against terrorism, freedom has always exacted a high price. For those of us who are free in Christ, we must never forget the good news that our freedom is the result of Jesus sacrificing His life on the Cross for us. Then He defeated death by rising from the grave. It was the most epic battle in all of history, and Christ's victory secured an eternity of freedom for us. Let's not forget at what price our freedoms have come. As our troops fight for freedom all throughout the world, let us remember the cost of freedom and thank God there are men and women who are willing to pay that price for freedom. More importantly, let us thank God He was willing to pay the price for our freedom on that old rugged Cross. That is definitely good news.

January 11
Too Busy, Too Rushed to Notice

"Let us not become weary in doing good, for at the proper time we will reap a harvest if we do not give up"
(Galatians 6:9).

'VE HEARD of seminaries that give their students a unique test. On the day of a quiz or mid-term or final, one of the staff members disguises himself as a homeless person and hangs around on campus as students rush to their tests. However, the real test isn't how well they can answer questions, but whether or not they stopped and tried to help a person obviously in need. Surprisingly, only about 10 percent of students—seminary students mind you, students learning to be ministers—actually paid any attention to the homeless person in their midst. It's very easy for us to put up the Somebody Else's Problem Force Field to make those who are suffering and less fortunate disappear from our sight. After all, we're busy serving God and have to be on time. Besides, will stopping really make all that much of a difference? Will helping somehow change their lives over night? Probably not, but we shouldn't be worried about results, especially instantaneous results. That's a sure way to grow weary in well doing. Instead, we should concentrate on taking every moment, every opportunity to share the compassion and love of Christ and leave the results to God. Let's take what we know about the good news and put it into action so that people, especially people in need, might see and feel the good news of Jesus Christ in action.

January 12
Growing Fast and Shallow Roots

"But since he has no root, he lasts only a short time.
When trouble or persecution comes because of the word,
he quickly falls away"
(Matthew 13:21).

AT THE RADIO STUDIO where I used work, we have weak trees. The day after we experience high winds, I'd come in to work and see either several branches or an entire tree had blown over. Apparently when the area around the studio was landscaped, someone decided to use trees that would grow quickly. That seemed like a good idea, because the trees quickly became quite beautiful and provided plenty of shade. But when it got windy (as it often does here in New Mexico), many of those lovely shady trees fell because their roots weren't very deep and they weren't strong enough to stand against the wind. Sometimes we as Christians can be like those trees. With all of the teaching resources available to us in this country, we can grow quickly because we're watered with the Word all the time. But if all we do is listen to what other people have to say, like those trees, our roots won't run very deep, our branches won't be very strong, and when the winds of adversity come, we'll be easily blown over. The good news is if we take the time to really study God's Word for ourselves, if we invest in the time to root ourselves deeply in thorough Bible study and fervent prayer, then no matter how strong the winds may be, we may bend and strain, but like the mighty oak tree, the strength of God's Word rooted deeply in our hearts will keep us from ever breaking. So, which sort of tree do you want to be?

January 13
The Secret to The Secret

*"This is the confidence we have in approaching God:
that if we ask anything according to his will, he hears us.
And if we know that he hears us—whatever we ask—
we know that we have what we asked of him"*
(1 John 5:14-15).

IT'S A SECRET that's been used by the greats of science, such as Newton and Einstein. Oprah and Larry King think very highly of this secret. It's a very basic principle for supposedly living life to the full: ask, believe, receive. To many Christians that may sound familiar. In fact, it may sound a lot like faith. But that's the problem with this secret, which became a book known, rather unoriginally as The Secret, not to mention other exciting phenomena like it. It may contain a nugget of truth, but it takes that truth and truly distorts it. When we take a closer look at The Secret and at what the Bible actually says, you'll see one key difference. Where The Secret tells us to ask and seek and believe for whatever we want, the Bible tells us to ask and seek and believe for what God wants. That's a pretty key distinction. But the good news is when you seek after God's will instead of your own, you'll truly discover the secret to what it means to live life to the full.

January 14

Victors, Not Victims

"One night the Lord spoke to Paul in a vision: 'Do not be afraid; keep on speaking, do not be silent. For I am with you, and no one is going to attack and harm you, because I have many people in this city'"
(Acts 18:9-10).

FROM POPULAR BELIEFS like *The Secret* to hearing there's only one true church, then add those things to all the depravity and lack of moral values we see in today's society, and it can be easy for us as Christians to feel like we're all alone and under attack. The major problem is when we start feeling like everyone is against us, we start living with a victim mentality. But when have we ever seen anyone in the Bible act like a victim? Even when Jesus Christ died on the Cross, He didn't act like a victim; He acted like a conqueror. Despite all that happened to Paul, he didn't give in to a victim mentality. Instead he remained determined to actively spread the Gospel of Jesus Christ. Christians are not victims; we are victors. But the fact of the matter is not everyone likes the winner. Besides, you aren't alone. No matter what you may see around you at work or school or at home, you aren't the only Christian. No matter how much it may look like the influence of Christianity is disappearing, you can be sure there are plenty of Christians who aren't cowering as victims, but courageously proclaiming the victory in Christ. You aren't alone. When you make a stand, know there are Christians both where you live and all over the world who are standing for Christ just like you. Isn't that good news?

January 15
It's Not About Medals, but They're Nice

"Serve wholeheartedly, as if you were serving the Lord, not men, because you know that the Lord will reward everyone for whatever good he does, whether he is slave or free"
(Ephesians 6:7-8).

NO MATTER WHAT you may think of war, especially some of the recent ones, I think we can all agree it's nice to see soldiers who not only come home safely, but who are also recognized and awarded for their efforts. I certainly felt that way not long ago when a solider from Kirtland Air Force Base here in New Mexico not only came back safely, but was awarded the Bronze Star. While many of the soldiers I know say they don't do what they do for pats on the back or medals, it still must be gratifying to have someone say thank you every now and then. As Christians who are also engaged in an ongoing war, we should remember and remind each other that someday we'll also receive a reward for what we do. While that shouldn't be our only motivation for living the Christian life, I still find it encouraging that God will give us something in return for our efforts and a life of service to Him. Just as a soldier getting a medal for his heroic efforts, the fact that we'll be rewarded by God is definitely good news.

January 16
Who Said Christians Are Supposed to Be Dumb?

"I am sending you out like sheep among wolves.
Therefore, be as shrewd as snakes and as innocent as doves"
(Matthew 10:16).

WE LIVE IN A DANGEROUS WORLD. From the virtual world to the real world, everywhere we turn, everywhere we look, danger lurks. At times, it almost seems as if we're surrounded by ravenous wolves salivating over the chance to tear us to shreds. Why on earth would Jesus send His innocent children into such a world? Why wouldn't He take us someplace safe instead of risk us being hurt in such a place? Because this world needs to be saved, and that won't happen if we cower and hide. I always found it fascinating that Jesus told His disciples, and, by extension, us to be as shrewd as serpents. *The Message* version of that verse tells us to be "as cunning as snakes." You see the good news is that even though we are being sent out into a world full of wolves, we aren't going into it with wide-eyed naiveté, or at least we shouldn't be. Jesus told us to be cunning, sly, and shrewd as we go into the world, while at the same time maintaining our pure innocence. So, as you go into the world to share the good news, know it's okay to be smart, to be intelligent, to be aware, and to be prepared for the dangers you'll face. Best of all, know that God himself will be with you to help as you move forward to fulfill that mission. When we realize that, the dangers of this world don't seem quite as scary and intimidating.

January 17
It's All About the Money

"About that time there arose a great disturbance about the Way. A silversmith named Demetrius, who made silver shrines of Artemis, brought in no little business for the craftsmen" (Acts 19:23-24).

YOU KNOW WHAT really makes people angry with Christians? It's not when we claim Jesus is the only way to Heaven, although they don't like that. It's not when we tell them they're sinners in need of grace and forgiveness, although people really don't like hearing that. No, people will really get angry when we cut into their profits. Some of the biggest opponents of revivals are businesses such as bars that lose their patrons, once those patrons realize Christ is really what they're looking for and He isn't found at the bottom of mug. And that's just one example.

When we're bold with the good news of Jesus Christ, eventually that's what's going to happen—some people will make less money, and they won't like that. In ancient Ephesus the Gospel of Christ put a dent in the idol-making business, and when people start realizing Jesus is *still* the answer they're looking for in the twenty-first century, it's going to affect the purveyors of drugs, alcohol, porn, online shopping, the makers of antidepressants, and much, much more. Although there are a lot of reasons why people don't like Christianity, I'm willing to bet at the root of those attitudes is some kind of dollar figure. And you know what? I'm okay with that, because the good news of Jesus' love is far more valuable than anything else in this life.

January 18
What Can We Learn From a Monkey on a Treadmill

"So God created man in his own image, in the image of God he created him; male and female he created them"
(Genesis 1:27).

NOT LONG AGO some scientists tried an interesting experiment. They believed they'd be able to unlock some of the mysteries of evolution by (and I'm not making this up) putting a chimp on a treadmill. Scientists hoped that by watching a chimpanzee walk on a treadmill it would help them figure out why we decided to walk upright as a part of the evolutionary process. I can tell you why we walk upright, and I don't need a monkey on a treadmill to figure it out. We walk upright because God created us to do so; He made us that way. Isn't that much more uplifting than thinking we were just monkeys who decided to walk on our hind legs? It's really no mystery why there's so much depression and dissatisfaction in today's society: we're constantly told we're just animals, a more advanced monkey. That's depressing. But to know we were created in the image of God—that's exciting, that's good news. So I say let the scientists play with a monkey on a treadmill; that will probably be pretty entertaining. But they really aren't going to discover any secrets as to how we came to be. All the answers to that question are found in the Bible.

January 19
What Are You Worthy Of, Really?

"What is man that you are mindful of him, the son of man that you care for him? You made him a little lower than the heavenly beings and crowned him with glory and honor"
(Psalm 8:4-5).

A FRIEND OF MINE recently got a very precious gift for his birthday, which made him feel rather depressed. You see, this gift was so extravagant, so precious to him, and also so expensive, he felt he wasn't worthy of such a gift. Well, being the type of friend that I am, I told him if he's going to start worrying about not being worthy, he might as well just give up and go to hell, because that's really the only thing he's actually worthy of. I know that sounds harsh, but it's true and it's true of us all. I'm blessed with a lot of things in my life I'm certainly not worthy of, and first and foremost among them is salvation. I'm so far from being worthy of salvation I can't even see *worthy* from where I'm standing. But you know what the good news is? The good news is even though I'm not worthy, God loves me so much He sees me as worthy of grace, forgiveness, and salvation. So instead of worrying about how unworthy we are of the blessings we have received, perhaps we should just start being grateful that God sees us as worthy of the blessings we're given, In fact, instead of wallowing in our worthlessness, we could, if we so desired, start striving to live in such a manner that, at least in small ways, we would be worthy of the favor we have received.

January 20
TGIF

"The Lord will rescue me from every evil attack and
will bring me safely to his heavenly kingdom.
To him be glory forever and ever. Amen"
(2 Timothy 4:18).

THERE'S A TODD AGNEW SONG that got me all choked up the first time I heard it and still gives me chills whenever I hear it. It's called "Martyr's Song." Now I'm not generally the mushy emotional type who cries at Hallmark commercials or when I see puppies, but this song, for whatever reason, really moved me. It was a song from God's perspective about how excited He will be when He finally gets to welcome us home in Heaven. As I thought about that, my heart and soul filled with joy and longing and I couldn't wait for that day to actually get here. I first heard the song during a stretch when life hadn't been the easiest. But as I imagined what it would be like to have God himself welcome me into His arms in Heaven, suddenly all the weighty problems and difficulties of this life seemed light and trivial. We all love Friday because it's the day before the weekend. Well, the good news is this entire world, this entire era, is currently living out a Friday. We are on the cusp of Jesus' return, and the long weekend He'll bring with Him is known as eternity. So thank God it's Friday, and I'm looking forward to that eternal weekend when God himself will wipe away every tear and dance with me in joy and laughter. That's definitely good news.

January 21
Free is Not Free... Usually

"Was it a sin for me to lower myself in order to elevate you by preaching the gospel of God to you free of charge?"
(2 Corinthians 11:7).

A WHILE BACK, my wife decided to use a coupon for a free sandwich from a fast food restaurant. Her thinking was it would be a cheap way to get dinner. Unfortunately, what she didn't realize (because she didn't read the fine print) was there were certain conditions that had to be met before she could get the free sandwich. Needless to say, our inexpensive dinner turned out to be not all that inexpensive because, as one of my co-workers once said, "Free isn't free." The good news is when God gives us something free, He actually gives it to us . . . for free! There's no fine print, no conditions, no other terms for us to meet. God gives us grace and forgiveness free. It's a gift from Him that has no requirements on our end except for one thing—we have to accept it. Now why would He be willing to do such a thing? Because of His love. God's grace is unlimited and His love for you and me is unfathomable. You see the sandwich place didn't love my wife, so they weren't really interested in providing her something for nothing. But God's loves us so much He does want to give us something for free. In fact, He renews that gift of love and grace each and every morning. Now that's good news that can make you want to live a life of obedience, gratitude, and love in return.

January 22
Rigging the Game and Eternity
"There is surely a future hope for you,
and your hope will not be cut off"
(Proverbs 23:18).

A FEW YEARS AGO the NBA faced an interesting crisis: Could they trust their referees? Although allegations were brought against only one of them for rigging games through his calls, there was concern there might have been more corrupt officials determining the outcome of NBA games. I find it interesting that people don't want the outcome predetermined, or rigged, in sports but when it comes to life, we find it scandalous not to know what the outcome will be. In fact, people will go to extraordinary and unusual ends to try and figure out what the outcome of their lives will be. While we may never be able to really learn specifics of what our life will be like at the end, there is one outcome we can know for sure—where we will spend eternity. In fact, you might even say that outcome has been rigged for us when Jesus Christ died on the Cross and rose from the dead to pay the price for our sins and to bring us eternal life. This rigging of eternity wasn't a scandal. In fact, it was one of the greatest acts of love in all of history, and one of the greatest gifts ever given to humanity. The question is what have you done with this gift? How have you cherished this gift? And how have you shared this gift of good news?

January 23
Pimp the Ride, Still Can't Hide

"But the Lord said to Samuel, 'Do not consider his appearance or his height, for I have rejected him. The Lord does not look at the things man looks at. Man looks at the outward appearance, but the Lord looks at the heart.'"
(1 Samuel 16:7).

DID YOU KNOW you could turn the rims on your car into video advertisements? That's right, you can have video images or phrases flashing across your hubcaps while you drive. I don't get it. People are willing to spend so much money on the outside appearance of their cars when they spend most of their time on the inside. And of course, depending on how your car looks, people automatically begin to make assumptions about what type of person you are. I certainly understand the appeal of appearing a certain way to the people who see you drive by in a fancy, expensive, sleek-looking, aerodynamic, top-of-the-line, high-tech car with video hub caps, but I also know ultimately such appearances are hollow. The cars we drive may present a certain front to the people we come across, but no matter what our cars looks like, God knows who we really are. We won't impress Him by what we drive or what we wear or how physically fit we are. God knows who we really are because He doesn't judge us based on our looks like people do. God sees us as we really are on the inside. And you know what? He still loves us. Not only is that really good news, but in the long run, it may even save us some serious money.

January 24
Simpson, eh?

*"For you created my inmost being,
you knit me together in my mother's womb"*
(Psalm 139:13).

ONE OF THE THINGS I've always thought was pretty funny about *The Simpsons* is how Mr. Burns never remembers Homer's name. Homer Simpson has been working for Mr. Burns for . . . I don't know how many years, and yet every time Mr. Burns meets Homer or hears about him, he uses his familiar catch phrase, "Simpson, eh?" Because to Mr. Burns, that's the first time he's ever heard that name. Perhaps you know some people who are like that, who just feel like you aren't important enough to remember. No matter how many times you meet them, they still treat you like a stranger. That doesn't make you feel all that special, does it? Well, here's the good news: the Mr. Burns of this world may not feel you're important enough to remember, but the God of the entire universe not only thinks you're important enough, but He loves you so much He'll never forget who you are. You matter to God. You matter so much that God knows and remembers every detail about you, from your name to how many hairs (or lack thereof) are on your head. So don't let it bother you when a Mr. Burns looks at you with a lack of recognition and says, "Snyder, eh?" or "Smith, eh?" or "Simpson, eh?" Take comfort in the fact that God, the same God that created all the stars and knows all their names, knows your name as well. No matter what anyone else says, that's good news that ought to make you feel pretty special.

January 25
The Pain of Credit Cards and Sin

" . . . But now he has appeared once for all at the end of the ages to do away with sin by the sacrifice of himself. Just as man is destined to die once, and after that to face judgment, so Christ was sacrificed once to take away the sins of many people . . . "
(Hebrews 9:26-28).

USING A CREDIT CARD is almost too easy these days. You hardly even have to swipe it anymore, you just have to tap it and off you go without even thinking about how much it's costing you. Fortunately, not too long ago, I sat on my credit card and almost bent it in half, so it doesn't swipe any more. If I want to use it, it's very inconvenient. The store has to dig up one of those old credit card machines and clack-clack it in order for me to use it. But really, that's how using credit should be—painful and inconvenient. That sound should remind me of how much credit costs me. Sin is a lot like our credit cards. We can come up with all kinds of rationalizations for why we should get away with some pet sin. We think up tons of reasons why it's not all that bad, and before you know it, we no longer think about how much sin is costing us anymore because it's become so convenient. The truth, however, is sin should be like those old credit card machines—an inconvenient and painful reminder of how much it costs. It'd be helpful for me if every time I sinned I heard some sort of clack-clack sound to remind me of how much that sin is really costing. Fortunately, the good news is that Jesus paid the price of sin for us, which is like having someone else pay your credit card bill. Now that doesn't mean we should run up a huge bill, but rather, we should strive to keep that bill clean out of our gratitude to Him.

January 26
The Tears of God and the Comfort They Bring
"Jesus wept"
(John 11:35).

EW THINGS ARE MORE DIFFICULT than watching someone you love suffer. I remember when my wife had her wisdom teeth removed. Sitting in that waiting rooming hearing the sounds of drills and metal being used on my wife was one of the most torturous moments of my life. Then taking her home and watching her move in a listless, slow, and painful manner all the while knowing there wasn't really a lot I could do to help her just tore me up inside. I would have done anything to take that pain from her, but the best I could do was tenderly care for and help her through it. This was around the same time some people in Minnesota were experiencing that same feeling magnified a hundred fold. When a bridge on a major highway collapsed and the search went on for the living and the dead, the agony of the families who were waiting to hear about loved ones and the devastation of those who had already heard was hard to imagine. I find it comforting in the midst of moments like those to know that Jesus wept. Jesus, God in the flesh, saw the suffering and death we endure, and wept. It was hard for me to see the wife I love suffer. It was hard for those families in Minneapolis to endure the pain and death caused by that collapsed bridge. Now imagine what it would be like to see the suffering of a beloved creation you made with your own hands. God's heart breaks with ours in the moments of pain and suffering; perhaps more than we'll ever know because He doesn't just love us, He made us to be loved by Him. So hearing that Jesus wept, odd as it may sound, is very good news to me.

January 27
Learning to Swing a Golf Club

"I am the vine; you are the branches. If a man remains in me and I in him, he will bear much fruit; apart from me you can do nothing"
(John 15:5).

GOLF IS A SPORT I've never quite understood. There's just something about all the mechanics involved in hitting that little, dimpled ball that I can't quite get. However, we had an annual golf tournament at the radio station where I used to work, and while I still don't get it, I think I'm closer to getting it than I was before playing golf once a year. You see I've learned I can let the golf club do a lot of the work for me. I used to think I needed to swing as hard as I possibly could, not only to hit the ball far but also to prove my manliness to my fellow golfers. The only problem with doing that was my ball never landed on the fairway. It usually ended up someplace like Juarez, Mexico. Eventually I decided to try pulling back and rely more on the club than my own strength, and, lo and behold, I actually got the ball on the fairway. This same principle also applies to our spiritual lives. When we try to do everything in our own strength, our efforts will go awry. When we let God do the work for us through the Holy Spirit in us, we will hit the mark far more often than when we just swing it with all our strength. You might say the Holy Spirit is our club of choice for coming in under par in the game of life. Any way you put it, the fact that we don't have to rely on our own strength in order to achieve success in life is definitely good news.

January 28
I Told You So

"Paul stood up before them and said: 'Men, you should have taken my advice not to sail from Crete; then you would have spared yourselves this damage and loss. But now I urge you to keep your courage, because not one of you will be lost; only the ship will be destroyed'"
(Acts 27:21-22).

HAVE YOU EVER BEEN IN A MESS? Especially some sort of trouble someone else warned you about, but you didn't listen. And now you're in a big mess and all that person who warned you about it can do is say, "I told you so." That's not very helpful, is it? I think we can learn two important things from Paul's journey to Rome and the subsequent shipwreck that took place. One, when God's people talk, we should listen. All of us at some point in our lives are seeking God's direction and will for our lives, but we think God will tell us in some dramatic, miraculous way. However, the fact is He may use your friend, or family member, or neighbor, or co-worker to help point you in the right direction. It may not be dramatic, or even seem all that important, but then neither did the warnings of the prisoner on that Roman ship. The second thing we learn is God doesn't just say, "I told you so," after we get in some sort of trouble He warned us about. Because of His mercy, love, and grace, He's still willing to help us. The results may not be as pleasant as they would have been if we had listened in the first place, but God loves us too much to just say, "I told you so," and not help. I find that to be very good news and it's also an attitude I want to emulate. I want to be a helper, not just an "I told you so-er."

January 29
Sprained Ankles and Hurt Lives
"I know that my Redeemer lives, and that in the end he will stand upon the earth"
(Job 19:25).

PAIN IS A FUNNY THING. Not funny ha-ha, but *it-makes-you-think* funny. I've twisted my ankle a few times playing basketball and it always takes a bit of time before I can get back on the court to play. However, before I can play again, I usually have to overcome a problem: I have to remember how to run. After a sprained ankle and some time on crutches, I have this strange hobble movement that makes me look like Igor trying to play basketball. I'm not sure if the problem is that my body doesn't remember how to run or if it's trying to purposely keep me from running in order to keep me from getting hurt again. Whatever the reason, it's awkward and frustrating. Pain can have the same impact on our spiritual lives as well; it can make us forget. In the midst of pain and suffering we can forget the good news that God loves us, cares for us, hurts with us, rejoices with us, and will never leave us or forsake us. Pain can wipe out our memories of all those things, and when we come out on the other side, God suddenly seems like a stranger. Pain may make my body forget how to run and play basketball, but that doesn't mean I don't try to remember. I'll go out on the court every day until those old reflexes and movements return. In the same way, when we're in pain or suffering let's make sure we still pray and read our Bibles and talk with fellow believers. Let's make sure we don't forget God in our pain, because the good news is, if we seek Him in times of suffering, we won't forget and have an awkward time getting reacquainted. And we'll find that during those times, that's often when He's the closest to us.

January 30
Talking About Daddy
"For I am the Lord, your God, who takes hold of your right hand, and says to you, Do not fear; I will help you" (Isaiah 41:13).

I'VE OFTEN WONDERED why God often refers to himself in the third person in the Bible. He doesn't just say *I* said such and such, but He will often say this is what *God* says. Now I'm sure there are a lot of really good theological reasons for that, but one night while talking to my daughter I stumbled across what I think is another reason. We were talking about how she behaved during her first couple days of kindergarten, and I caught myself saying, "Well, Daddy is very proud of you for . . . blah de blah." As soon as those words were out of my mouth, I stopped at the realization I was referring to myself as *Daddy* instead of just as *I*. So what does that tell me about how God talks to us? Well, it tells me He refers to himself sometimes in the third person because that's how all parents talk to their children. I know this is a rather odd observation, but here's the point: the good news is God treats us as His children. Not as business associates, not just as servants or friends or partners, but as His beloved children. Just as my kids have a need to hear tender words from Daddy, so we all as God's children need to hear tender words from our heavenly Daddy. Isn't it awesome that He gives us those tender words just like a loving father would?

<hr />

January 31
How to Avoid Getting Tired of Work

"Whatever you do, work at it with all your heart, as working for the Lord, not for men, since you know that you will receive an inheritance from the Lord as a reward.
It is the Lord Christ you are serving"
(Colossians 3:23-24).

HAVE YOU EVER NOTICED that work has a way of wearing you down? It doesn't matter what kind of work it is. You could have the most glamorous job in the world, but doing it day after day will cause it to eventually lose its luster. However, whether it's a glamorous job or something totally dull and mundane, whether it's homework or busy work, believe it or not we can prevent our work from wearing us down. How? It's all a matter of perspective. Why are you doing this work? If it's just to make sure you don't flunk, or just to make sure you don't get fired, that's going to get tiring. However, if you're doing your work because you want to please God with everything you do, if you realize that how well you do things here has an impact on what you'll receive when Christ returns, suddenly work isn't so much *work*. I'm not saying we'll always be happy about what we have to do, but I do know the good news is when you work for Christ, you can be assured that no matter what, it's worth doing.

February

From the chamber of the south comes the whirlwind, And cold from the scattering winds of the north.

Job 37:9

February 1
Holy Spirit: Stunt Coordinator

"That is why, for Christ's sake, I delight in weaknesses, in insults, in hardships, in persecutions, in difficulties. For when I am weak, then I am strong"
(2 Corinthians 12:10).

ONE EVENING when I didn't have anything better to do I watched the Taurus Stunt Awards, which is like the Academy Awards for stunt men and women. It was actually a pretty spectacular show, and it was cool to see big-time Hollywood actors pay tribute to the no-name, hardworking, life-risking stunt people that help make so many movies exciting and thrilling to watch. It also got me thinking it would be nice to have a stunt double in life. Not that I do a lot of dangerous work, but you have to admit, every now and then it would be nice to have someone else stand in to face all the difficult times we have in life. But, on the other hand, it's always cool when an actor does his own stunts. That's pretty much the way my life is, I do all my own stunts—which really isn't as cool as it sounds. The good news, however, is I'm not really doing all these stunts alone. Thanks to the power of the Holy Spirit, God has equipped and enabled me not only to face the difficult moments in life, but to get through them in spectacular ways. You might say the Holy Spirit is my stunt coordinator, walking me through the stunts in life to make sure I get through to the other side safely.

February 2
Predicting the Future . . . With a Tiger

**"'For I know the plans I have for you,'" declares the Lord,
'plans to prosper you and not to harm you,
plans to give you a hope and a future'"
(Jeremiah 29:11).**

WE LIKE TO KNOW what's going to happen in the future, and sometimes we try to find out what will happen in the future through a variety of ways. One of the most popular is to rely on a giant rodent to tell us if we'll have a longer winter. However, in Nebraska they don't rely on a groundhog, they use a tiger instead. Yep, on the same morning the famous rodent does his thing, this tiger comes out to have breakfast, and depending on which bowl it eats from—green for spring or white for winter—it determines what the forecast will be. It's about as reliable a forecast as you can hope to get without using Doppler radar. Regardless of whether the tiger gets the forecast right (he has a fifty-fifty chance), there's one who is 100 percent accurate in His predictions: God. God has predicted things thousands of years in advance, not just six weeks, and He's been right every single time. More than that, He has plans for you. He has a future all planned out and ready to go for you. Isn't that good news? Wouldn't you like to know what that future is? There are two things you can do: read the Bible and ask Him. I think you'll find His predictions for the future far more reliable than a groundhog's . . . or a tiger's.

February 3
Putting Mondays Into Perspective

" . . . God opposes the proud, but gives grace to the humble.
Humble yourselves, therefore, under God's mighty hand, that
he may lift you up in due time"
(1 Peter 5:5-6).

HEARD a very interesting statement from our pastor one Sunday: the humble don't think little of themselves, the humble don't think of themselves at all. That's a definition of humility I haven't heard before, and it's also a definition that actually makes a lot of sense to me. It especially made sense to me on the Monday after I heard it in church. You see Monday is often the day when we think about ourselves the most. We think about all we have to do this week, we think about how short our weekend was, we think about how much we dislike going back to work or school. Monday is often a pretty miserable day, but the reason it's miserable is because we're thinking so much about ourselves. Imagine what Monday would be like if we weren't so wrapped up in our own worries, but were actually concerned about the needs of others. Instead of asking people how their weekend was as we walk by in a hurry to get to the next event in our day (that we really aren't interested in), what if we took the time to actually listen to how a person's weekend was? What if we were humble enough to make Mondays about others instead of about ourselves? You know, the good news is the Bible tells us if we humble ourselves, God will lift us up in due time. So if

God is taking care of us, that should leave plenty of time to not think about ourselves at all and instead think about how we can minister to the people around us.

February 4
Why Complaining Doesn't Work and How To Stop

"Do everything without complaining or arguing, so that you may become blameless and pure, children of God without fault in a crooked and depraved generation . . . "
(Philippians 2:14-15).

DO YOU REMEMBER as a kid when you tried to whine and complain to get what you want? Did it ever work? Depending on what kind of parents you had, I'm willing to bet it didn't—at least it never did for me. My parents refused to give me what I wanted if I grumbled and complained about it. I've noticed, however, that once we grow up past our elementary years, we suddenly seem to think our fortunes will change. Once we hit our teens, then into our college years, and on into adulthood, for whatever reason, we once again seem to think that complaining and grumbling is a good way for us to make things happen. And for the most part, there isn't anyone who can tell us to stop. However, I've also noticed that even as an adult, complaining really doesn't get things done. In fact, I've discovered what my parents told me as a child still holds true in my life as an adult: you never get what you want by complaining. About the only thing I've seen complaining and grumbling actually accomplish is to make me feel worse. So here's the good news: God gives us a reason not to complain. It's just a matter of perspective. If we only focus on what isn't working, what's not going our way, or otherwise isn't what we want, all we'll see are reasons to complain and grumble. But, if we fix our eyes on God and all the ways He's provided, cared for, and otherwise watched out for us, if we'll remember His great love and grace He shows us every day, and if we'll remember He wants to bless us so we can be a blessing to others, suddenly we'll find plenty of reasons to do exactly what the Bible tells us—do everything without complaining.

February 5
Scientists Find Nothing; Make Major Announcement

"Salvation is found no one else, for there is no other name under heaven given to men by which we must be saved"
(Acts 4:12).

DID YOU KNOW a few years back scientists discovered a giant hole in the universe? It's an area of the universe where there aren't any stars, galaxies, quasars, nebulas, matter, or even dark matter. I thought it was weird that scientists could make a major announcement, and the announcement was—they found absolutely nothing. Just as there is a hole in our universe, there's a hole in all of us as well. A great void of nothingness out of which leaks a desperate desire to know who we are, whether or not we have a purpose, or if we even matter. We can try and fill that void with all manner of things we think will satisfy, but ultimately we'll find the void too great to be filled with anything from this world. So what do we do? We turn to the only One who can fill that hole in our life: Jesus Christ. We all have a God-shaped hole, and God is the only one vast enough to fill it. Just because scientists can't detect anything in a certain area of the galaxy doesn't mean there isn't anything there. God is great enough to fill that void. The good news is the same God loves you so much He wants to fill the hole in your universe as well. If God has already done that for you, then share your discovery with others. Just think; you'll be able to announce to people that you've found something, something eternal, instead of being like one of those scientists who announced they found absolutely nothing.

February 6
Does God Laugh?

"The Lord is my strength and my shield; my heart trusts in him, and I am helped. My heart leaps for joy and I will give thanks to him in song"
(Psalm 28:7).

HAVE YOU EVER NOTICED the Bible never really talks about God laughing all that much? The only passage I can really think of that mentions God laughing is one where He's laughing at someone, and it wasn't because He found something funny. I've often wondered about that; does God not find anything funny? Does He even have a sense of humor? On a seemingly unrelated point, have you ever been around a truly joyful person? Someone who is obviously full of the joy of the Lord? I've noticed truly joyful people like to laugh a lot, plus they're just pleasant to be around all the time, even when something isn't funny. Reading through the Bible, I get the impression God must be the most joyous being in the entire universe, and apparently that joy is infectious. The Bible constantly talks about how anyone and everyone who gets around God is filled with joy, and I'm sure at times that leads to joyous laughter. If God truly is the source of joy in our lives, I'm willing to bet He likes to have a good laugh with us every now and then. I like the fact that the Bible talks about joy more than laughter. Laughs are usually contingent on circumstances; joy is contingent on the eternal nature of God, so it's something we can always have, no matter what the circumstances are. I find that to be way better news than to know whether or not God laughs.

February 7
Ready for the Weekend?

"No one knows about that day or hour, not even the angels in heaven, nor the Son, but only the Father . . . Therefore keep watch, because you do not know on what day your Lord will come" (Matthew 24:36, 42).

WHAT WOULD LIFE BE LIKE if the weekend could happen at any moment? Imagine how that would change the way we go to work or school or run errands or anything else we do during the week. If the next day could suddenly be Saturday without any warning, what would you do differently today? I for one would have to stop being a procrastinator, because if surprise weekends happened at any time, I'd have to be sure I got my work done during the days I'm at work. On the flip side, I'd also want to make sure I was ready for the weekend by having my Bermuda shorts and Hawaiian shirt packed and ready to go at a moment's notice. While I don't think it'll ever happen, wouldn't it be cool to suddenly have your boss or teacher burst into the room and say, "That's it folks, the week's over. Go home and enjoy the weekend"? Well, the good news is someday that's exactly what's going to happen. When Jesus Christ returns, He's going to bring the greatest and longest weekend of all time with Him. The trick is we don't know when that's going to happen. It could be tomorrow, or next Monday, or right now, or in the next thirty seconds, or four hundred Thursdays from now. So if you don't know when the weekend of eternity is going to get here, the question then becomes: Are you ready regardless of when it arrives?

February 8
Being Angry at God
"The Lord is slow to anger, abounding in love and forgiving sin and rebellion"
(Numbers 14:18).

HAVE YOU EVER BEEN SO ANGRY with someone you didn't want to talk with them anymore? You know, you're not on speaking terms because you're just so mad at them? Have you ever been that mad at God? I know it's not very Christ-like to say it, but I'm willing to admit I have been mad at God, and I've even been angry enough to say we weren't on speaking terms. Once I cooled down, however, I realized what a silly thing that is to say about God, "We're not on speaking terms," because there's never a time when God will ever feel that way with us. Isn't that great news? God never gets so angry He doesn't want to talk with us, and no matter how angry we are with Him, He always wants to hear what we have to say. It's actually kind of humbling to think the God who created the entire universe could love us so much He would show us that kind of patience and grace. Yes, I have been angry with God. I have been so angry I didn't want to talk to Him anymore. But when I remember how much He loves me and He always wants to listen and speak with me, no matter how angry I am, suddenly my anger dissipated and in humility and submission I came before the throne just to rest in His great love. The fact that He's always there and always loves me enough to allow me to do that is about the best news I can think of—even when I'm angry.

February 9
Life Lessons From Tom and Jerry

Therefore we do not lose heart. Though outwardly we are wasting away, yet inwardly we are being renewed day by day. For our light and momentary troubles are achieving for us an eternal glory that far outweighs them all. So we fix our eyes not on what is seen, but on what is unseen, since what is seen is temporary, but what is unseen is eternal.
(2 Corinthians 4:16-18)

'VE ALWAYS LOVED TOM AND JERRY. One of my favorite pastimes is to sit in front of the TV watching one of their DVD collections and laughing. Even though I can see most of the gags coming a mile away, they're still funny to me. For instance, when Tom's chasing Jerry and Jerry spreads several rakes all over the ground and Tom runs around and steps on one, gets smacked in the face, stumbles back, and steps on another, and then stumbles forward and gets smacked by another—priceless. Sometimes my life feels a lot like a Tom and Jerry cartoon. Not that I feel like a cat or mouse, but rather there are times in my life when it feels like I'm walking into one disaster after another. There are times where it feels like I'm just stepping on one rake after another. Ever had a day or week or month or year like that? Fortunately, when we keep in mind what the Bible tells us about our daily troubles, that they're light and momentary, and one day we will enjoy eternal glory, suddenly those rakes we keep stepping on feel more like cartoonish inconveniences instead of overwhelming disasters. Compared to eternity our life lasts about as long as a Tom and Jerry cartoon, so even if we have a few hurts along the way, the good news is God's gift of eternity can help us keep things in proper perspective, and maybe even help us have a few laughs along the way.

February 10

Downloaded Videogames and Disappointment

"Hope deferred makes the heart sick, but a longing fulfilled is a tree of life"
(Proverbs 13:12).

HAVE YOU EVER really been looking forward to something, only to have it not happen? Sure you have. It happens to me all the time, like when I spent most of the afternoon downloading an exclusive demo to a new video game, and then when I finally sat down to play it . . . it didn't work. There was some sort of error and I was told I'd have to download the game all over again. That was disappointing to say the least. I had been looking forward to playing that game all afternoon, and when I couldn't do it, I was pretty upset. I felt let down. I felt cheated. I felt like my time had been wasted. (Of course some of you may say that actually playing videogames is a waste of time.) My point in bringing this up is once again the Bible is right; hope deferred does indeed make our hearts sick. And yet, we keep putting our hope in temporary, unreliable things that only disappoint and upset us. This world is in desperate need of a hope that will not fail, of a longing that will fulfill. You and I know exactly where that can be found. Time is growing short, so we need to get busy in sharing the good news of the hope of Jesus Christ, for that's a hope that will not fail, will not disappoint, will not be deferred, or make our hearts sick. It's a hope that brings life, joy, peace, and salvation to our hearts. I was really upset when the game I spent all afternoon downloading didn't work; but what would be even more disappointing would be to not share an everlasting hope with people who need it so desperately. And I definitely don't want to disappoint God.

February 11
Never Say Never in Prayer

"No longer will a man teach his neighbor, or a man his brother, saying, 'Know the Lord,' because they will all know me, from the least of them to the greatest," declares the Lord. "For I will forgive their wickedness and will remember their sins no more" (Jeremiah 31:34).

F EW THINGS IN LIFE are as frustrating and stressful as having a loved one who just doesn't seem to understand why it's so important to follow Christ. I suffered through that torture for years with one of my close friends. He'd go out and do something stupid, end up regretting and feeling bad about it, and I'd share how he could make it better. He'd nod his head sadly and say "I know, I know that's what I need to do, but . . . " and some sort of extravagant and lame excuse would follow. I never understood. It's like someone saying "I know, I know I need immediate open heart surgery to live, but now's just not a good time and I don't think I'm really prepared to go that route now." It just doesn't make any sense. Now at this point you're probably expecting me to have some profound way to magically help you get that loved one of yours to understand their need to accept Jesus Christ. Unfortunately, I don't. So what did I do with my friend? I prayed. I prayed for years and years through arguments and heartache. You know what the good news is? My patience and love and prayer paid off. But it wasn't anything I did; it was all about my friend and God finally coming to terms. I could offer advice and encouragement here and there, but really it was up to God to get him to understand why He was so important in his life. Prayer is far more powerful and effective than we give it credit for, and even if you do it for years and years, never give up. The result—eternal life for your closest loved ones—is well worth it. Isn't that good news?

February 12
Transformative Goo

"Therefore, if anyone is in Christ, he is a new creation; the old has gone, the new has come!"
(2 Corinthians 5:17).

I'VE LEARNED some very interesting things by visiting the butterflies over at the Botanic Gardens here in Albuquerque, New Mexico. I learned when my daughter was two years old, that for some reason she was terrified of butterflies, and I also learned some things about

48

butterflies I never knew before. Did you know that a butterfly completely changes from a worm or caterpillar into a beautiful butterfly while it's in its cocoon? Okay, maybe you did, but did you know during that transformation the caterpillar dissolves into living goo? It's not only really bizarre, but it's also true. Everything that is even remotely caterpillar-like dissolves into nothing but goo, and out of that goo emerges a completely different creature. It's amazing to me that God has put in nature such an accurate picture of what happens when we come to Christ. Isn't it awesome that our old nature, our sin nature, dissolves into goo and no longer exists, and we emerge completely changed in Christ as a whole new creature? That's amazingly good news. And you know what? Just because every now and then we behave like the worm we were instead of the butterfly we are doesn't mean we've once again become a worm. The worm is gone, dissolved into redemptive goo, and we are now nothing but a beautiful, redeemed butterfly. So when we mess up, let's just clean ourselves off and fly back to God and live the new life we've been given.

February 13
Where to Find True Romance in Life

"The Lord appeared to us in the past, saying: 'I have loved you with an everlasting love; I have drawn you with loving kindness'"
(Jeremiah 31:3).

DO YOU HAVE enough romance in your life? Would you like more romance in your life? Romantic novels bring in over a billion dollars each year, and they make up 39 percent of all fiction written and sold. Lest you think that's just a fetish of the world, romantic stories are also the most popular genre of Christian fiction. It's obvious we all thirst for a little romance in our lives; the problem is we aren't sure how to get it. We confuse romance for lust, and lust for love. We try to fill our romantic need with all sorts of things that ultimately prove to be unfulfilling. When you reach that point, it's time to turn to God. There is no greater romance than our relationship with God. If you look through the Bible, the way God feels for us is incredibly romantic. History is filled with great romances: Romeo and Juliet, Kermit the Frog and Miss Piggy, my wife and me. But the greatest romance of all is of an Almighty God wooing His beloved creation. God loves you, and when you enjoy a relationship with Him, you will experience what romance truly is. Doesn't that sound like good news?

February 14
Best. Valentine's. Ever.
**"This is how we know what love is:
Jesus Christ laid down his life for us"
(1 John 3:16).**

AH, LOVE. It's one of those ideals we all say we hold in high regard, yet a rampant divorce rate, domestic abuse, date rapes, and abundant pornography only show that we don't really know what love is. Do you know what the greatest Valentine ever was? It wasn't flowers or dinner by candlelight or poetry or even chocolates. No, the greatest Valentine was a man beaten to a bloody pulp, slowly suffering and dying on a crude, wooden Cross. You may be wondering how that is the greatest Valentine ever. Well, it's the greatest because it shows us what love is. Love is sacrificial, love is a choice and a determination, love is often painful, and love is all about others. Jesus Christ displayed all of this and more on the Cross, and when He rose from the dead, He invited us to follow His example so that we too might know true love. Now I'm not saying you need to die on a cross to prove your love to someone this Valentine's Day, but maybe it's time we started to learn to die to ourselves and to choose to love others. Better yet, this Valentine's Day, let's share God's love with the people we know who need it. They may just find it to be good news.

February 15
Never-ending Valentine's

"A new command I give you: Love one another. As I have loved you, so you must love one another. By this all men will know you're my disciples, if you love one another"
(John 13:34-35).

WELL, MEN ALL OVER THE NATION are breathing a sigh of relief now that Valentine's Day is over. Of all the holidays on the calendar year, Valentine's Day generally brings the most pressure to do something truly special, something truly thoughtful, something truly romantic. Now that we've gotten that out of the way, it's on with life as normal until next year, right? Not so fast. When we start thinking that way, we leave out one of the key elements of the Christian life. You see, as Christians we aren't to love just once a year, but all the time. Also, we aren't just supposed to show thoughtfulness and kindness to the people we like, we're supposed to show thoughtfulness and kindness to everyone we encounter. Of course I'm not saying we have to be romantic with everyone, but as Christians, we should show the same sacrifice, deference, and respect to everyone that we show to the people we are romantic with. In short, Valentine's Day shouldn't just be another day in a calendar year, but the entire year should be filled with days where we love others. I know that may not sound like good news for those of you who were feeling relieved the holiday is past, but it's definitely good news for those who may encounter God's love for the first time because you were willing to show them.

February 16
Finding Out What's Wrong
"Cast all your anxiety on him because he cares for you"
(1 Peter 5:7).

MEN AND WOMEN ARE DIFFERENT. I know that's an astounding revelation, but living with my wife I'm reminded of that fact on a regular basis. For instance, there are times when I know something is wrong with my wife, but when I ask if something is wrong, she says she's fine— even though I knew it isn't true. As it turns out in the particular example I'm thinking of, the reason she said this is because my question wasn't specific enough. (Fellas, I hope you're taking notes on this.) She thought I was only asking if something was wrong emotionally, and since there wasn't, technically she was fine. However, there was something wrong physically. I assumed my question of "Is there something wrong?" was good enough to cover all the bases. Wrong. In a man's mind "Is something wrong?" means is *anything* wrong? Apparently that's not how it translates in a female mind. Good to know. You know what else is good to know? God wants to hear what's wrong with us. Whether it's physical, emotional, or spiritual pain we're going through, God wants to talk about it with you because He loves you. Best of all, He doesn't have to play any guessing games with you because He knows everything about you anyway. That should make it easier to be up front and honest with Him, and also to enjoy the loving comfort of our Savior's arms in our times of suffering. That's definitely good news.

<hr />

February 17
A Hypocritical Argument

"God is not a man that he should lie, nor a son of man, that he should change his mind. Does he speak and not act? Does he promise and not fulfill?"
(Numbers 23:19).

ONE OF THE MOST COMMON REASONS people have for avoiding church and Christianity is because the churches are full of hypocrites. I once read about a state official whose job involved the prevention of drunk driving and yet he was apprehended under the suspicion of—you guessed it—driving drunk. My point is this: if you really want to avoid hypocrites, go live in a cave on Mars. Hypocrites are everywhere. Hypocrites are people. That's why I don't go to church for the people, or even for the pastor (that's shocking, I know). I go to church because I want to worship God, who is not a hypocrite, and His Son, Jesus Christ, who was the only man to ever walk the face of the Earth who also wasn't a hypocrite. The reason Jesus could ask us to be perfect as our heavenly Father is perfect is because He did it. The reason He could tell us to love even our enemies is because He did it. The reason He could tell us to sacrifice is because He did it. Jesus did everything He's ever asked of us. It's true the Church is full of hypocrites—I'm one of them—but the Church isn't about the people. The Church is about the God it worships. Jesus Christ was never hypocritical, and He doesn't avoid fellowship with us even when we are. He still loves us. That's good news worth going to church for.

February 18
It's Good to Have Friends

"Two are better than one, because they have a good return for their work: If one falls down, his friend can help him up. But pity the man who falls and has no one to help him up!"
(Ecclesiastes 4:9-10).

IT'S GOOD TO HAVE FRIENDS. When there's an angry swarm of zombie aliens descending upon you, it's nice to have friends to help back you up with some heavy firepower. Of course, that's a rather extreme case of why friends are nice to have around. I play a lot of online video games, and what I've found is when I have some friends online helping me out, I have a much easier time getting through the challenging sections than when I'm playing by myself. The same is true in getting through the challenges of life; it's nice to have friends to back you up. Of course, the friends we want in life need to meet different criteria than the friends you need online. I'm proud to say I have a handful of really good friends who I know I can rely on should life go bad. I know they would be there to help no matter what, and they would do so without expecting anything in return. It's almost like having several Christ-like figures constantly around to support, encourage, and help me. And I hope they know I'd do the same for them. Life is hard sometimes, more often than not really, but the good news is when you have true, godly friends, even the most difficult times can be a lot easier than when you try to go it alone. Treasure your friends as the blessings from God they truly are, and in return, always strive to be a Christ-like friend yourself.

February 19
Figuring Out Movies and the Bible
"Blessed is the one who reads the words of this prophecy, and blessed are those who hear it and take to heart what is written in it, because the time is near"
(Revelation 1:3).

HAVE YOU EVER WATCHED a movie and once it was over, if someone asked you what it was about you wouldn't be able to tell them because you weren't entirely sure. I have. Seriously, I watched a movie recently and I had no idea what took place aside from the fact that guys with swords literally flew all over the place wrecking things while trying to slice each other up. It sounds exciting, I know, and in truth it was, but I still couldn't tell you what the movie was really about or why anything that happened in it happened. A lot of people feel the same way about the Book of Revelation; they have no idea what's happening and would be hard pressed to explain it to anyone else. I understand how that feels, especially after watching certain movies, but here's the deal: Revelation is actually worth our time and investment to understand, unlike that movie I never really understood. Not only does it tell us what our ultimate fate will be, which is good news, but it provides certainty and comfort in an uncertain world. It also promises we'll be blessed if we take to heart what's written in this book. I know there are some difficult passages in the Bible, but rather than ignoring them, let's actually apply ourselves to understanding them. Then we can truly enjoy all the blessings God has promised us, which is always good news.

February 20
Trouble in Elementary School

"Whether you turn to the right or to the left, your ears will hear a voice behind you saying, 'This is the way; walk in it'"
(Isaiah 30:21).

IT'S BEEN A FEW YEARS since I've been in elementary school. Okay, maybe it's been more than a few years, but the point is I haven't been there for a while. When I went back to elementary school to pick up my daughter I ended up getting into trouble. Apparently I was doing it wrong—picking up my daughter that is—I didn't pick her up correctly. I wasn't even aware there was a wrong way to pick up a child, but I guess there was. I was told by a teacher, who made me feel like I was back in kindergarten, that I was going the wrong way. I apologized, to no avail, and went along my merry way. How interesting, I thought, the first time I go back to school in years, and I get in trouble during the short ten minutes I'm there. It's no wonder I'm glad to be out of school. I'm also glad God is always there to point me in the right direction. It's so easy in life to go the wrong way or make a wrong turn, yet the Bible tells us God is there to lovingly tell us which way we should go, which is not only good news, but much preferable to a grumpy teacher telling you you're going the wrong way.

<hr />

February 21

Know What You Love, Love What You Know

"For I delight in your commands because I love them.
I lift up my hands to your commands, which I love,
and I meditate on your decrees"
(Psalm 119:47-48).

ASK ME ABOUT SOMETHING I LOVE, and I'll tell you a whole lot about it. Ask me about *Star Wars* (I know, I'm a nerd) and I'll quote it for you. Ask me about the Broncos, I'll let you know all about them (except for when they lose; then I'm pretty quiet). Ask me about my wife, and I'll tell you all about how wonderful and amazing she is. You see, when we love something, we naturally want to know a lot about it. So how do you feel about God's Word? I've realized I don't really love God's Word as much as I ought, or even as much as I pretend. A startling realization, I know, and it's something I'm going to change. I'm not going to be one of those Christians who only read the Bible on Sundays, or one of those Christians who don't read the Bible at all. I want to be one of those Christians who love God's Word so much I meditate on it day and night, can quote it better than *Star Wars*, or know more statistics about it than I know about the Broncos. We say the Bible is the foundation for our lives as Christians, but the truth is many of us don't spend a lot of time getting to know that foundation. For me, it's time to change that. The good news is it's never too late to fall in love with God's Word, and with God, all over again.

February 22

Better to Be Wise Than Smart; Better Still to Be Both

"The fear of the Lord is the beginning of wisdom;
all who follow his precepts have good understanding.
To him belongs eternal praise"
(Psalm 111:10).

A PROFESSOR here at the University of New Mexico has for the past few years studied what parts of our brain make us smart. Whatever part that may be, I'm fairly sure I'm missing out on a large portion of it. I'm excited they're doing the research here because I'm fairly sure if they figure out what parts of our brain make us smart, they'll be able to invent some sort of pill that will give us an easy way to get smarter instead of doing it the traditional way: learning. Being smart is one thing, but being wise is totally different. There won't ever be any medical study that will lead to an easy way to become wise by just taking a pill. The Bible tells us the fear of the Lord is the beginning of wisdom. If you want to be wise, you don't start by learning a lot of nifty quotes from fortune cookies, you start by accepting the fact God knows everything and you don't. That's not always easy for us, but when we take that first step, wisdom inevitably follows as we humbly submit to the loving guidance of God's hand. It's nice to be smart, but even smart people can be unwise. The really good news is that even not-so-smart people, such as myself, can be wise simply by listening to our Almighty God.

February 23
Treasure in a Cereal Box

"The kingdom of heaven is like treasure hidden in a field. When a man found it, he hid it again, and then in all his joy went and sold all he had and bought that field"
(Matthew 13:44).

ONE MORNING as I was eating my chocolaty sweet cereal, I found a Spongebob Squarepants pencil topper in my cereal box that changed color when you made it warm with your hands or when you breathed on it. Now this may sound silly, but I still love getting that kind of stuff in my cereal. In fact, when I do the shopping, I don't buy any cereal that doesn't have some silly little toy in it. Now some may feel that an adult still getting enthusiastic about some plastic trinket in their cereal box is a sign of immaturity, or perhaps other more serious issues. I say it's a sign of a person who still takes joy even in the simple and small things in life. In fact, the good news is God has treasures for us to discover each and every day. The question is how hard are we willing to look for them? Are we willing to set aside our business at various points during the day to enjoy the simple, beautiful blessings God gives us? Are we willing to invest time in studying God's Word, and through prayer, diligently seek out the deeper treasures of having a relationship with Him?

The treasures of God don't come in a cereal box (which is too bad because they'd be a lot easier to find), but they last far longer and are much more useful. That's good news and worth seeking after.

February 24
Never Say Never in Playoffs or Salvation
"This is good, and pleases God our Savior, who wants all men to be saved and to come to a knowledge of the truth"
(1 Timothy 2:3-4).

A FEW YEARS BACK the Colorado Rockies made it into the MLB playoffs for the first time in over twenty years. Now I'm not really a big baseball fan, but the Rockies are from my beloved home state of Colorado, so I couldn't help getting a little excited. It's always exciting when an underdog team in any sport, that no one ever expects to make it, gets to the playoffs. It reminds me that people can be the same way. We can look at certain people and quickly make the judgment they'll never get saved because of such and such a reason. However, that's really saying there are certain people God just doesn't want or even love, and we all know that isn't true. The Bible tells us God doesn't want anyone to be lost, but would love it if everyone would turn to Him and be saved. He loves everyone, and He's entrusted us with the important task of telling people that fact. You know in professional sports there are teams that are just so bad you'll never see them in the playoffs, but isn't it fun when they surprise you? In the same way, we may feel there are certain people who won't ever want to get saved. But how much more exciting is it when we share the good news of God's grace with them anyway and they surprise us by accepting? All the more reason to share the good news with everyone we meet. You just never know.

February 25
Girls, Games, and Talking Trash

"Do not let any unwholesome talk come out of your mouths, but only what is helpful for building others up according to their needs, that it may benefit those who listen"
(Ephesians 4:29).

HAVE YOU EVER HEARD of Trixie from Xbox Gamerchixs? No, well this is a young woman who got fed up with the way women were being treated when playing games online and decided to start a place where girls could play games without being bugged. One of the conditions of joining this community, however, is you can't trash talk about another woman. That's not just when you're playing games online; that's anytime, anywhere. Even when you're not playing games, you have to agree not to trash talk about anyone (badly behaving female celebs included) at anytime. This isn't a Christian club mind you, but I found it fascinating they understood the importance of a very biblical principle, a principle many Christians seem to ignore: speaking nice about each other. Few things make Christians look quite as petty as gossip, and even the Gamerchixs realize talking trash or talking bad about other people doesn't make anything more fun or help people to feel good about themselves. If we truly take what Ephesians says about our words to heart, imagine what sort of impact it would make on our society. Eliminating trash talking is already changing the online gaming world thanks to Gamerchixs. Perhaps it's time we as Christians started changing the world. Wouldn't that be good news?

<hr />

February 26
Letting the Kids Win
"So we say with confidence, 'The Lord is my helper; I will not be afraid. What can man do to me?'"
(Hebrews 13:6).

MY DAD NEVER let me win at games. In fact, he never let anyone win. It didn't matter if it was Candyland, Chutes and Ladders, or Monopoly; if he could win the game, he would. My mom would try to explain to him that some of these games are kids games and the point is to let them win every now and then. But that never seemed to make sense to my dad. If you don't win legit, you don't win. While I have a similar competitive spirit, I still remember how it felt to never be able to win at Candyland, so I've learned it's okay every so often to just let my kids win, and even to help them win (on the sly of course). People have similar opinions about God. There are some who feel that God is someone who's determined to make sure we don't win at life. However, I think God is the kind of indulging father who really wants us to win. In fact, after looking through what God has done for His people all throughout the Bible, I get the impression

He is the type of father who's willing to arrange things so we can win. (He does it subtly in many cases, and in other cases very obviously, such as Jesus on the Cross.) Now that's what I call really good news.

***

February 27
What Freedom Is and Isn't

"So whatever you believe about these things keep between yourself and God. Blessed is the man who does not condemn himself by what he approves"
(Romans 14:22).

"YOU CAN DO WHATEVER YOU WANT as long as it doesn't hurt anyone." "Love means never having to say you're sorry." These are fairly common statements when it comes to most people's perception of what true freedom is, but it's a rather childish way to view freedom. I remember as a kid wanting to be an adult because I thought adults got to do whatever they wanted without anyone telling them what to do. Boy, was I wrong. There's more to freedom than doing what we want, which brings me to Romans 14. This is a passage that's often misused by Christians to defend their behavior. It's their "I can do whatever I want because the Bible says so" verse. You know what this passage is really telling us and why I don't always really like it? It's telling us that sometimes we have to give up our freedoms in order to help others—which I admit I occasionally struggle with. When what we're doing is confusing or problematic for another person, we don't defend that action and keep doing it by saying, "Oh well, Romans 14." No, we're called to surrender that action so we might build others up. I know that doesn't really sound like good news, but when you consider all Jesus Christ gave up on our behalf, any sacrifice we make doesn't really compare. Yes, we are free in Christ, but let's make sure we use that freedom to bring the good news to others and not to indulge our own desires.

February 28
Worshiping God . . . and Elvis?
"No one can serve two masters. Either he will hate the one and love the other, or he will be devoted to the one and despise the other"
(Luke 16:13).

THERE'S A PRIEST in Italy who also happens to be a professional Elvis impersonator. I know that sounds like an odd combination, but according to this priest, there's nothing wrong with worshiping Elvis and God. In fact, he believes because Elvis sang so much about love that makes him an appropriate inspiration for Christian worship. Regardless of how you feel about Elvis, the simple fact of the matter is the Bible is very clear about whether or not we can worship anything or anyone else along with our worship of God. It just can't be done. It's like having two favorite football teams who play against each other and you say you want them both to win. That's not going to happen. There's nothing wrong with being passionate about things like Elvis' music or football, but we need to be careful that the things we love don't crowd out our love for God. We may not have little golden statues lying around our house, but that doesn't mean we aren't idol worshipers. Let's make sure we aren't cluttering our lives with the idols of today's culture: music, celebrities, money, status, careers, electronics, clothes, pastors, or whatever it may be. God wants to be worshiped because He's worthy of our worship. That's not arrogance; it's fact. Nothing in this life can even begin to compare to Him. So save your worship for the only One who's worth worshiping. It'll make your life a lot less complicated, which is always good news.

February 29

Storm Season

*"He got up, rebuked the wind and said to the waves,
'Quiet! Be still!' Then the wind died down and it was
completely calm. He said to his disciples,
'Why are you so afraid? Do you still have no faith?'"*
(Mark 4:39-40).

WHENEVER HURRICANES slam ashore they produce lots of wind, lots of rain, and lots of fear. People often evacuate and prepare for those storms days before they arrive, and, of course, there are also some who decide to stay and ride out the storm. Someone once said Jesus doesn't always calm the storm; sometimes He calms us as we go through the storm. That doesn't sound nearly as miraculous. We'd much rather have Jesus just make the storms of life go away so we don't have to go through them. There have been times in my life when we've had particularly active storm seasons and during them I've seen God do a little bit of both. He's calmed storms and He's calmed me as I go through the storms. While it's nice when the storms are calmed, the truth is I've learned far more when God calms me and I still have to go through the storms. That's when I've grown the most, where I've learned the most, and when I've been better equipped to help others when they face storms in their own lives. Here's the good news: regardless of whether God calms the storm or He calms you as you go through the storm, the result is still exactly the same. God will be with you to make sure you get through to the other side. That's a truth I find to be very good news indeed.

March

He shall come down like rain upon
the grass before mowing,
Like showers that water the earth.

Psalm 72:6

March 1
Reimbursements and Paybacks

"This is love: not that we loved God, but that he loved us and sent his Son as an atoning sacrifice for our sins"
(1 John 4:10).

REIMBURSEMENT IS A FUNNY THING. It's a process in which you spend your own money, but don't care about it as if you're spending your own money, because you'll get reimbursed. My problem is I'm not very financially disciplined, so by the time my reimbursement comes in for the money I originally spent out of my own pocket, I've forgotten it's supposed to pay me back for what I've already spent. I think of the reimbursement as extra money and I spend it on something else. So, technically I'm never really reimbursed because my account is still short the original amount I spent. Yeah, I know that sounds confusing, but I have some good news: we don't need to reimburse God. When He paid the price for our sins, He didn't do it with a reimbursement form in hand, and He didn't do it on an installment plan for us to pay Him back. He paid in full without any expectation of us paying Him back simply because He loves us. And it's a good thing we don't have reimburse Him because we couldn't afford it anyway. So if you're busy trying to fill out a reimbursement form for God, relax. It's totally not necessary. Isn't that good news?

March 2
All Alone in L.A.

"Help, Lord, for the godly are no more;
the faithful have vanished from among men"
(Psalm 12:1).

SPENT A WEEKEND IN L.A. not long ago and it was really lonely. Not just because I missed my family, but because looking at the people there and how they lived I sort of felt the same way David did when he penned this Psalm. Perhaps you've noticed it feels like Christian influence is sorely lacking in our culture, our media, our workplaces, and our schools. In fact, you've probably felt like David did in the Psalm 12 or like I did in L.A., where you feel like you're the only Christian around. Perhaps you feel like everyone else lives they way they want and you're the only one trying to please an Almighty God. Elijah also felt that way right after defeating the prophets of Baal, and when he complained to God that he was the only one left, God told him there were seven thousand others. You see, the good news is whenever we feel alone as Christians in our culture, schools, workplaces, or wherever, we can be sure that we aren't. For one, there are more believers in this world than we realize. Sometimes all we need is to be bold enough to identify ourselves as son or daughter of Christ so others will know who we are. Secondly, God has promised to never leave us or forsake, so even if we were the last believer on Earth, we still wouldn't be alone.

So take heart, my fellow Christians. You are not alone. Isn't that good news?

March 3

Finding the City of Gold

"The wall was made of jasper, and the city of pure gold, as pure as glass"
(Revelation 21:18).

THE CITY OF GOLD. Cortez searched for it. Custer took his last stand trying to find it. It's been the quest of explorers for centuries, and that quest was revived in the 2007 film *National Treasure: Book of Secrets*. It's easy to understand why a treasure like the City of Gold would capture the imagination of so many adventurers, but here's the interesting thing: a city of gold can actually be found . . . by anyone, including you. I know that sounds like a strange thing to say, especially about something like a fabled City of Gold, but it's true. You see, Jesus said He was the way, the truth and the life. Have you ever wondered what He was the way to? Well, in short, He is the way to His city of gold—the New Jerusalem, also known as Heaven. You see, you don't have to follow obscure clues and evade deadly traps to find the city of gold. All you have to do is believe God loved you so much He was willing to sacrifice His only Son to pay the price for your sin because you couldn't. When we accept the gift of redemption and grace, we will find the way to our city of gold. Now, granted that may not sound quite as exciting as something you'd see in *National Treasure*, but it's a whole lot easier this way, and the end result is a discovery that will last for all eternity. That's what I think is really good news, good news we need to share.

* * *

March 4

Inconvenient Truth is Good

"To the Jews who had believed him, Jesus said, 'If you hold to my teaching, you are really my disciples. Then you will know the truth, and the truth will set you free'"
(John 8:31-32).

THE TRUTH HURTS SOMETIMES. I'm sure you've heard that. Well, the fact is that one way you can tell when something is the truth is that it makes you uncomfortable. You see, truth doesn't pander to our every desire in an effort to tell us only what we want to hear. Truth doesn't change to suit our needs; truth reveals what we need to change in order to avoid danger and to mature. For example, the truth is there's a thing called gravity, and it will make you fall if you walk off a cliff. Now that may be inconvenient for you. That may be something that doesn't make you happy because it keeps you from doing and going where you want. But the truth of gravity isn't going to change just to make you feel better. However, once you understand the truth of gravity, you can change and use a hand glider or even a parachute to walk off that cliff and still actually get somewhere without being killed. The truth of the Bible won't always make us feel good, and sometimes it may even upset us. But if we're willing to accept the truth of God's

Word and let it change us, it will not only help us discover true freedom like Christ said, but it will also lead us to eternal life. That's what I call good news.

March 5

Spidey's Brand New Day

"We were therefore buried with him through baptism into death in order that, just as Christ was raised from the dead through the glory of the Father, we too may live a new life"
(Romans 6:4).

AMAZING Spider-Man #546 was a landmark moment in Spidey's career. Granted, you may not really be all that interested in comic books, but the substance of that issue was rather fascinating. It marked the beginning of a "Brand New Day" for Spider-Man. Through some very contrived and controversial events, Spider-Man's world was reset. He was no longer married, a bunch of bad stuff never happened, and some people who were dead were now alive—it was all reset and renewed to give Spidey a fresh start. That's nice. You want to hear some good news? You can have a fresh start too. It won't be quite as magical as Spidey's, things from your past won't magically disappear as if they never happened, but you can experience a brand new day through Jesus Christ. When Jesus died on the Cross and rose from the dead, He made it possible for all of us to start over and enjoy a brighter future. The past may not be gone, but it's forgiven. I can't really say the way Spider-Man was given a new start really works for me. It all seems kind of silly really, but I can tell you that starting over with Jesus Christ works every time, and that new day can last forever. Doesn't that sound like good news?

March 6
Generation X, Y, Z and Then What?
"This is the generation of those who seek Him . . . "
(Psalm 24:6, NASB).

W E'VE HEARD ABOUT GENERATION X, and we've heard about Generation Y. So, what happens after Generation Z? Do we start over at the beginning of the alphabet, or is that one of the signs of Christ's return, that we run out of letters for the generations? This may not seem like a big deal to you, but I'm really concerned about what happens when we run out of letters. I'm hoping someone has thought this through. Of course, more important than what letter your generation happens to be is what your generation will be known for. What will *this* generation be known for? What will Generation Z be known for? As I was reading through the Psalms, I found what I want my generation to be known for, and if my not my generation, it's at least what I want to be known for: that we are a generation who seeks God. Just a brief glimpse shows our nation and our world are in desperate shape. What's it going to take to change it? It's going to take a generation of people who seek God first in their lives. Regardless of whether you're a member of Generation X, Y, or Z, let's all be a generation that seeks God. The result of doing that can only be good news for us all.

March 7
The Holy Spirit is My Caddy
"I will ask the Father, and He will give you another Helper, that He may be with you forever" (John 14:16, NASB).

ONE OF THE GREAT THINGS about the Nintendo Wii is for sports like golf, you actually have to perform the real moves to play the video game version of it. However, seeing as how my golf swing is really not so great, that means I don't do any better at video game golf than I do at real golf. I played one golf game and I had a caddy who was shaped like a paper bag. I'm not sure what that was all about, but I can tell you that he was absolutely no help at all. I thought a golf caddy was supposed to give advice to help you get close to the hole, not look like a sack lunch with a cute bunny face painted on the front. In any event, it got me thinking. Did you know that one of the definitions for sin is to miss the mark? If that's true, then I sinned a whole lot on the back nine in that game because I was definitely missing the mark. However, the good news is when it comes to the game of life, we have a caddy who will actually help us hit the mark. You see, the Holy Spirit is in each one of us who has come to Christ, and He's there to help us avoid sin and embrace holiness. The trick is we have to actually listen to His advice. Having a caddy who will help me get a birdie instead of a bogey is good news any time, and having the Holy Spirit in my life to help me hit the mark instead of miss it is definitely good news. Now all I have to do is listen.

March 8
Going Fast to Slow Down
"But Jesus often withdrew to lonely places and prayed"
(Luke 5:16).

WHAT DO WE NEED TO DO in order to slow down in today's busy world? According to one commercial, in order to slow down in this hectic, fast-paced world what we need is to get some gadgets that are even faster than we are so we can get things done. How does that make sense? Things are moving too fast, so to slow down let's make gadgets that will help us get things done even faster? I don't think that's going to help. In reading through the New Testament one of things I've noticed is despite being a very busy person, Jesus knew the best way to slow down was to take a moment in a quiet place to pray. I know that seems counter-intuitive in the "faster we move, the more we do" type of world we live in. But even our gadgets need to be set down every now and then to re-charge, so why not set ourselves down every now and then to do a little recharging ourselves in the presence of God? In this fast-paced world, moving even faster isn't the solution to finding rest and peace. It's stopping and being still that will help us do more in our busy lives. This sounds like good news to me.

March 9

Wrecks and Restoration

"The Lord sustains all who fall, and raises up all who are bowed down"
(Psalm 145:14, NASB).

"BURNOUT PARADISE" is one of my all-time favorite racing games. In it, you race around the gigantic Paradise City as you try to win events and pull off crazy stunts. The catch is since you're doing this in the city, you have to watch out for traffic or you'll crash, and crash in spectacular fashion. (Actually, half the fun of the game is seeing the crazy wrecks you cause.) Of course, being a video game, after you crash, your car is magically restored and you can continue on your way. Life may not be a video game, but isn't it good news to know whenever we have a wreck God is always there to restore us? Isn't it nice He loves us so much that even when we fail, goof up, or otherwise make a mess of things, He's always willing to help repair the damage and give us a new start? There's no wreck too big, no person too damaged that God's love can't reach out and give them a new start. When we look around at all the wrecked lives in today's world, I hope you realize that's good news we need to share.

March 10

Money Talk

"Provide purses for yourselves that will not wear out, a treasure in heaven that will not be exhausted, where no thief comes near and no moth destroys"
(Luke 12:33).

THIS PASSAGE FROM LUKE took on new meaning during the recent economic turmoil. As the Dow has bounced up and down and the economy lagged overall, people worried a lot about money. Some worried about the thousands they lost in the stock market, and some worried the economic help from the government wouldn't come soon enough. Apparently it didn't seem odd to anyone else that our solution to the economy's woes was to go into debt to give money to people to help them go into debt. With all of that money talk, it's easy for us to forget what's truly valuable. We worry about losing what's temporary instead worrying about storing up that which is eternal. The good news is the treasures we store in Heaven are completely unaffected by housing slumps, rising oil prices, an unpredictable Wall Street, or even recession. Our treasures in Heaven are everlasting. So instead of concern about your investments here on Earth (although we certainly should be wise about those), let's make sure we don't forget to invest in economy of Heaven. How do you do that? Go share the good news of salvation with someone today. In times of bad economic news, it may be the best thing they've heard all week.

March 11

Where Do You Put Your Trust?

"To you, O Lord, I lift up my soul; in you I trust, O my God"
(Psalm 25:1-2).

TRUST IS EASILY BROKEN. I'm sure you've noticed that. Many people have trusted in the American economy, which has faltered in recent years and cost people money instead of making them money. Some people trusted their four-wheel drive SUVs to get them to work on icy mornings here in Albuquerque, New Mexico (which don't occur very often). But ice is still ice no matter how many wheel drives you have and there are always plenty of accidents on those mornings. Perhaps you've trusted a specific person for fulfillment and comfort, only to find they're human and therefore will eventually let you down. It's no wonder we live in such a jaded, cynical society. So many of the things we put our trust in only end up being untrustworthy. Fortunately, I have good news: trust in God will never disappoint you. God is the only One we can trust and be sure our trust won't be broken. So let's be like David in his Psalm and lift up our souls to God and trust Him knowing He will never let us down.

March 12

Suing the Dead

"But he said to me, 'My grace is sufficient for you, for my power is made perfect in weakness'"
(2 Corinthians 12:9).

A BUSINESSMAN IN SPAIN was driving his luxury car a little too fast when he hit and killed a young man on a bike. However, in an obscene twist to this tragic story, the Spanish businessman ended up suing the family of the dead boy to pay for the damage done by the boy's body to his luxury car. It's the type of story that almost makes you want to secede from the human race. Sadly, some people treat God the same way. We killed God's Son, or at least our sin killed Him and is the reason He died. Yet, God doesn't hold us responsible. In fact, He wants to make us a part of His family. Jesus Christ willingly died for us, stepped in front of the oncoming vehicle of our sin, and paid the price we could never pay. It's an amazing gift, and yet some still feel God owes them something more—money or success or instant gratification. It's almost as if they feel the same way as that Spanish businessman: you got in my way and caused problems, therefore you owe me. The fact is God doesn't owe us anything. We owe Him, but He doesn't ask us to pay. All I know is this: Jesus died for me so I wouldn't have to die for my sins, and all He asks in return is my love and devotion. If that's all I were to ever receive from God, it would be far more than I deserve, and more than I could ever ask. That's grace, that's all I need, and that's good news.

March 13

Rely On What's Really Reliable

"Who among you fears the Lord and obeys the word of his servant? Let him who walks in the dark, who has no light, trust in the name of the Lord and rely on his God"
(Isaiah 50:10).

THE BIBLE SAYS our God heals, yet we usually rely on medicines that have gone through clinical tests. The Bible says our God protects, yet we usually rely on the advice of warning labels to know what's really dangerous. The Bible says our God provides, yet we usually rely on what's happening with the Dow or the hope of winning the lottery to take care of our needs. What's my point? All I'm saying is that in my own life, I've noticed a pattern in that I say I trust and rely on God, but when I examine my actions they reveal that what I really rely on are things I believe are more tangible and substantial. To be honest, I was shocked that I thought this way and realized it was kind of silly. Am I really going to believe the stock market is more reliable than an Almighty God? Am I really going to trust medicine more than an all-powerful God? Am I really going to rely on anything more than an all-knowing God? I'm not saying doctors and savings accounts and home security systems or any of that is bad; they can be quite helpful. All I'm saying is I need to be more careful about believing what I can see and touch as being more reliable than the God I say I love. God keeps His promises. God does what He says. And best of all, God loves me, and He loves you. That's why he's so reliable and trustworthy. In our uncertain world, that's good news.

March 14
The (Almost) Perfect Super Bowl
"Be perfect, therefore, as your heavenly Father is perfect"
(Matthew 5:48).

PERFECTION DOESN'T COME EASY. The New England Patriots discovered that in the memorable Super Bowl XLII as they watched their perfect season disappear with a gutsy, determined win by the New York Giants. Now the Patriots are a part of history as a team that fell one game away from perfection. If perfection is that difficult to attain in sports, how could Jesus ever expect us to do better in real life; especially when we have an opposing force like Satan and all of his minions determined to keep us from perfection? The answer is He doesn't expect us to do it at all. He expects us to let Him do all the work in us through His Holy Spirit. Granted, completely surrendering yourself to someone else isn't all that easy either, but if we are to have any hope of being perfected, it's the only way we'll ever achieve it. Perfection is a lofty goal, both in life and professional sports, and it's a goal most will never attain. That's why I find it good news to know I don't have to try and get there on my own; I can let Christ take care of that for me. The trick is to remain in

Christ and never try to do it on our own, because once we start trying to be perfect in our own strength, we'll end up just like the New England Patriots of Super Bowl XLII. Close, but not quite there.

March 15
A Time of Devotion

"In the morning, O Lord, you hear my voice; in the morning I lay my requests before you and wait in expectation"
(Psalm 5:3).

WHAT DO YOU DEVOTE YOUR TIME TO? I'll be honest, I devote a lot of time to video games and as a result I'm pretty good at them. (I want to make sure that I'm always better than my kids when it comes to video games.) I also devote a lot of time to reading and as a result I know a lot of useless but amusing stuff, which you'd think would make me very popular at parties, but I never get invited to any parties so I wouldn't know. We all devote time to things like school, sports, careers, families, or hobbies, so whether we admit it or not, we know what a devotion time is like. I've heard from several different sources about how important my devotion time is with God. We need Him, His power and presence, and most importantly His love and grace in our lives, but we'll only get that through time devoted to Him. And let's not be silly and try to deceive ourselves by saying we don't have the time to devote to Him. That's a lie. I like being good at video games and basketball, so I don't mind devoting time to them. But what I really need to be good at is following Christ. I like knowing things, so I don't mind reading. But what I really need to know is Jesus and His Word. The good news is, the more time I devote to Him, the better I'll know Him, and the bigger my impact will be on the world around me.

March 16

The Secret to True Beauty

"Know that the Lord is God. It is he who made us, and we are his; we are his people, the sheep of his pasture"
(Psalm 100:3).

WAS LOOKING through the CNN.com news site when an article caught my eye. I didn't even really read through the article itself, it was just the title that I found fascinating. The article was entitled "Stars Expose Who Makes Them Beautiful." I think it's pretty bold for celebrities to admit it takes the efforts of someone else to make them beautiful and they're not effortlessly beautiful. That's like a magician revealing how he does his tricks. Still, the point is it takes the work of someone else to make us beautiful. Hairstylists and fashion advisers, even plastic surgeons can only make you beautiful on the outside. Jesus pointed out it's what's on the inside that reveals who we really are. If you really want to be beautiful, you don't need an exterior makeover, you need an interior makeover, and only the Holy Spirit can make that happen. The sad fact of the matter is no matter how hard you work, or how much money you spend to have other people make you look beautiful, eventually that beauty will fade. When the

Holy Spirit comes in to your life, the beauty He brings with Him will last for all eternity, and that's good news. So the question truly is: Who makes you beautiful?

March 17
The Reality of Dragons
"No one is fierce enough to rouse him. Who then is able to stand against me?"
(Job 41:10).

HAVE YOU EVER WONDERED whether or not dragons were real? Think about it; just about every region of the planet has some sort of dragon mythology, just like they all have some sort of flood mythology. We all know the biblical flood was real, so what about dragons? Plus, God compares himself to a creature that sounds a lot like a dragon in Job 41, and I've never really been able to understand why a real God would use a fake creature for an illustration of His real power. Regardless of whether or not the creature is a real dragon, a creature from Canaanite mythology, or just a crocodile, the fact of the matter is God is fierce and powerful, and that's good news. I know we prefer a tame God, but that's just not in His character. The reason it's good news for our God to be ferocious and untamed is because that means we can be sure He's bigger, more powerful, and fiercer than any power or any challenge that may come against us. Even when we don't understand what's happening in our lives, we can be sure the God we serve has the situation well in hand. I think it would be cool if dragons were real creatures, but I find it far cooler to know my God is not only a real God, but He's far more powerful and fierce than any creature to have ever walked the Earth. And He loves me.

March 18

What's Wrong With Perfect?

"It is God who arms me with strength and makes my way perfect"
(Psalm 18:32).

READ A BOOK some time ago where the author suggested the main problem with Christians today is we have our halos on too tight. This author believed Christians are too righteous, too good, and too perfect to be relatable to ordinary, everyday sinners. In order to be more approachable, Christians should adjust their halos so they're just a little crooked. I personally found that to be one of the stupidest things I've ever heard. Granted, Christians can be pretty annoying when they're legalistically holier than thou, but the solution isn't to behave in an unabashedly worldly fashion knowing God's grace will cover it. Some believe Jesus told us to be perfect like God to demonstrate we can never do that on our own. But that doesn't mean we shouldn't try. Being a disciple of Christ means learning to be like Christ, and the good news is as we do that, we will slowly be perfected by Him. As for being too perfectly righteous and therefore unrelatable to people, Jesus was perfectly righteous and yet sinners flocked to Him and wanted to be around Him. Righteous perfection doesn't scare sinners; it piques their curiosity and draws them to the good news of salvation. Don't be a "holier than thou" Christian, because they are pretty annoying, but be a Christian who is trying every day to live more and more like the perfect example of righteousness we see in Christ by the power of the Holy Spirit.

March 19
Hot, Cold and In Between

"I know your deeds, that you are neither cold nor hot. I wish you were either one or the other! So, because you are lukewarm—neither hot nor cold—I am about to spit you out of my mouth"
(Revelation 3:15-16).

DO YOU KNOW what the second most common complaint in the office is? The office is too hot. Do you know what the most common complaint is? The office is too cold. Those are the two things complained about most in the office, but when it comes to our lives, Jesus Christ has a different complaint: you're not hot, you're not cold, you're just *meh* . . . also known as lukewarm. Part of the problem is our society is very much a "good enough is good" enough type of society. We thrive in mediocrity. Businesses hire fancy PR firms to produce slick ads that give a look of excellence to what they do, but let's be honest, most of us are content to do just enough to get the job done and no more. It's time for Christians to set the pace when it comes to excellence. From the work we do to our studies at school even to our worship and Bible study, it's time we set the bar higher for doing the absolute best we can. Quite frankly, I can't think of better compliment than to have people complain I'm too hot in my passion for Christ. I think that would be very good news, and it's certainly better than Christ wanting to spit me out because of my mediocrity.

March 20
Missing Without a Trace?

What do you think? If a man owns a hundred sheep, and one of them wanders away, will he not leave the ninety-nine on the hills and go to look for the one that wandered off? And if he finds it, I tell you the truth, he is happier about that one sheep than about the ninety-nine that did not wander off. In the same way your Father in heaven is not willing that any of these little ones should be lost.
(Matthew 18:12-14)

WITHOUT A TRACE was a popular television show about the FBI's search for missing people. At the end of one particular show, the main character was asked what kept him going in such a tough job. He thought about it a moment and then said it was the people they got back, but there didn't seem to be enough of them anymore. Take a look around you. How many of the people you see are missing people? How many of them are the missing children of God? Jesus said our heavenly Father is not willing for any of them to be lost, but I'm sure He sometimes feels like the main character on *Without a Trace*: there just aren't enough of them being found. The good news is that it can be changed. The good news is that God's missing children are far easier to find than the missing people the FBI is searching for. The good news is we can bring them home and celebrate with the Father over those who were lost but now are found because of our efforts. The question is: Are you willing to put in the time to look for, find, and rescue God's missing children?

March 21
Talking About What You Know

"I am angry with you and your two friends, because you have not spoken of me what is right . . ."
(Job 42:7).

IT NEVER CEASES to amaze me how much useless information we acquire during our lives. We know stats about our favorite teams and players, we know facts about our favorite celebrities, we know things about our favorite games, or even our favorite periods in history, but how much do we know about God? Although we say as Christians we love God, how often do we treat Him as one of our favorite people—one of those favorite people we know everything about? Some Christians try to fake it so they can at least look like a good Christian, but do we really want to talk about God if we don't really know Him? God didn't seem too happy with Job's friends when they spoke about Him as if they knew what they were talking about—when they really didn't. The good news, however, is we can know God. We can know Him better than any celebrity or sports star. We can know all about Him, and that's knowledge that isn't useless. If we're going to talk about God let's make sure we talk about Him knowledgably like we do about our favorite anything. Besides, when we speak accurately about God, others will want to hear more about this good news that we know all about.

March 22

What Is a Hero?

"The reason my Father loves me is that I lay down my life—only to take it up again. No one takes it from me, but I lay it down of my own accord. I have authority to lay it down and authority to take it up again"
(John 10:17-18).

WHAT IS A HERO? The 2007 movie *Beowulf* seems to believe true heroism lies within one's own power. In fact, this film went so far as to suggest that the Christ God was responsible for the extinction of true heroes. Because of the Christ God, men were no longer bold and fierce and courageous, but in the words of one character, "They have become nothing more than whimpering, weeping martyrs, full of shame." That's one of the dumbest thing I've ever heard. You want to know what true courage, true heroism is? Read the gospels. There has never been a more courageous or heroic act than the sacrifice of Jesus Christ on the Cross for our sin. He was innocent, we were not, and yet He chose to die on our behalf that we might be saved. If that isn't heroic bravery, I don't know what is. More than that, Jesus also chose, through His own power, to take up His life again and thereby defeat death forever. If that isn't strength—being able to conquer death—then I don't know what is. The fact of the matter is there is no hero, real or fictional, that can ever come close to the power, courage, and bravery of Jesus Christ and His heroism on the Cross. The good news is He can be your hero. In fact, He would very much like to be your hero because everything He did, everything He suffered, He did not for glory or to be written about in songs and legends. No, He did what He did because He loves you so very much. That is heroism with heart that Beowulf will never understand.

March 23

Your Life on Display Like a Float in a Parade

**"Serve the Lord with fear, and rejoice with trembling"
(Psalm 2:11).**

A FEW YEARS BACK people here in New Mexico weren't too happy with the design choice for the state's float entry in the Tournament of Roses of Parade. The float design featured a spaceport and aliens flying through in a UFO. According to a poll in the *Albuquerque Journal*, 62 percent of New Mexicans resented the fact that little green men were chosen to represent New Mexico in a nationally televised parade. The whole debate brought to my mind a very important question. What are you known for? When people think of you, what do they say? People might say of me that I play basketball, I love video games, and I know a lot of useless, obscure information. That all may be true, but what I really hope people notice about me is that I love

God. This Psalm tells us to serve God with fear and joy. That's what I hope represents my life. Granted, I'm not going to be in a parade, but it's still important for me to occasionally examine how I represent myself and especially how I represent God. Why? Because I may be the only way some people get know God. I may be the only way someone hears the good news. You may not be a float in a parade, but make no mistake; you are on display, especially if you claim to follow Christ. That can either be good news or bad. It's your choice.

March 24
Feeling Tired? Want a Solution?

"But those who hope in the Lord will renew their strength. They will soar on wings like eagles; they will run and not grow weary, they will walk and not be faint"
(Isaiah 40:31).

WE LEAD BUSY LIVES, which often leads to us feeling pretty wiped out . . . all the time. In fact, four out of every thousand Americans suffers from chronic fatigue syndrome, many of them without even realizing it because they don't recognize the symptoms. I don't think I have chronic fatigue syndrome, but I am busy and I do feel tired quite often. If you're like me you want to know if there's a solution to that tired feeling. I was in church when the answer swatted me upside the head. It was one of those *duh!* moments where a Scripture you've heard all the time suddenly has real relevance for your life. Isaiah tells us that if we'll hope, wait, and trust in the Lord (depending on which translation you read), we will run and not grow weary. Isn't that good news? It's possible for us to not be weary, but in order to do so, we need to slow down and trust and wait on the Lord. Waiting isn't easy in today's busy society. Trust and hope seem too nebulous in a culture that's more reliant on fact. There's no denying that life today is busy, but there's also no reason for me to be constantly weary . . . if my hope and trust is in the Lord and I wait on Him. I find that to be really good news.

<hr />

March 25
Breakfast Cereal and Free Grace

"For all have sinned and fall short of the glory of God, and are justified freely by his grace through the redemption that came by Christ Jesus"
(Romans 3:23-24).

WAS EATING MY BREAKFAST CEREAL one morning and reading the back of my cereal box, which had one of those so-called free offers. Have you ever looked closely at those? It says whatever little trinket it's offering is free, but you have to have three hundred and ninety two proofs of purchase to send in to get the "free" trinket. I'm pretty sure buying all that cereal costs way more than a little piece of plastic that makes a funny noise. Here's the good news: God's grace really is free. You don't have to collect anything, you don't have to do anything, you don't have to pay anything. Jesus Christ paid the price with His death and Resurrection. I think sometimes we forget that. We try to collect proofs of purchase to turn in to God so we can get *free grace.*

God doesn't need nor want our box tops—be they good works, charity, perfect attendance at church, or whatever they may be. All He wants is to love us and for us to love Him back. Funny how an offer on the back of my breakfast cereal can remind me just how good the good news really is. Now I need to go and share that good news.

March 26
Expect the Unexpected

"And we know that God causes all things to work together for good to those who love God, to those who are called according to His purpose"
(Romans 8:28, NASB).

IFE DOESN'T ALWAYS GO AS PLANNED. Maybe you've noticed that. Whether it's a trip with unexpected delays, a pop-quiz you're not prepared for, or a guest canceling at the last minute for a radio show that you host. (Well, maybe that hasn't happened to you, but it's happened to me.) If there's one thing that's certain in life, it's that life is uncertain. The question is what will we do about it? When the unexpected happens, when life doesn't go as planned, how will we respond? There are some who think that as a Christian everything should be magically and miraculously fixed to be exactly the way we want it, and let's be honest, we're usually pretty disappointed when that doesn't happen. But if life always went the way we wanted it to, we'd never have a chance to grow and never have a chance to exercise our faith. There are two things we can be sure of: God is far bigger than any mess and any unexpected circumstance in life, and His plans always work out according to His design. So, when we pursue His plans, and when we face the unexpected and the unplanned in our lives, we can be sure God will bring something good out those situations. Doesn't that sound like good news to you?

March 27
The Sherpas of Our Lives
"Carry each other's burdens, and in this way you will fulfill the law of Christ"
(Galatians 6:2).

IF YOU EVER CLIMB the Himalayan mountains (not sure how many of you are planning on doing this, but just in case), odds are that you'll hire a Sherpa to help guide you and carry some of your gear. For many decades, these Tibetan people have helped travelers attempting to scale the mountain as guides and porters. Although you don't see the word used in the Bible, Sherpa is a good way to describe how we ought to treat one another. We ought to be each other's Sherpas. One of the things I've been most grateful for when it comes to my family and the people I work with is the fact I know I'll never have to carry any burden alone. I'll always have people around me ready to help me carry that burden, and I would do the same for them. But that's not the good news. The good news is we can help others carry their burdens because Jesus Christ is willing to carry ours. We're told to cast all of our anxiety on Him because He cares for us, but that's not just so we can live a worry-free life. It's so we'll be free to help each other by being

Sherpas to our fellow believers and to those who need to hear the good news.

March 28

All About Love

"And so we know and rely on the love God has for us. God is love. Whoever lives in love lives in God, and God in him" (1 John 4:16).

THERE'S A LOT OF CONFUSION about what love really is today. Some confuse love for lust. Some confuse love for sex. Some confuse love for wanting a cute puppy dog. The point is, not everyone knows what love really is. There's a sure-fire way for you to discover true love, and you don't even need an account on Match.com. If you want to know love, get to know God. When you do that, you'll be able to test every other relationship against your relationship with Him in order to tell if it's truly love or something else. You may be surprised to know that the Bible actually has the ultimate love test (that's right, all those magazines didn't come up with the idea on their own). Look at 1 Corinthians 13. See if what you're feeling fits the criteria of being patient, kind, not envying or boasting or being rude or self-seeking or easily angered or . . . well, read it for yourself and take the test. The good news is we can know love because we can know God. And we can know God because Jesus Christ paved the way for us with His death and Resurrection. Which, when you think about it, was the ultimate expression of love and therefore the best way to learn what love really is.

March 29

Get Some Satisfaction

"I know that there is nothing better for men than to be happy and do good while they live. That everyone may eat and drink, and find satisfaction in all his toil—this is the gift of God" (Ecclesiastes 3:12-13).

ACCORDING TO A SURVEY by Career Builder.com, around 25 to 30 percent of people are not happy with their jobs. I can certainly identify with that . . . not because of the job I'm doing now, but because of some of my previous jobs. As I look back, however, I realize I didn't really have any reason to be unhappy. After all, God was providing for my family through steady work, I had the opportunity to share Christ with many of my co-workers, and, in general, I was given the opportunity by God to set an example as a faithful employee. The more I look back on my previous jobs, the more I realize what a blessing they were. Here's the good news: God wants us to have satisfaction in whatever we do, but the only way we can do that is when we focus less on ourselves and more on Him. No matter what your job is, or what your studies for school are, when you toil for the Lord you're much more likely to find satisfaction.

March 30

Welcomed Home by Dad

"But while he was still a long way off, his father saw him and was filled with compassion for him; so he ran to his son, threw his arms around him and kissed him"
(Luke 15:20).

A FEW YEARS BACK I can vividly remember seeing a picture of a soldier in the morning paper holding his two-month-old baby for the very first time. Sometimes I think it's easy to forget the personal and emotional cost of having troops deployed overseas, but when we see a picture of a father holding his child who was born while he wasn't home, it's a vivid reminder of that cost. As I looked at that picture, I wondered how God would feel when He finally gets to hold His kids. I mean, when we come to Christ, the Bible says we become the children of God. Yet as long as we're in this world, we are away from our heavenly Father. Some feel that when they get to Heaven God will be busy going over all the wrong they did and everything they should have done better. I don't get that impression. In fact, if anything, I think when we get to Heaven God will have the same reaction that any loving father would have when finally seeing his child for the first time. I believe He won't be able to contain himself, but will rush up to us, hold us, hug us, and whisper with such gentle kindness, "Welcome home, my beloved child." How I ache and yearn for that day whenever I think about it. But I know until that day comes, there are a lot of people who need to know God will welcome them in the same way, and that really is good news.

March 31

A Lesson Learned

"When Jesus landed and saw a large crowd, he had compassion on them and healed their sick"
(Matthew 14:14).

WHEN MY DAUGHTER was just five years old, I received a humbling lesson from her in having childlike faith and Christ-like compassion. We were at the grocery store and as we were walking in, we saw a man on crutches with a huge cast on his leg. I noted it and moved on with my tasks, but my daughter kept looking at him. Finally, she asked my wife if she could pray for the man. My wife explained that we need to wait for the Holy Spirit to tell us when and who to pray for, but my daughter insisted that He did. So we let her go up to the man with the broken leg and ask if she could pray for him. The man said this was the first time in his life anyone ever asked that, and he was so touched my daughter wanted to do that for him. So she prayed that he would be healed, and then we went and finished our grocery shopping. I don't know what happened to that man. I believe he was healed and that his life was forever changed by the compassion and child-like faith of one little girl. The lesson I learned was that I've slowly stopped viewing the world with Christ-like compassion, that I've stopped seeing and feeling the needs of this desperate world. But, praise God,

He used my daughter to remind me of what I should really be doing with my every day—sharing the good news of Christ's compassion and love.

April

Then He also said to the multitudes,
"Whenever you see a cloud rising out
of the west, immediately you say,
'A shower is coming'; and so it is."

Luke 12:54

April 1
Extreme Foolish Makeover

*"The LORD appeared to us in the past, saying: '
I have loved you with an everlasting love;
I have drawn you with loving-kindness'"*
(Jeremiah 31:3).

OKAY, THIS IS JUST PATHETIC. A woman in China recently underwent surgery so she could look more like Jessica Alba in order to get her boyfriend back. Apparently he constantly hinted that he wished she looked more like the actress, and the Alba obsession eventually became so intense she dumped him. However, this woman missed her boyfriend so much, she went through plastic surgery anyway to look like Jessica Alba and get her boyfriend back. So, for those of you taking notes, let me point out this isn't true love. Anyone who loves you should love you for who you are, not who they want you to be. Now, I know we all want to feel loved, and it's nice to have a "someone"—a boyfriend, girlfriend, husband, or wife. However, don't ever forget the fact that God loves you. God loves you the way you are. God loves you for who you are. God loves you so much He died for you. God doesn't want you to be anyone but who He made you to be. If you want love, turn to God, because if God's love can't satisfy you, no one's love will. You don't want to end up doing something foolish like making yourself look like someone That's just the shallow affection from someone who couldn't appreciate you for who you are.

April 2
It Never Hurts to Talk

"Be wise in the way you act toward outsiders; make the most of every opportunity"
(Colossians 4:5).

ONCE READ A STORY about how a woman led another woman to Christ when she simply sat next to her on a bench at the zoo. After sitting down, they started talking and they ended up praying for the woman to receive Christ. We hear stories like that and we often think, "Wow, that's amazing, nothing like that ever happens to me." Really? Not Ever? As I thought about that story, I realized something important: the woman didn't really do anything special. She didn't share four spiritual laws or the original Greek of a verse or an apologetic analysis. She simply sat down and started talking with someone. How many times do we pass by somebody without talking to them? We think leaving a gospel tract as we hurry off to our next pressing appointment is evangelism. But is it? People need to know that Jesus cares, and the only way they'll know that is if those of us who represent Him are willing to sit down and talk with them, learn about them, and find out what their needs are. Would you like to share the good news? Talk to the person next to you. You may be surprised where the conversation leads.

April 3
Do Gods Retire?

"Jesus Christ is the same yesterday and today and forever"
(Hebrews 13:8).

NOT LONG AGO an eleven-year-old girl in Nepal who was revered as a living goddess, decided to retire. It's never occurred to me before that gods or goddesses could retire. What sort of retirement benefits do you suppose they have for that kind of gig? Do they get Social Security? Is there a *retirement for eternity* option as part of their 401k or IRA, assuming of course that all gods and goddesses are immortal? Seriously, I found it rather depressing to learn that a goddess could retire, which means the people in Nepal had to scramble to find someone to replace her. Isn't it good news to know our God never retires? Isn't it nice to know He's been on the job since before time began, and that He'll continue to be on the job long after time has ceased? Best of all, He does His job because He loves you. That's right; the God of the entire universe will never retire, will never quit, and will never "go in a different direction," all because He loves you. To know God loves me so much that He would never even think of retiring is what I call very good news.

April 4
Confessions of a Bad Driver
"For it is God who works in you to will and to act
according to his good purpose"
(Philippians 2:13).

HAVE A CONFESSION TO MAKE: I'm an annoying driver. I don't always obey speed limits, sometimes I cut off other drivers, and other times I purposely do irritating things to other drivers (usually because they did something dumb or did something irritating to me first). This driving behavior of mine used to be very embarrassing to my wife. Well, it still is, but not as much as it used to be. You see, we used to have a Jesus fish on our car, and it embarrassed my wife when I would do some not-very-Christian-things in a car that had a Christian symbol. Now obviously the correct solution wasn't to remove the symbol so I could get away with stuff—and that's not what happened. Somebody stole it. Still, the issue isn't whether or not our cars have Christian symbols or we wear Christian symbols and therefore should be careful how we act. The issue is that Christ lives in us as Christians and therefore our entire lives should be a Christian symbol—we should look and act like Christ. I admit my behavior when driving should change, regardless of whether or not my car has a Jesus fish. The good news is that by the grace of God I can change. In fact, we all can change and be more like Christ by letting the Holy Spirit do His perfecting work in us. After all, our lives and the way we act will often be the only way many people will ever be introduced to the good news. So drive carefully.

———⋅◦•◦⋅———⋅◦•◦⋅———

April 5

Here Today, Gone Tomorrow ... Maybe

"Just as man is destined to die once, and after that to face judgment, so Christ was sacrificed once to take away the sins of many people ... "
(Hebrews 9:27-28).

AS IF WE DON'T have enough to worry about, scientists are now telling us that Earth may be in the line of fire of a binary star system that's about to go supernova. If that happens, the system could send out an intense beam of focused gamma rays that would turn everyone on Earth into the Incredible Hulk. Just kidding. Actually, those gamma rays could destroy up to half our ozone layer, exposing the Earth to much more of the deadly space radiation it's normally protected from. While all of this is a concern, what's more of a concern is whether you know where you're going to go when you die. (Whether it's from a supernova blast of gamma radiation or from being hit by a bus.) What about your neighbors: do they know? Of all the crucial decisions in life, this is one we only get one chance to get right. We can either go to our death uncertain of what happens, or we can go to our death with the secure knowledge that Christ paid the price for our sin on the Cross and made the way for us to enjoy eternal life through His Resurrection. Do you know people who are unsure about what happens after death? Don't keep them in suspense. Share the good news with them. We may have hundreds of thousands of years before a supernova irradiates the Earth, but I guarantee someone you know will not have that many tomorrows.

April 6
Talking Smack

"Therefore, as it is written:
'Let him who boasts boast in the Lord'"
(1 Corinthians 1:31).

SPRING IS IN THE AIR; can you feel it? I love the spring because it means it's basketball time. It means the weather's finally nice enough and warm enough to lace up my sneakers and hit the courts. I love basketball, but unfortunately the sport does involve a certain amount of smack talk, especially when you play on the street like I do. Smack talk is the intellectual side of the game where you try to intimidate your opponent with bravado and boastful words. No, it's not very Christ-like, but I must admit I have occasionally given in to the habit of talking smack and boasting on the basketball court. Although smack talk is more prominent on the basketball court, I think we could all admit to being boastful at times, to talking a little bit of smack every now and then. The question is: What are we boasting in? If we boast in anything other than the Lord, all of our smack talk is really nothing but empty talk. There's nothing we've done that's really worth boasting about because in comparison to eternity, all of our accomplishments are meaningless. However, when we boast in the Lord and what He has done in our lives and through our lives, well, then we're boasting about something that's eternal. So whether it's on the basketball court at school or in the corporate world, let's not boast about ourselves, but rather boast in the Lord. It may be exactly the good news someone we know needs to hear.

April 7

The Seriousness of Sin

"Therefore, my brothers, I want you to know that through Jesus the forgiveness of sins is proclaimed to you"
(Acts 13:38).

NOT LONG AGO the Vatican added some new sins to the list of deadly ones that people should avoid. Among the new entries were ruining the environment and performing morally debatable scientific experiments. The Pope said he was concerned about the "decreasing sense of sin" in today's world. Some probably felt this expansion of the list of deadly sins a rather severe move by the Vatican, but I think we could all agree that sin isn't treated nearly as seriously as it should be in today's society. Let's never forget God takes sin very seriously. No matter what the offense is, big or small, sin is a grievous offense to God, and we're all guilty of it. The good news, however, is God also provided a way for us to be free from sin. Sin was such a serious problem God had to sacrifice His one and only Son to pay the price for it, and yet He did so because He loves us so much. Better yet, Jesus didn't stay dead. He arose in victory so not only can we be free from sin, but we can also enjoy eternal life. During the Easter season, let's never forget just how serious, how wretched sin really is. Let's also never forget the good news—in Jesus Christ God took care of the serious problem of sin.

April 8
Dwelling on the Problem of God's Love

" . . . And I pray that you, being rooted and established in love, may have power, together with all the saints, to grasp how wide and long and high and deep is the love of Christ . . . "
(Ephesians 3:17-18).

ONE MORNING as I rolled out of bed and began my quiet time, I had an interesting thought: "God loves me more than I'll ever love Him." I'm not sure why this thought flashed across my mind, but I wasn't able to think about anything else that entire day. I really struggled to understand what it meant. At first, I felt sad and guilty because I knew it was true; I would never really love God as much as He loves me. I thought maybe I should do something about it and force myself to love Him more. But, then again, when love is obligatory it isn't really love. Slowly, it dawned on me what an amazing thing it is that God loves me so very much. In fact, because He loves me more than I'll ever love Him, my feelings slowly turned from sad to something to glad. What an amazing gift, what a wonderful feeling to know I'm so loved by God. Eventually, I realized the reason I should want to love Him more is because He already loves me more than I'll ever know. And you know what? He loves you just the same. That's good news—and definitely worth dwelling on.

April 9
The Challenge of Forgiveness

"Bear with each other and forgive whatever grievances you may have against one another. Forgive as the Lord forgave you"
(Colossians 3:13).

'M LEARNING A LOT ABOUT FORGIVENESS. It's funny, because as a Christian I thought I understood forgiveness pretty well. As I've found out, however, that's not entirely the case. I've discovered there's a lot more to forgiveness than just the trite *forgive and forget.* I think if we were all honest, we'd admit to having trouble with forgiveness from time to time. There are lots of reasons why we might feel like we can't forgive someone or we shouldn't forgive someone. In fact, the number one misconception I've had to deal with when it comes to forgiveness is that it's what we offer when someone is sorry. That's not necessarily true. In fact, forgiveness is something we need to do even when the other person *isn't* sorry. After all, that's what Christ did for us when He died on the Cross. He didn't wait for someone to say sorry before He prayed " . . . forgive them." He didn't wait for the world to apologize for sin before He offered himself as a sacrifice for sin. No, He died and rose again to forgive us, then left it up to us to accept that forgiveness. When the Bible says we need forgive like the Lord, that's what it's talking about. It may not be easy, but when we forgive like Christ forgave us, it's just one more way we can demonstrate the good news.

April 10

Hearing Voices

"Then I heard the voice of the Lord saying, 'Whom shall I send? And who will go for us?' and I said, 'Here am I, send me!'"
(Isaiah 6:8).

HAVE YOU EVER told someone that God spoke to you? Depending on who you're talking to, you may get a sympathetic nod, a confused look, or a submission slip to a psych ward. For whatever reason, it's not considered normal to hear from God. In fact, if you dare claim to hear from God, you may get treated the same as Horton in *Horton Hears a Who*. Many of Horton's fellow jungle creatures didn't treat Horton very nicely when he claimed that he could hear the desperate cries of all the Whos in Whoville, but that didn't stop Horton from caring or listening. Just like Horton, we shouldn't stop listening to God just because the idea of God speaking to people makes others uncomfortable. The good news is God does still speak, and He wants to speak to you. Our choices are to either refuse to listen so other people won't think we're weird, or not worry about what other people think. Let's just enjoy the fact that a loving God wants to have relationship with us and talk to us on a daily basis.

April 11

Counting the Birthdays

**"Teach us to number our days aright,
that we may gain a heart of wisdom"
(Psalm 90:12).**

TODAY IS MY BIRTHDAY. Assuming I live to the average age of seventy-something that most Americans reach, I've already lived over half my life . . . which is kind of astounding . . . and a bit depressing. Everyone has different feelings about birthdays; some really like them, some really don't. Me, I guess it depends on the year. This year I've been fairly neutral as I've tried to decide if I'm numbering my days aright, if I'm truly making the most of every day God has given me to serve Him. We each have a set amount of time to do what God has called us to do, and birthdays give us a chance to evaluate just how well we've done as we check off one less year we have to accomplish our tasks. However you look at it, the fact that God wants to use each and every one of us to do the work of His Kingdom is a pretty amazing privilege; and it's a privilege I've come to appreciate more and more each year of my life. Am I numbering my days aright? I hope so. I really want to. After all, I want my days to count for something in eternity. And the fact God wants to help me do that each year I'm alive is definitely good news. So, happy birthday . . . to me, and to all of you.

April 12
Multiplying Like Rabbits
**"As for you, be fruitful and increase in number;
multiply on the earth and increase upon it"
(Genesis 9:7).**

WE HAVE A LOT of rabbits where I used to work. Every morning I would come in and I see them all over the grassy area in front of the radio station. In fact, it seemed like there were more and more of them every morning. I began to wonder if that joke about how rabbits multiply is more fact than fiction. In any event, as I looked at the ever-growing number of rabbits I saw every morning it got me thinking about our main job as Christians. Even more than rabbits, Christians should excel at multiplication. Jesus called each and every one of us to share the good news with everyone we encounter. God told us to multiply, and although that pertained to making babies, I think it also applies to making disciples as well. Sharing the good news isn't just the job of the evangelists and preachers. It's the job of everyone who calls Christ Lord. Just like those rabbits I saw every morning on my way in to work, we should see the children of God multiplying on a daily basis, and you can help make that happen in a very simple way: tell someone God loves them. You may be surprised how many people will be glad to hear that good news.

April 13

Going Retro

"Forget the former things; do no dwell on the past.
See, I am doing a new thing!
Now it springs up; do you not perceive it?"
(Isaiah 43:18-19).

LOVE IT WHEN CEREALS, like those from General Mills, go retro and sport a vintage look on their boxes. It's always interesting to see Golden Grahams, Lucky Charms, and Honey Nut Cheerios with their original artwork and compare them to the way they look today. But going retro isn't always a good idea. In our walk with Christ, we should never want to go back to our original look. Whether we call it going retro, looking vintage, going old school, or whatever, there's no reason for us to return to the old life. In fact, that's one of the most dangerous things we can do. Besides, Jesus Christ didn't die on the Cross and rise from the dead so we could be constantly looking back, but rather so we could look forward to spending an eternity with Him. When it comes to cereal, there's really not a lot to look forward to (except maybe a new marshmallow shape . . .) so it doesn't hurt to look back. In our Christian walk, however, we have everything to look forward to—Christ's return, eternity in Heaven, reuniting with loved ones, and meeting Bible heroes—and that's such good news, I don't ever want to look back.

April 14
Always at Home

Do not let your hearts be troubled. Trust in God; trust also in me. In my Father's house are many rooms; if it were not so, I would have told you. I am going there to prepare a place for you. And if I go and prepare a place for you, I will come back and take you to be with me that you also may be where I am.
(John 14:1-3)

HOME IS WHERE THE HEART IS, or at least that's how the saying goes. Sadly, many people don't have a home, or are away from their homes. Some don't have a home because of problems with their spouse or parents. Some don't have a home because they're living on the streets. Some are away from home as they serve our country overseas. Some are away from home simply because they're studying at college. There are a lot reasons why people don't have a home or are away from it, but I have good news for all of you. No matter where you are, no matter the reason, no matter if you have a home here or not, you'll always have a home in Heaven. That's right. When you come to Christ, when you make Him the ruler of your heart and life, you can know that you'll always have a place, a home, with Him. Whether you're away from your earthly home or you don't have one, never forget that God is preparing a place for you so when Jesus Christ returns, He'll welcome you to your true home, your eternal home. Would you like to come home? Come to Jesus. Would you like to be at home? Be with Jesus. If home is where the heart is, let's make sure our hearts are always with Christ.

April 15

Taxes and Blessings

Bless the Lord, O my soul, and all that is within me, bless His holy name. Bless the Lord, O my soul, and forget none of His benefits; Who pardons all your iniquities, Who heals all your diseases; Who redeems your life from the pit, Who crowns you with lovingkindness and compassion . . .
(Psalm 103:1-4, NASB)

TODAY IS NOT A DAY that people usually count their blessings. It's usually a day when they're counting their costs. That's right, it's tax day—time to pay up; or if you're lucky, get back some of that money you've already paid. Either way, it's not the favorite day of most Americans. That's why I thought it was so interesting that today of all days my Bible reading was Psalm 103. It's a reminder that there are eternal costs and rewards, which are far more important to consider than anything we pay or receive on tax day. So today, do not forget all the benefits of the Lord; do not forget you don't have to pay the price for your sin because Jesus Christ paid it for you. Today, bless the Lord with all your soul, and then do it again tomorrow, and the day after that, and the day after that . . . doesn't that sound like good news?

April 16
Forgetting to Forget
**"They forgot what he had done,
the wonders he had shown them"
(Psalm 78:11).**

WAS THINKING THE OTHER DAY about elephants (don't ask why, just go with me on this). I was thinking about the common belief that elephants never forget and I was wondering what it would be like to have that kind of memory. For one, I certainly know I would have done better in school. Two, it'd be nice to actually remember people's birthdays (like my wife's). And finally, I think it would have a big impact on my relationship with God. Reading through the Psalms, it seems humanity's number one problem is we constantly forget just how wonderful God has been to us. Every year we love to celebrate Easter, but how long does it take after the last chocolate bunny is gone before many of us are already letting the joy of the celebration to fade into the back of our minds until we're reminded of it again next year. Well, I've decided I want to be more like an elephant when it comes to my relationship with God. I don't want to forget the good things He has done for me. So, apart from getting some elephant DNA transfused into me, I guess I'll just have to work on taking the time daily to think about God and to thank Him for all of His loving kindness and for sharing His good news with me.

April 17

Myths, Fables, and Resurrections

"After his suffering, he showed himself to these men and gave many convincing proofs that he was alive"
(Acts 1:3).

A QUICK GLANCE BACK through history shows that just about every culture has some sort of resurrection myth. Even in our modern world, we have our own resurrection myths about superheroes. (Anyone remember when Superman died and came back to life?) Since this idea of a hero dying and coming back to life is so common in the stories and fables of world cultures, including our own, what makes the Resurrection of Jesus Christ so special? Have you ever wondered about that? We've all heard the question of whether art is imitating life or life is imitating art. In the case of Jesus' Resurrection and all those other resurrection myths, it's art imitating life. Jesus Christ was a real person of history; that fact is not disputed. He really walked, talked, and died on this Earth. But what sets Him apart from every other figure in history is that He didn't stay dead. He rose from the grave and proved to His followers that He was alive. Then He told them to go and tell everyone the good news, a charge that we need to continue to carry out today. Jesus Christ is no mythological figure, He's not a fable, and He's not a comic book character in tights and a cape. He was and is very real, and His tomb is empty. Isn't that good news worth sharing?

April 18
Car Repairs and Life Repairs

**"Speak tenderly to Jerusalem, and proclaim to her
that her hard service has been completed, that her sin has
been paid for, that she has received from the
Lord's hand double for all her sins"
(Isaiah 40:2).**

CARS ARE EXPENSIVE. Everything about them costs money, from buying them to driving them and especially fixing them. I remember once when our car broke down how blessed we were to have very kind and loving parents who still desired to help their kids out whenever possible. They were kind enough to give us a blank check for our car repairs. While that was a big blessing, it was also a big responsibility: we didn't want to abuse the trust and kindness our parents had showed us with such a gesture. When Christ died on the Cross for our sins and rose from the grave, He did essentially the same thing for the repairs in our lives. He wrote a blank check of forgiveness that covers all of our sin and opens the way for us to have the Holy Spirit perform repair work in us, to remove our sin nature, and makes us more like Christ. While that blank check of forgiveness is a big blessing, we also must be careful not to abuse the trust and kindness our heavenly Father has shown us in giving us such a gift. It's tough when you're faced with an expense you aren't sure how to pay, and a blessing when someone steps in and helps. Jesus Christ stepped in and completely paid the debt we couldn't begin to pay. As the old song says, "Jesus paid it all, all to Him I owe, sin had left a crimson stain, He washed it white as snow." That sounds like good news to me.

<hr />

April 19
The Trials and Sufferings of Allergies

"Dear friends, do not be surprised at the painful trial you are suffering as though something strange were happening to you. But rejoice that you participate in the sufferings of Christ, so that you may be overjoyed when his glory is revealed"
(1 Peter 4:12-13).

LOOKED UP THE WORD *trial* from today's verse because I was sure the original Greek would reveal that Peter was talking about allergies, but that's not what I discovered. Still, whenever allergy season rolls around, especially when it does so with a vengeance, this verse often comes to mind. I know that may seem kind of weird, but it's true. I don't know why, but for some reason, despite the fact that I endure it every year, I'm always surprised when allergy season gets here. I guess I have an expectation that *this* year I'll be spared (which has yet to really happen), so I grumble and complain like suffering from allergies is something unexpected for me. We often treat the hard times we go through the same way. We grumble and complain about how difficult things are and how we deserve better, how we deserve everything to go our way. The Bible never guaranteed an easy life here on Earth, but it did promise we would face trials and tribulations, and we would face them on a regular basis. Just like allergy season, they're bound to come around, so we shouldn't be surprised when they do. And just like allergy season, they won't last forever, which I think is definitely good news.

* * *

April 20
The Big Give
**"And God is able to make all grace abound to you,
so that in all things at all times, having all that you need,
you will abound in every good work"
(2 Corinthians 9:8).**

A WHILE BACK Oprah had a show called *The Big Give*. One thing that really stuck out to me was how the people on the show were so willing to give . . . because they knew Oprah would provide everything they needed. They had transportation, I presume they had lodging and food, they were even given the right corporate contacts, and the money to give and to give big. I think people on that show found it so easy to give because they knew all of their other needs were being met. That got me thinking about my own life and who I thought was bigger: Oprah or God. If people could rely on the phenomenally rich Oprah to provide what they needed in order for them to give, why couldn't I rely on the Creator of the universe to provide for my needs in order for me to give? The good news is the Bible says I can; only it's going to take a little more faith because God doesn't have His own TV show like Oprah. Still, God blesses us so we can be a blessing to others. That doesn't mean we'll all have wads of cash to spread around to people, but it does mean God has equipped us with exactly what somebody else needs to be blessed with today. The question is: Are we going to look for the opportunity to be a blessing? I know I will, because it's just one more way for me to share the good news of God's love with people, which quite frankly is the biggest "give" of all time.

April 21

Real Thieves and Real Treasure

Do not store up for yourselves treasures on earth, where moth and rust destroy and thieves break in and steal. But store up for yourselves treasures in heaven, where moth and rust do not destroy, and thieves do not break in and steal. For where your treasure is there your heart will be also.
(Matthew 6:19-21)

THAT PASSAGE OF SCRIPTURE took on new meaning for me when a thief really did try to break into our house and steal our stuff. We were lying in bed reading one night when we heard a strange sound at the front of our house. It turned out to be someone tearing up a screen on our front window. Then we heard someone in our back yard removing the cover to the crawl space under our house. That's when I did something not so smart. I grabbed a sword (yes, I have a real sword . . . long story) and headed outside. Like I said, not the smartest move. As I headed into the backyard, a car out front peeled out and sped away. Later, when the police arrived, they said to make sure we had anything of value put away. It was at that moment I realized all my stuff wasn't really all that important to me. I realized I wasn't upset because someone wanted to steal my things, but I was upset because my family was home and potentially could have been in danger. I treasure my wife, and I treasure my daughters. The rest of it is just junk that won't last. In any event, I was reminded of what I really valued that night, and I was also reminded of how nice it will be someday to live somewhere where thieves aren't trying to break in. So I guess you could say our attempted break-in was good news; but I still would have rather learned the lesson some other way.

April 22
Identity Theft in the Church

"My sheep listen to my voice; I know them, and they follow me.
I give them eternal life, and they shall never perish;
no one can snatch them out of my hand.
My Father, who has given them to me, is greater than all;
no one can snatch them out of my Father's hand"
(John 10:27-29).

READ ONCE of a pastor in Pennsylvania who confessed to using the personal information of people in his congregation to obtain credit cards. The real tragedy wasn't just that a pastor was stealing identities from his congregation, although that is a tragedy, but rather in the end the church disbanded and ceased to exist. My heart breaks when I hear news like that, but fortunately I do have some good news. Although we may live in a world where even our identities are at risk, no one can ever steal our identity in Christ. We are safe in His hands, and we don't have to worry about anyone taking that identity from us to use for their own benefit. In fact, the only way we can get to Heaven is to come to Jesus Christ ourselves. We can't rely on our parent's faith, or the faith of our friends, or, if it were possible, on the faith stolen from someone else. We must to come to Christ through our own faith. Someone once said quite appropriately that God doesn't have any grandchildren, only children. Better yet, He won't lose a single one of us, or let anyone take us, or our identity in Him.

April 23
Having Tea With God

"Here I am! I stand at the door and knock.
If anyone hears my voice and opens the door,
I will come in and eat with him, and he with me"
(Revelation 3:20).

WAS EXPLAINING to someone one day about my personal relationship with a loving God. To my surprise, he was rather skeptical of my description of that relationship. He mockingly asked if Jesus came over for tea and talked about His day. He asked me just how personal could that relationship be? It's an interesting question, and certainly I can understand how someone would be wary of anyone claiming to know God personally. However, that's the wonderful miracle we're given through Jesus Christ: we can know God like we know any of our good friends. And in fact, it *is* almost like He comes over for tea to talk about our day, on a daily basis in fact. Granted I don't serve tea—mainly because I prefer hot cocoa and I'm not sure God drinks tea—but we do hang out and converse, also known as prayer and Bible study. I tell Him about my day, the ups and the downs, and He provides comfort and guidance. The truth is it's one of the best relationships I've ever experienced, followed closely by my relationship with my wife. And you know what the good news is? Anyone can enjoy that kind of relationship with God. But in order to do so, we need to let go of our hard-hearted cynicism and come to God with simple, child-like faith. I pray the person I was talking to will do that someday, because despite his harsh and mocking words, I think he was really longing for that kind of relationship with a loving God. In fact, many people are. So it's up to us to tell them they can have it.

April 24
Rules and the No Fun League

"Do not think that I have come to abolish the Law or the Prophets; I have not come to abolish them but to fulfill them"
(Matthew 5:17).

HAVE RULES RUINED THE NFL? If you've ever seen the movie *Leatherheads*, you'll know what the makers of that movie think. Even today, many commonly call it the No Fun League. Me, I'm not so sure. I mean I've always been a big fan of Calvinball (you know, where you play a game without any rules at all), but I don't know how much fun that would be to watch. Still, the perception persists that rules have ruined the NFL, and in fact, often ruin life as well. That's one of the main complaints people have about Christianity; they feel there are too many rules and it ruins any possibility of fun. Interestingly enough, Jesus didn't feel that way. In fact, despite the fact He came to bring us grace, Jesus also said He didn't come to get rid of the rules, but to fulfill them. Why? Because it's only by following God's rules that we'll find true freedom. So Jesus Christ died and rose again to make a way for us to do what we could never do on our own. I don't know about the NFL, but from personal life experience, I can say life is a lot more fun following the rules of God then trying to live without them. That's why it's such good news that God made it possible for us to not only to follow them, but to want to follow them because of our loving relationship with Him.

* * *

April 25
Choosing the Right Addiction
**"Everything is permissible for me—but not everything is
beneficial. Everything is permissible for me—
but I will not be mastered by anything"
(1 Corinthians 6:12).**

WE ARE A SOCIETY OF ADDICTS. Does that sound shocking? Maybe, but I think it's true. We may not all be addicted to illicit drugs or alcohol, but we live in a society that's designed to get us addicted to something. From gambling to shopping, from sports to videogames, our culture wants us to get hooked on something, even if it's something as simple as our fancy coffee in the morning. I can't say I've been immune to these influences; I, too, have my addictions. However, it doesn't have to be that way. In fact, Paul says we don't have to let anything master us.

That's why Jesus Christ came, died, and rose from the grave, so we can be free from everything that would master our lives. In fact, Jesus Christ gives us the freedom to choose what, or who, will master us. That's one of the greatest gifts of all time, and as I've thought about it, I've realized I really don't want anything to master me except Christ. I only want to be addicted to Jesus, and the really good news is I'm free in Christ to make that choice. We may be a society of addicts, but at least in Christ we can choose the right addiction.

April 26
Real Long Distance Communication
"This is the confidence we have in approaching God: that if we ask anything according to his will, he hears us"
(1 John 5:14).

NOT LONG AGO the radio station where I used to work hosted a prophecy conference in Jerusalem. All that week, I spent a lot of time coordinating broadcasts with fellow DJs in Israel. Think about that. I was talking instantaneously to people thousands of miles away and nine hours removed from where I was, yet I could talk to them like they were next door. More than that, thanks to the Internet and other technologies, people all over the world had a chance to watch that prophecy conference in Jerusalem live on the web. I just find it amazing that we can know in real time what's happening anywhere in the world at any time. About the only thing that's more amazing than that is the fact we have access to Almighty God who created the entire universe and exists beyond our dimension of reality. We can talk to Him anytime, anywhere, and the Bible says He hears us. We can talk to Him like He's standing right next to us. In fact, the Bible says He lives inside all those who have accepted Jesus Christ. Think about that for a moment. Instant communication across the globe is pretty cool, but instant communication with a powerful and loving God who wants to talk with us like a friend is absolutely astounding. Now that's what I call good news.

April 27
God Particles and Knowing God's Mind
"For who has known the mind of the Lord that he may instruct him? But we have the mind of Christ"
(1 Corinthians 2:16).

AN ALERT LISTENER of the radio station where I once worked sent me an article about a British physicist who believes it's only a matter of time before the so-called God particle will be discovered. The reason scientists are excited about discovering this particle is because they believe it will help humans "know the mind of God." Well, I have some very good news for those scientists, and for you all of you. You don't need a huge particle accelerator that smashes atoms together in order to discover a theoretical particle that may reveal the mind of God. All you need in order to know the mind of God is Jesus Christ. Jesus Christ is God. Jesus Christ walked on this Earth and shared His mind with His followers, and Jesus Christ resides in the hearts of all those who have decided to follow Him. We can know the mind of God through Jesus who reveals what that mind is, which when you think about it, is pretty mind-blowing. Not only that, but it's also good news because one of the first things we'll discover when we know the mind of God is that He loves each and every one of us very much.

April 28
Batman for the Win

"For the message of the cross is foolishness to those who are perishing, but to us who are being saved it is the power of God"
(1 Corinthians 1:18).

WAS TRYING TO EXPLAIN to someone how Batman, who doesn't have any super powers, could beat Superman in a fight, as he often does in the comics and TV series. The person I was discussing this very important topic with just couldn't understand how someone as powerful as Superman could ever be beaten by a mere mortal like Batman. And yet I insisted that's what consistently happens because of Batman's superior intelligence and strategic thinking. (Also, Batman isn't afraid to cheat and use kryptonite.) You're probably wondering why I'm even bringing this up. Well, as I thought about this inane debate we were having, I suddenly realized that trying to explain how Batman can defeat Superman is like explaining how the Cross is the most powerful symbol of victory the world has ever known. It's hard for the world to understand how a piece of wood used for torture and execution could be powerful enough to be used to defeat sin and death, and yet that's exactly what happened on the Cross. It may not make a lot of sense for something so ordinary to overcome something so powerful, like Batman defeating Superman or the Cross of Christ defeating death, but God seems to take delight in using the ordinary and weak to overcome the extraordinary and the powerful. He did it with the Cross, and He can do the same with you. Isn't that good news?

April 29
You Look Like Dad

"You were taught, with regard to your former way of life, to put off your old self, which is being corrupted by its deceitful desires; to be made new in the attitude of your minds; and to put on the new self, created to be like God in true righteousness and holiness"
(Ephesians 4:22-24).

DON'T KNOW IF YOU'VE NOTICED, but sometimes kids are tiny, mirror images of their parents. For instance, my daughters sound a lot like my wife when they get upset. They have the same vocal inflections and even the same facial expressions. They also sound like my wife when they're tickled (not that I make a regular habit of tickling my wife). Sometimes it's almost spooky how much my girls are like my wife, and even me. Well, if it's true that kids are often reflections of their parents, what does that say about us? Does our behavior as Christians reveal who our Father is? Does the way we react to certain situations remind people of Christ? Do they look at us and say, "Sometimes those kids act and look just like their dad"? Here's the good news. The Holy Spirit is constantly at work in us to do just that: to make us look like our heavenly Father. Of course, we need to be willing to let that change happen, and more than that, we have to actually want to look like our dad. I know that's not always the case with kids; they don't always want to look or act like their parents. But in this case, why wouldn't we? After all, the more we look like Him, the more we'll be able to share the good news with others.

April 30
The Curse of Haircuts

After this I looked and there before me was a great multitude that no one could count, from every nation, tribe, people and language, standing before the throne and in front of the Lamb. They were wearing white robes and were holding palm branches in their hands. And they cried out in a loud voice: "Salvation belongs to our God, who sits on the throne, and to the Lamb."
(Revelation 7:9-10)

THE RADIO STATION I worked for held a Christian prom for the city every year, and every year that meant I needed to go get my hair done *nice*. One year, as I was sitting in the chair watching some stranger cut my hair, a thought occurred to me: the need to style our hair must have be a result of the curse. The fact that we have to take care of our hair is probably just one more of the results of the fall of humanity when Adam and Eve sinned and rebelled against God. I'm willing to bet while they were in the Garden, Adam and Eve never had worry about their hair. They never had to get it cut, get it permed, colored, curled, straightened, or highlighted or anything. I think they had perfect hair. Then they sinned, the curse fell over the Earth and their bodies, they were kicked out of the Garden of Eden, and they started looking for a good salon the first time they woke up with "bed hair." Okay, so I don't know for sure that's the case, but I really dislike haircuts, so I can't see how the need to get them is anything but the result of the curse. I do have good news, however. There's going to come a time when we won't have to worry about our hair, our appearance, or anything else. When Jesus comes to take us home to Heaven all we'll be concerned with is praising God. Won't that be nice? No haircuts (I hope) equals good news to me.

May

His thunder declares it,
The cattle also,
concerning the rising storm.
Job 36:33

May 1
Growing Old Ain't So Bad

"In this same way, husbands ought to love their wives as their own bodies. He who loves his wife loves himself. After all, no one ever hated his own body, but he feeds and cares for it, just as Christ does the church . . . "
(Ephesians 5:28-29).

TODAY IS MY WIFE'S BIRTHDAY. She's something-something years old, and I'm so proud of her. It's been such a blessing for me to celebrate her birthdays with her over the years we've been together, and every year I find I cherish her even more. Why do I tell you this? Well, I just thought you'd like to know in a world where a "permanent" marriage is one that lasts five years or so, there are people who actually enjoy growing old together . . . not that we're old . . . yet . . . but, we like celebrating our birthdays together. I absolutely believe it's possible to love someone for a lifetime, and to enjoy being with them for a lifetime. Why? Because Jesus Christ has shown us what real love is, and when we emulate that in our marriages, well, growing old together becomes a blessing and not a reason for filing for divorce. Marriage is the greatest blessing two people can know other than salvation through Christ, and I know if my wife could have one birthday wish, it would be for more people to finally understand that good news.

May 2
A Hero's Job is Never Done

"When he had received the drink, Jesus said, 'It is finished.'
With that, he bowed his head and gave up his spirit"
(John 19:30).

HAVE YOU EVER NOTICED how a superhero's job is never done? As soon as one super villain's maniacal evil plot is stopped, another is out to try and take over the world, or rob banks. Not only that, but there are all those people who are special to the superhero—friends, family, loved ones—who constantly need saving. It just seems to me that being a superhero could get really frustrating after a while because no matter how much you do, it's never enough. That's what sets Jesus Christ apart from every other hero, super or otherwise. He actually finished the job. When Jesus died on the Cross and rose from the grave to save us from our sins, He completed the task. All it took was that one sacrifice from God's only Son to save all of us from our sins and to bring us eternal life. There isn't another superhero out there who has ever been able to say of their task, "It is finished." So while those other heroes constantly scramble around fighting the so-called "Never ending fight against evil," know there is one hero who finished the fight against evil, who saved us once for all, and one day will return to celebrate His victory with us. Doesn't that sound like good news?

May 3
The Big, Scary Universe

**"By faith we understand that the universe was
formed at God's command, so that what is seen
was not made out of what was visible"
(Hebrews 11:3).**

OVER THE YEARS, the Hubble Space Telescope has shown us some amazing sights in our galaxy. Among the most spectacular were pictures of distant galaxies colliding with each other. They're beautiful, amazing images that show galaxies of hundreds of millions of stars slowly smashing into one another. These events are so enormous and are happening at such a vast distance and involve forces of such power that it's almost beyond our comprehension. This is why I think the Bible says we need faith when we look at creation. Despite the advancements in science, there's still so much about the universe, and even our own world, we just don't understand, and which could be rather scary. However, when you can look at the sky through a telescope and see far off galaxies collide or simply see birds returning for the spring and acknowledge that God commanded all of that into being, it doesn't make you any less intelligent, but it will certainly make you a whole lot less anxious. And that's definitely good news.

May 4
A Guarantee That Means Something
"Give thanks to the Lord, for He is good;
for His lovingkindness is everlasting"
(Psalm 118:29, NASB).

IT MAKES ME NERVOUS that so many things have warranties these days. It's as though companies are conceding that whatever it is they make is going to break within a certain amount of time. When it does, they'll fix it or replace it after you waste forty-five hours of your life talking to various people about exactly what the problem is in order to establish that their product is indeed broken, and it broke within the specific parameters as explained in your 570-page warranty manual. Even guarantees aren't always a guarantee that you'll get what you were guaranteed. It's enough to make a person cynical. Fortunately, I have good news. The Bible gives us a simple promise in Psalm 118. It tells us the lovingkindness of God is everlasting. That's it. No conditions. No "It's everlasting as long as you fulfill these requirements." No quid pro quo. Just the simple statement, *His lovingkindness is everlasting.* In a world full of warranties and guarantees jam-packed with fine print, I find it refreshing to find a promise that simple and straightforward.

May 5

The Present of God's Presence

"Where can I go from your Spirit? Where can I flee from your presence? If I go up to the heavens, you are there; if I make my bed in the depths, you are there . . . even there your hand will guide me, your right hand will hold me fast"
(Psalm 139:7-8,10).

THE BIBLE makes many wonderful promises to us, but I think one of the most precious is the promise of God's constant presence. No matter how far we try to get away from Him, either physically or spiritually, He's always right there with us. He's there, not because He wants to keep track of everything we do wrong, and He's not there to keep a tally of our mistakes so He can rub them in our faces later. He's there because He loves us. God loves us so much He doesn't want to be apart from us. That's why He sent His Son Jesus to die on the Cross for our sins and to rise again on the third day—so we can simply be in the presence of God. Sometimes it feels like God is far away, but the truth is He loves us too much to ever be far away. That's something we all need to remember every day, in every situation. No matter what your circumstances are, God is always there loving you. That's good news.

May 6

Good News in a World Full of Bad

When he saw the crowds, he had compassion on them, because they were harassed and helpless, like sheep without a shepherd. Then he said to his disciples, "The harvest is plentiful but the workers are few. Ask the Lord of the harvest, therefore, to send out workers into his harvest field."
(Matthew 9:36-38)

HERE'S SOMETHING THAT MAY SHOCK YOU: around 95 percent of American Christians have never helped another person discover salvation through Christ. In short, most Christians aren't sharing the good news. That's just about the saddest thing I've ever heard. In world with so much bad news being reported on a constant basis, you know people are desperate to hear something good. We as Christians are sitting on the best good news that world has ever known—freedom from sin, forgiveness, love, eternal life—and yet we're not telling anyone because . . . what? We'll be uncool? People might be rude? It's awkward to share about Jesus? When I look at the headlines every morning and see all the despair, the hurt, the suffering, the pain, and hopelessness this world experiences on a daily basis, I realize there is no good reason for me not to share the good news of Jesus Christ. So this week, let's pray that God will give us all an opportunity to share His good news with at least one person. If we can do that, then perhaps this world will begin to change, one person at a time, through the good news of the gospel.

May 7
From the Crib to the Big Bed

In fact, though by this time you ought to be teachers,
you need someone to teach you the elementary truths of
God's word all over again. You need milk, not solid food!
Anyone who lives on milk, being still an infant, is not
acquainted with the teaching about righteousness.
But solid food is for the mature, who by constant use
have trained themselves to distinguish good from evil.
(Hebrews 5:12-14)

REMEMBER when I had to disassemble a crib and set up a bed for one of my daughters. It was the first time in many years our home no longer had a crib. It was the first time in a looooong time our home no longer had any babies. I confess that it's kind of sad to reach that point, but the fact is kids grow up no matter how much we wish they wouldn't. Of course, if they didn't grow up, they wouldn't mature, and if they didn't mature, they wouldn't be able to face and conquer the world around them. The same is true for us as Christians; we all need to grow up. However, Christians seem much more likely to cling to their cribs rather than move on to a big bed. Granted life is easier in the crib, but God has work for us to do—lives for us to change, people for us to help, and the only way we can do that as Christians is when we grow up and mature. So don't be afraid of growing up as a Christian. Take the time to really learn the good news for yourself and learn why you believe what you believe. It's always sad to leave childhood behind, but it's exciting to move on and face new adventures, especially when those adventures involve sharing the good news of God's grace.

May 8
Absolutes and Crossword Puzzles

"Salvation is found in no one else, for there is no other name under heaven given to men by which we must be saved" (Acts 4:12).

ANYONE WHO BELIEVES there's no such thing as absolutes and that everything is relative has never done a crossword puzzle. I do one every day, and I'm telling you there are absolutely right answers and absolutely wrong answers. The answer for the clue "bird" when there are only four letters isn't *yellow-bellied sapsucker*, no matter how sincerely I believe it is. I could try to force it in, but then it would affect all my other answers, and they would be wrong, and by the end of it I'd have nothing but gibberish (which I sometimes do). There's only one way to fill out a crossword puzzle, just like there's only one way to get to Heaven. The odd thing is people don't seem to mind being told there's only one way to fill out a crossword puzzle correctly, but they *do* mind being told there's only one way to Heaven. It's not that the makers of the crossword puzzle are trying to be mean, it's just a fact that the puzzle only works if you fill it out properly. Well God isn't trying to be mean either, it's just a simple fact that eternity only works when you have a proper relationship with God through Jesus Christ. It just doesn't work any other way. So the next time you're told Christianity is all right for you, but that doesn't mean it's right for everyone, pull out a crossword puzzle and help that person fill it out. It might be useful in sharing the absolute fact of the good news.

May 9
Being Neighborly
"... And who is my neighbor?"
(Luke 10:29).

ATTENDED a neighborhood meeting a while ago regarding what we could do about a string of robberies that had taken place in our neighborhood. (It was around this same time someone tried to break into our house while we were at home). It was very interesting because one of the solutions for this problem, suggested to us by a crime prevention specialist, was really quite simple: get to know your neighbors. We were told to get to know the people we live next door to and across the street from, to learn to recognize their daily pattern, what their cars look like, when they're going to be out of town and so forth. In general, just be more neighborly with our neighbors. I found this to be a rather intriguing solution because one of the things we've been learning in church is if we want to fulfill the Great Commission and go and make disciples of the world, for many of us that starts by simply going next door. We can improve the security of our neighborhoods and help people discover eternal security for their souls simply by getting to know our neighbors. Don't you think that's good news?

May 10
The Super Power of Forgiveness
"Be kind and compassionate to one another, forgiving each other, just as in Christ God forgave you"
(Ephesians 4:32).

FORGIVENESS CHANGED THE WORLD. Did you know that? When Jesus Christ hung on the Cross for our sins and said, *"Father forgive them . . . ",* the world was changed forever. Now you've probably noticed comic book movies routinely rule at the box office, which just goes to show how much audiences love superheroes—and why wouldn't they? These are characters who do things we've always wanted to do. They fly, they fight against overwhelming odds for right and justice, and they have cool super powers. I've recently come to the conclusion that forgiveness is the greatest super power of all time, and you know what's really exciting? We get to use it. The same power Christ used to forgive the world when He died on the Cross and rose from the dead is within all of us who call ourselves Christians. We, too, can change lives, save lives, and, in fact, change the world with the awesome power of forgiveness. Granted, forgiveness isn't the easiest thing in the world to do. But when we're willing to follow Christ's example of forgiveness, we get a chance to be super—but without the tights—and that's good news.

May 11

The Arithmetic of Grace

"If you, O Lord, kept a record of sins, O Lord, who could stand? But with you there is forgiveness; therefore you are feared" (Psalm 130:3-4).

F I WERE TO ASK my older daughter the number of times her sister has played with her dollhouse without permission, she wouldn't even hesitate in telling me. But it's not just children who remember the number of offenses that have been committed against them. Most adults have refined that art and are capable of holding on to an offense for years. One of the things I've learned about forgiveness recently is how amazing it is that God, the only One who really has any right to do so, doesn't keep a tally of all our mistakes. Instead, He forgives them and doesn't count them anymore. That means it's rather presumptuous of us to think we have the right to count the wrongs other people commit against us. After all, if God doesn't keep count, who are we to judge and keep count? Quite frankly, I'm relieved God doesn't keep a record of my sins, and if He's willing to do that for me, I should be willing to do the same for others, and to teach my daughters to do likewise. Why? Because forgiveness is good news, and it's good news we can practice on a daily basis.

May 12
Why Do Siblings Fight?
**"How good and pleasant it is when brothers
live together in unity!"
(Psalm 133:1).**

MY BROTHERS AND I didn't always get along. In fact, I can remember a few times where we made the WWE look like a friendly pillow fight. Siblings fight, and part of the reason we did is because we were all so different. Now that we're older, I'm proud to say we truly are best friends and our differences actually strengthen our bond instead of being reasons for division. The same needs to be true of us as Christians, especially in the times we live. I've learned in recent months that unity doesn't mean uniformity; we can be united without being the same. As long as we agree on the basic essentials of the gospel, there's really no reason for us to fight among ourselves, especially when there's a world perishing in desperate need of the good news of Jesus Christ. Yes, siblings will fight sometimes, and there's probably no avoiding it all the time among our brothers and sisters in Christ. But let's make sure it only happens infrequently. The rest of the time, let's celebrate our differences, use our various strengths and talents, and get out there and share the good news of Jesus Christ. We can't do it alone, but together we can't be stopped.

May 13
The Horn of Help

"I lift up my eyes to the hills—where does my help come from? My help comes from the Lord, the Maker of heaven and earth" (Psalm 121:1-2).

IN the movie (and the book) *The Chronicles of Narnia: Prince Caspian*, the land of Narnia is in trouble and Susan's horn is used to summon help. The only problem is, no one in Narnia is sure where that help might come from or who it will be. We all would like help when we face difficult or dire circumstances, and I'm sure there are times when you thought it would be nice to have a magical horn to summon that help. Fortunately, we have something much better and more reliable: prayer. Any time we need help, we don't need to aimlessly blow a horn into the air and hope that some sort of aid arrives. All we need to do is drop to our knees and turn our eyes toward Heaven to the Maker of the entire universe who loves us so much that He's concerned about what happens in our lives and wants to help us. Help is always there for those of us who call on the Lord. Sure, it might be more exciting if it came in the form of a roaring lion (and who knows, there may be times when God helps us that way), but fact is God loves us and is always there to help us. And that's what I call good news.

May 14
Indiana Jones and the Treasure of God's Love

"For God, who said, 'Let light shine out of darkness' made his light shine in our hearts to give us the light of the knowledge of the glory of God in the face of Christ. But we have this treasure in jars of clay to show that this all-surpassing power is from God and not from us"
(2 Corinthians 4:6-7).

TALK OF A FIFTH MOVIE about Indiana Jones has continued ever since he returned seeking one of the legendary crystal skulls that supposedly holds mystic powers. I don't know if that movie will ever get made, especially after so many fans disliked the fourth one, but during his career, Jones has sought after many valuable and iconic treasures, from the Lost City of Atlantis (one of his video game adventures) to the Lost Ark. However, there's one treasure even the great Dr. Jones has yet to discover. It's a treasure that's hidden in the most obvious of places: the treasure of God's love. There is nothing so valuable or so remarkable as the love of God, and this precious treasure isn't hidden in an ancient temple filled with traps, but rather in each of us who follow Christ. Why would God place such a valuable treasure in such an obvious spot? So everyone, from Dr. Jones to our neighbors next door would have an opportunity to discover it. So while Indy may or may not set off on another adventure, his films should serve as a reminder to all of us to begin an adventure of our own: the adventure of sharing the light, that eternal treasure God has put in us all. It's time to begin the adventure of sharing the good news.

May 15

Video Games, Fitness, and Your Spirit

"For physical training is of some value, but godliness
has value for all things, holding promise for both
the present life and the life to come"
(1 Timothy 4:8).

WHEN NINTENDO introduced its unusual video gaming console known as the Wii, it also brought to the gaming world a whole new genre, one most people probably would have never associated with video games: exercise. That's right, video games suddenly became one more way to help you get into shape and have fun doing it thanks to *Wii Fit* and its eventual successors *Wii Fit Plus* and *Wii Fit U*. Now, how much difference these games make in the physical fitness in the ones who play them is probably all a matter of perspective, but I do know this, we need more than just physical fitness, we need spiritual fitness. It's important to keep our bodies fit, but we also need to remember these bodies are temporary. Our souls, however, are eternal, and therefore we need to make sure we keep them in tiptop shape. How do we do that? Prayer, Bible study, discipleship, fellowship with other believers, attending church, and, of course, by sharing the good news. Millions of people have turned to video games to help them get fit, but in the spirit of health consciousness, let's get people to consider their spiritual fitness as well. In other words, let's share the good news that a relationship with God is the healthiest habit you can form.

May 16
We All Scream for Ice Cream

"The wicked man flees though no one pursues, but the righteous are as bold as a lion"
(Proverbs 28:1).

DID YOU KNOW that the United States accounts for 93 percent of the ice cream consumption in North America? It's true. Canada and Mexico make up the other seven percent, but they don't even come close to the American love of ice cream. Not that I'm surprised; ice cream is pretty tasty. I've even had ice cream for dinner on occasion—one of the benefits of being a grown-up. What is surprising, however, is that same statistic also represents the number of Christians in America who have never led anyone else to Christ. Isn't that strange? We're perfectly happy to proclaim our love for ice cream, but when it comes proclaiming our love for Christ, we choose to remain silent. Now I'm not suggesting we all need to start thumping Bibles on people's heads or starting pointing the condemning fingers of fiery doom at people, but I do think we need to start letting people know we love Christ as much as ice cream, and more importantly that Christ loves them. (Which is something you really can't say about ice cream.) Besides, ice cream eventually melts, whereas a relationship with Christ will last for all eternity. Forgiveness, love, and eternal life: don't those sound like much more exciting topics than chocolate or vanilla?

May 17
Loves, Likes, and God

"Do not love the world or anything in the world. If anyone loves the world, the love of the Father is not in him"
(1 John 2:15).

THERE ARE A LOT of good things in this world. I know it doesn't seem that way sometimes because all we usually hear about is the bad, but the fact is there are a lot of good things in this world. Just some of the simple pleasures I enjoy and see as the "good things" in life include going to the movies with my wife, playing a board game with my kids, and grilling in my back yard on a cool summer evening (I love doing all these things). In fact, there are a lot of things in this world I love, which always makes me nervous when I get to 1 John. It's one of those passages of Scripture we'd like to explain away or ignore, but we know we can't do that. Personally, I like it when the Bible causes me to squirm a little bit. It's good to examine and question our lives to make sure we're doing what we were called to do: to love God with all our hearts, and to love our neighbors as ourselves. When I think about it, nothing should compare with the love I have for God because nothing compares with the love He has for me. I suppose that means I just really *like* many of the good things in this world, but there's only one God whom I really *love*. I just need to be more selective in how I use that word—love.

May 18

Earthquakes, Movie Stars, and God's Judgment

"Therefore judge nothing before the appointed time; wait till the Lord comes. He will bring to light what is hidden in darkness and will expose the motives of men's hearts. At that time, each will receive his praise from God"
(1 Corinthians 4:5).

IN MAY 2008, China was hit with one of the deadliest earthquakes in its history. In the aftermath, a prominent movie star stated he believed China got what it deserved. He said it was karma because of the human rights violations China committed in Tibet. In what may have been another act of karma, China banned all of that star's movies. Maybe it's just me, but I have a hard time assigning blame when events like that earthquake take place. When the death toll is in the tens of thousands, I wouldn't be comfortable saying whose fault it is or that anyone got what they deserved. I don't think I'm in any position to pass that sort of judgment. In fact, the only one who's really qualified to pass judgment on anything is God. He's the only one who's all-knowing. He's the only one who's truly just and righteous. He's the only one who is completely holy and perfect. I've found when I'm willing to let God handle the judgment stuff while I just take care of trying to help meet the needs of people who are hurting, life is a whole lot simpler. It's nice not to have the responsibility of passing judgment on everything that happens in this world, and even nicer not to worry about other people reporting on my actions. Besides, who am I and who are any of us, to say we could be a better judge than God?

❖•❖•◆──────◆────────◆•❖•❖

<h2 style="text-align:center">May 19</h2>

Let's Make Beautiful Music Together

"The body is a unit, though it is made up of many parts; and though all its parts are many, they form one body.
So it is with Christ"
(1 Corinthians 12:12).

ONE OF MY FAVORITE special outings is when we attend the New Mexico Symphony Orchestra. We are certainly lucky to have such a talented symphony right here in New Mexico. I especially enjoy it when they do the Symphony Under the Stars concert at the Rio Grande Zoo. Once as we were sitting there in the cool evening listening to animals add their own music to the music being produced from the stage, a thought occurred to me: a symphony orchestra is a lot of different people with different instruments playing different notes but all doing so in harmony. In fact, I became quite fascinated in watching the coordination of so many different people and instruments in order to produce the wonderful music we were hearing. It got me thinking about the Body of Christ. We sometimes confuse unity for uniformity; we think we have to all be the same to be united. But in truth, I think we need to be more like a symphony: each doing our part with our unique talents, but all working in harmony together for one purpose—to share the beautiful music of the gospel with a world audience. The symphony wouldn't have been nearly as enjoyable if everyone on stage was playing the same instrument and the exact same notes, nor would the Body of Christ be nearly as beautiful if we were all the same. So let's work together in harmony, just like an orchestra, so we can better share the good news of Jesus Christ with our world.

May 20
Faithfulness for Life
"And after he become the father of Methuselah, Enoch walked with God three hundred years and had other sons and daughters"
(Genesis 5:22).

WHEN MY AUNT MARGERY DIED, one of the things we all remembered about her was her enduring faithfulness to God. At her funeral, the pastor read from her Bible and, up to that time, I had never seen a Bible that looked like that. It was worn and torn, taped and patched, and every page had notes and underlines, not to mention all the bookmarks and odd pieces of paper stuck here and there. It was the Bible of a woman who loved being with her God every chance she got, and she had walked faithfully with him for decades—as long as I knew her, in fact. Another inspiring figure is Enoch. He walked with God for three hundred years. Can you imagine what that must have been like? In our world, it's often expected of us to walk with God a few decades and then give up. Many people think that backsliding and rebellion will inevitably come, that it's impossible to walk consistently and faithfully with God for an entire life. My Aunt Margery and Enoch prove otherwise. We can walk faithfully with God, and we can do so for life, whether that's three hundred years or eighty years. That's what I call good news.

May 21
Playing With the Jenga Blocks of Life

"Therefore everyone who hears these words of mine and puts them into practice is like a wise man who built his house on the rock. The rain came down, the streams rose, and the winds blew and beat against that house, yet it did not fall, because it had its foundation on the rock"
(Matthew 7:24-25).

DO YOU REMEMBER the game Jenga or have you ever played with blocks? Sometimes our lives can feel like a stack of Jenga blocks or a tower made out of old fashioned blocks—they can feel wobbly and unstable and all it will take is one little nudge for the tower to come tumbling down. That may be the way we *feel*, but the truth is when our lives are built upon the rock of Jesus Christ and the solid truth of the Bible, no matter what tragedy may strike, no matter how crazy life may get, the blocks of our lives will never tumble. They may sway a bit, a few pieces may be removed, but with a solid foundation in Christ we can be sure they'll stay together. As the old hymn says, "On Christ the solid rock I stand, all other ground is sinking sand . . . " That sounds like good news to me, especially considering how crazy life can be sometimes.

May 22
How Much Fun is Church?
"What has happened to all your joy?"
(Galatians 4:15).

WE WERE DROPPING OFF our daughter at VBS, and the little boy my wife watched on a regular basis was with us. He was amazed at what he saw because it looked like so much fun. In fact, he was so impressed that he wanted to go. He wanted to go so badly he begged his parents to let him, and so eventually my daughter and this little guy were both going to VBS. How cool is it that this kid took at look at what was going on at church and thought it looked like so much fun he wanted to go? Why doesn't that happen more with adults? Why isn't church something adults naturally find exciting and fun, so much so that when they see it they can't wait to go? When you look in the Bible, you'll notice how much people actually liked being around Jesus. There are probably several reasons for this, including the fact that He was so kind, gracious, and loving, but secretly I think one of the reasons people liked being around Him was because He was fun to be around. Some people feel like we need to make church more appealing and *seeker friendly*. I say if we're living out the good news and walking with Christ, we won't have to try and do anything; the appeal will naturally be there because Jesus naturally drew people to himself. How do you view church? Is it fun? Is it exciting? Is it a place where you can't wait to be? That VBS experience made me realize it was time to recapture that same excitement my daughter had for church, and make sure she didn't lose it as she grew up. Church and being a Christian is supposed to be fun. Besides, if we want people to accept the good news, first they need to see that it's actually good for our lives. What do they see when they look at you?

May 23
A Case of Mistaken Identity?

"But if you fail to do this, you will be sinning against the Lord; and you may be sure that your sin will find you out"
(Numbers 32:23).

SOME GOOD FRIENDS OF OURS had to take their son to the doctor's office. Unfortunately, he didn't understand *he* was the one going to the doctor; he thought daddy was going to see the doctor and he was just coming along. Needless to say, that little kid was surprised when the doctor tried to stick a needle in him instead of his dad, and he cried out, "You've got the wrong guy!" Many of us react in the same way when sin finally catches up with us and sticks us with the consequences of our actions. We turn to all sorts of other people to blame yelling out, "You've got the wrong guy!" It's been like this since the Garden of Eden. Fortunately, it doesn't have to be that way. There is a way to be free of sin, but it's not by blaming someone else. You see, when Jesus Christ hung on the Cross to die for our sins, He didn't yell, "You've got the wrong guy!" Although He could have because He was completely innocent. No, He simply said, "Father, forgive them." Sin will always find us out. There's no hiding from it. But the good news is that because of the death and Resurrection of Jesus Christ we don't have to be slaves to it. The next time you see someone being stung by sin, take the time to share the good news with them.

May 24
The Fixed Price of Eternity
"For it is by grace you have been saved, through faith— and this is not from yourselves, it is the gift of God . . . " (Ephesians 2:8).

I'M SURE YOU'VE PROBABLY NOTICED the cost of just about everything has gone up in recent years. Fuel costs have gone up, and because fuel costs have gone up, so has the cost of shipping food and merchandise, and because shipping all that is more expensive, all those products that are being shipped are more expensive. Basically it all adds up to making life a lot more expensive than it used to be, which makes me glad the cost of eternal life is always the same. Despite the fact that forgiveness of sin and the gift of eternal life cost God the life of His only Son, He offers those things to us for free; and that price will never change. God will never hike up the price, will never alter the fee, and will never demand we pay more because it cost Him more. The gift of salvation, the gift of grace, the gift forgiveness and love is just that: a gift. With all the talk about how much everything is costing these days, finding out that something as valuable as eternal life and forgiveness is actually free is probably good news a lot of people you know would like to hear. Are you willing to tell them?

May 25
Building a Better Babel

"The Lord said, 'If as one people speaking the same language they have begun to do this, then nothing they plan to do will be impossible for them'"
(Genesis 11:6).

THE STORY OF THE TOWER OF BABEL has always intrigued me. I always found it fascinating just how much people were able to accomplish when they were united in spirit and intent. In fact, our potential was so great that God felt that it was better to confuse our languages so we wouldn't be able to work so effectively together. Don't you find that interesting? It's also left me wondering what would happen if we were to truly unite sharing the gospel with people. If we were to finally set aside our petty differences about things that really don't matter, if were to start speaking the same language, as it were, the language of the gospel, what might we accomplish? As with the Garden of Eden, I've always wondered what would have happened at Babel had the people chosen differently. What would our world be like had they done something together to honor and glorify God rather than themselves? Would we all understand each other today? Would our combined, united efforts have produced a better world? We'll never know, but we still have a chance now to know what would happen if we were all to work together, overcome our differences, and unite in sharing the good news. Perhaps it's time we tried that. After all, it looks as though time is running out.

***

May 26
One of Those Days

"Praise be to the God and Father of our Lord Jesus Christ, the Father of compassion and the God of all comfort, who comforts us in our troubles, so that we can comfort those in any trouble with the comfort we ourselves have received from God"
(2 Corinthians 1:3-4).

EVER HAVE ONE OF THOSE DAYS? You know, one of those days filled with problems and stress. One of those days you wish would just go away. Well, I'm here to provide you with a different perspective when we have one of those days. The truth is it's good for us to have one of those days every now and then. Yep, that's right, I said it's a *good* thing, and here's why: if we never had days full of problems or days where everything seemed to go wrong, we could never tell anyone how God was able to carry us through those kinds of days. You see, it's the days we enjoy the least when our faith is required the most. Those are the days when we get to see just how faithful, caring, comforting, and powerful our God is. Without having one of those days every now and then, we'd never get to experience that. More importantly, if we never experienced that, then we would never be able to tell other people about how our loving God cared for us when everything else in life failed. Those types of experiences equip us to be used by God to help comfort others. So remember, whenever you have *one of those days*, it may be an experience that will not only help you lean more on God, but later it may be an experience that will give you an opportunity to share the good news with someone else.

<hr />

May 27

Time to Grow Up

"Then we will no longer be infants, tossed back and forth by the waves, blown here and there by every wind of teaching and by the cunning and craftiness of men in their deceitful scheming"
(Ephesians 4:14).

HAVE A CONFESSION TO MAKE: I like to misinform my kids. I like to tell them blue is red or round is square or clouds are made of marshmallows. Why do I do this? I don't know, and don't worry, my wife doesn't let me get away with it. She's always there to provide the kind, loving voice of reason to my good-natured fun. The thing is that kids are innocent enough to believe anything you tell them. At times that can be fun, but at other times it can be very dangerous. That's why as Christians we need to grow up. We can't remain baby Christians forever, because if we do, we'll be easily led astray, we'll be easily confused, and we'll be easily deceived—and it won't be by someone like me who just thinks it's funny. So how do we grow up as Christians?

Well, for starters, read and actually study your Bible every day. Spend time in prayer every day. Join a church and a small study group. Whatever you do, don't be content to just learn what other people tell you about the Bible and Christianity; examine it yourself. More than ever, we need mature, grown-up Christians to share the good news. I don't know about you, but I know for me it's time to grow up.

May 28
Who Chooses Our Fate?

This day I call heaven and earth as witnesses against you that I have set before you life and death, blessings and curses. Now choose life, so that you and your children may live and that you may love the Lord your God, listen to his voice, and hold fast to him. For the Lord is your life . . .
(Deuteronomy 30:19-20)

IS OUR FATE PREDETERMINED or do we get to choose it for ourselves? That's one of the questions asked in Pixar's movie *Brave*, and it's a question we'd all like answered. It may be a surprise for you to know I come down on the side of both being true: our fate is predetermined and it's up to us to choose. Why do I say that? Because the Bible says so. When you look through what the Bible says, it tells us that we can either choose Heaven or hell. We're fated for one or the other, and we don't have any choice about that, but we do have a choice of where we'll spend our eternity, of which one will be our fate. Fate really isn't as complicated or mysterious as people or movies make it out to be. The Bible clearly tells us what our fate is and what choices we have when it comes to our destiny. Sure, it might be nice to have more choices, but the good news is that we're given a choice at all through the death and Resurrection of Jesus Christ. So, our fates are determined, we will all die, but we still have a chance to choose where we will spend eternity, thanks to Jesus Christ. That's good news I think we need to share.

May 29
What's it Like to Win the Lottery?
**"How great is the love the Father has lavished on us,
that we should be called the children of God!"
(1 John 3:1).**

HAVE YOU EVER WON THE LOTTERY, or have you ever wondered what it would be to win the lottery? Yeah, me too. Although, in one sense I think I can say I have won the lottery and I know exactly what it feels like: the day I married my wife and every day since. Winning the lottery is one of those pie-in-the-sky moments we'd all like to have but most us never really expect to experience. Well, try this on for size: what if someone gave you their lottery winnings? They just walked up to you and said, "Here, have this. I won it, but I want you to have it; no strings attached." What would you do? Well, naturally you'd be a little skeptical and wary. I think that's why some people react to the good news of Jesus Christ the way they do. It's like someone walking up to them and telling them they can have their lottery winnings. In fact, eternal life in Heaven is far more extravagant than anything you could ever win in a lottery, and it will last longer, too. I mention this because we shouldn't be surprised when people are wary and skeptical when we share the gospel. It really does sound too good to be true. However, just like the lottery, deep down it's something everyone wants, so we should never give up trying to give them the good news.

May 30
Going All In

"I eagerly expect and hope that I will in no way be ashamed, but will have sufficient courage so that now as always Christ will be exalted in my body, whether by life or by death. For to me, to live is Christ and to die is gain"
(Philippians 1:20-21).

ODDS ARE that you've gambled at some point in your life; if not in a formal sense at a casino (of which we have a plethora here in New Mexico), then at least in the sense that you were willing to take a chance on something. The fact is a lot of life is a gamble, which is why it's wise to be prepared and hedge our bets as much as possible in order to minimize the risks. Unfortunately, there's one area of life where we try to minimize the risk when we really should be risking it all: being a Christian. You see, Christ wants us to go all-in with Him, He wants us to risk it all, and that can be a scary prospect. After all, what do you do if it doesn't work out? Too often, we hedge our bets on Christ and make sure we have some sort of backup plan in case this Christian thing is a bust. However, if you really want to follow

Christ, you have to go all-in, hold nothing back, and be willing to risk it all—including in your life. There is good news, though, and it's this: betting on Christ is the safest, surest bet you can make. So go ahead, go all-in with Christ and see for yourself why it's worth the risk.

May 31
Following the One-way

"Salvation is found in no one else, for there is no other name under heaven given to men by which we must be saved" (Acts 4:12).

WHEN YOU SEE A ONE-WAY SIGN, you don't expect people to ignore it and go any way they want because that's going to cause problems. When you come to a freeway off-ramp, you wouldn't expect people to decide it should also function as a freeway on-ramp because that would really make things a mess. Why is it, then, when Jesus says He's the way, the only way to get to Heaven, people decide He doesn't really mean it and they can go any way they want and still get there? It's shocking to hear how many people believe all religions are basically the same and they all pretty much lead to the same place. It's like people driving in the opposite direction on a one-way street. Look, being told that you can only go one way on a street or one way on a freeway off-ramp isn't being restrictive or narrow-minded. It's just stating a fact. If you ignore that fact, you put yourself in danger. When Jesus said He was the way to Heaven, He wasn't being restrictive or narrow-minded. He was announcing good news. He was turning a dead-end into a one-way street. Where there wasn't a way to Heaven, He made a way through His death and Resurrection. And that's something only He has done.

June

"Now learn this parable
from the fig tree:
When its branch has already become
tender, and puts forth leaves,
you know that summer is near."

Mark 13:28

June 1

Is Cheating Ever Okay?

"... What made you think of doing such a thing?
You have not lied to men but to God"
(Acts 5:4).

WE'VE ALL CHEATED at some point in our lives, right? We've all tried to find the easy way out or the easy answer. After all, sometimes cheating is harmless, right? Especially when it comes to our Christian walk, there's nothing wrong with fudging things a bit to make ourselves look like better Christians, is there? I've been getting some exercise with a video game called "Wii Fit U." One day a little boy who was visiting our house pointed out that it would be very easy to cheat on "Wii Fit U" to get a high score in one of the exercises. Like a good parent, I pointed out that cheating is wrong, but I had to admit he had a point. Besides, it wouldn't really hurt anyone if I cheated on a silly little video game, right? But then I came to my senses and realized that whether or not anyone got hurt was missing the point. I was playing "Wii Fit U" to improve my health and fitness, and cheating wouldn't do anything to help that. It would only hinder it. The same is true for us as Christians. We put in the effort and the hard work to follow Christ because we know it benefits us. When we try to cheat at it, we're not doing ourselves or others any favors; something that Ananias and Sapphira found out the hard way. The saying that cheaters never prosper is true, but it's also true that persistent, consistent faith has everything to gain, everything to prosper. And that's good news.

***

June 2
What Do You Know?

"Now this is eternal life, that they may know you, the only true God, and Jesus Christ, whom you have sent"
(John 17:3).

LET ME GET PHILOSOPHICAL with you for a moment: How do you know anything? What makes you believe you know anything? Have you ever stopped to consider that? I bring this up because there's a growing consensus in our culture that would have us believe we can't *really* know anything for certain, nor should we bother trying. Nothing is knowable, and if you say you know anything, that's merely arrogance. This type of thinking has even leaked into the Church by saying we can't *really* know God, His Word or His Son. I'm not sure why people believe it's intelligent to say we can't truly know anything. Personally I think it's dumb, willful ignorance designed to release one from personal responsibility. I'm here to tell you the good news is as sure as you can know that two plus two is four. You can *know* God. More than that, God *wants* you to know Him. He wants you to know His character, His personality, and most importantly, to know of His love for you. Yes, the God of the entire universe wants to be known by you, and He's done everything possible to make that happen. So why would we refuse to know that which desires to be known?

June 3
Fish, God, and What Makes You Special

"O Lord, what is man that you care for him, the son of man that you think of him?"
(Psalm 144:3).

LOVE TO VISIT the aquarium we have here in Albuquerque, New Mexico (the city where Bugs Bunny always needed to turn left). It never ceases to amaze me that 1), we actually have an aquarium here in Albuquerque, and 2), there are so many varied and unusual creatures in the sea. We only have a small sampling at the aquarium, but even among the few species on display, there are a wide variety of abilities and skills in the various forms of marine life that are absolutely fascinating. In fact, the creatures of the sea have so many unique abilities I seem positively mundane by comparison. But then again, we humans have one unique ability no other creature, no matter how unusual, can duplicate. I'm not talking about thinking or reasoning or tool making or any of that. No I'm talking about the ability to have a relationship with God. We can know God as a Friend, as a Father, as a Comforter, as One who loves us deeply. In fact, He wanted to have a relationship with us so badly Jesus Christ willingly died for our sins and rose from the dead to make a way for us to have a personal, intimate relationship with a loving God. No other creatures on the face of the planet can make this claim: God's Son died for them. To think God would choose us out of all the species on this planet to be able to know Him—that's what I call good news.

<hr/>

June 4
Make Time to Rest

"Then he said to them, 'The Sabbath was made for man, not man for the Sabbath'"
(Mark 2:27).

DON'T KNOW ABOUT YOU, but I really enjoy getting an extra day off whenever there's a holiday. In fact, I'm starting to think it's necessary. I have to admit I don't really take time off during the weekends. I always have jobs at home and extra work I need to get done that I end up doing on the weekends. It's usually only when I have a three-day weekend that I actually find the time to just rest. I also have to admit I need to change that. When God rested on the seventh day of creation, He didn't do it because He was tired. He did it so He could have a chance to enjoy the fruits of His labor. More than that, He rested in order to set aside a day just to spend some time with us. I'm always humbled when I'm reminded that God so wanted to hang out with me He even set aside a special day in creation just to do that. So here's my point, if God loves us so much that He would create one day a week for us to rest and not having anything else to do but just spend time with Him, who are we to say we're too busy to do so? God found time while creating the universe to take some time off. We should be able to do the same, and a weekend is a good place to start.

June 5
Speaking With a Three Year Old

"With him I speak face to face, clearly and not in riddles; he sees the form of the Lord . . . "
(Numbers 12:8).

IT'S FUNNY HOW PARENTS understand their kids better than other people. When our daughter was three years old she talked . . . a lot. Now, I understood her just fine, but other people who didn't spend as much time around her didn't always know what she was saying. I understood her because I knew her well, I had a closer relationship with her, which made for better communication. However, the fact that someone didn't clearly understand what she said didn't mean she hadn't said anything. One simply needed to spend more time with her to better understand what she was saying. The same is true with God. He speaks to us all the time, but some of us understand Him better than others. Does that mean that He isn't speaking to everyone? Not at all. Rather, some of us just need to spend more time learning to hear and understand what He has to say. In short, we need a better relationship for improved communication. Look at Moses. He knew God so well that he spoke with Him face-to-face. Wouldn't that be amazing (and a little intimidating)? The very fact that the God of the entire universe would want to speak with us at all is something I find rather miraculous. And that is what I would call good news. God wants to talk with us. Let's make sure we learn to listen.

June 6

Bumps in the Night

*"Humble yourselves, therefore, under God's mighty hand,
that he may lift you up in due time.
Cast all your anxiety on him because he cares for you"*
(1 Peter 5:6-7).

FEAR AND ANXIETY are two of the toughest foes we will ever face. Can I be honest with you? I am a coward. Yep, it's true. I'm afraid of all kinds of things. Spiders, for one. Strange noises in the dark for another. Once my daughter fell out of bed at 1 a.m. and the bump I heard had me convinced for a split second that ninjas were in the house. (I'm not too bright when I'm half asleep). Of course those are just trivial things. There are other major concerns, like pretty much all the big events happening in the world today that provide plenty of reasons for fear and anxiety. But then I remember what it says in 1Peter. I remember the first time I came across this verse and how blown away I was. I found it so amazing the Bible said to give all of my anxiety to God because He cares for me. That verse could have said a lot of things, like give your anxiety to God because He's so powerful, or because He's bigger than anything you fear. But no, it says to do so because God cares. I don't know about you, but that warms my heart and gives me courage. God cares. God cares about me. God cares about you. In the face of so much bad news in this world, I find that to be really, really good news.

June 7
Is Too Much Always Bad?
"But godliness with contentment is great gain"
(1 Timothy 6:6).

DO YOU KNOW what "cupidity" is? It's eager or excessive desire. You may want to file that away and impress your friends with it later. I mention it, however, because we live in a society that's overflowing with cupidity. From sex to money to prestige, our culture tells us to grab as much as we want as fast as we can before it's all gone. The funny thing is, it's never enough. No matter how much money, prestige, possessions, or sex we might get, we'll always want more and we'll always feel dissatisfied. In short, cupidity will never lead to happiness and contentment. Fortunately, I have good news for you: there is a way to find true contentment, and it has nothing to do with getting more stuff from the world. To truly experience contentment we need godliness, and the only way to get that is through a relationship with God. Fortunately for us, Jesus Christ came and died on the Cross and rose from the dead in order to make it possible for us to have a relationship with God. And that makes it possible to have godliness in our lives, and thereby experience true contentment. So remember, cupidity only leads to discontentment, unless that cupidity is directed toward God. After all, there's no such thing as having too excessive a desire for Him.

June 8
Just How Bad is Hell?

"Do not be afraid of those who kill the body but cannot kill the soul. Rather, be afraid of the One who can destroy both soul and body in hell"
(Matthew 10:28).

THE ANTICIPATION of pulling off a band-aid is often far worse than actually doing so. The anticipation of getting a shot is often far worse than actually getting the shot. In fact, many of the things we dread aren't nearly as bad as our anticipation of them. We seem to have a special gift for making things far worse in our minds than they are in reality. There is one thing, however, that will always be worse no matter how bad our anticipation of it may be. I'm talking about hell. In fact, I think because we can never truly understand just how bad hell is, some go the opposite direction and try to make it not so bad. Some say it's going to be a party with all our friends, or it'll be nicer than Heaven because it won't have all of those self-righteous, hypocritical, stuffy saints. The reality is that hell won't be a vacation, and in fact is far worse than our darkest, most horrific imaginings could ever anticipate. Why do I mention this? Because we never want to trivialize hell. Jesus Christ died on the Cross and rose from the dead to make sure we never have to experience it, and that's not something to be taken lightly. Besides, even though our worst anticipation of hell could never come close to how bad it actually is, our best anticipation of Heaven pales in comparison to how wonderful it's going to be. And that is good news worth sharing.

June 9
The Summer of Superheroes

No king is saved by the size of his army; no warrior escapes by his great strength. A horse is a vain hope for deliverance, despite all its great strength it cannot save.
But the eyes of the Lord are on those who fear him, on those whose hope is in his unfailing love, to deliver them from death and keep them alive in famine.
(Psalm 33:16-19)

EACH SUMMER has more than its fair share of superheroes on the big screen. For whatever reason, the comic book genre of films continues to remain popular. I think part of that is because people like the idea of there being someone to save them. Specifically, people like the idea of a hero who is really strong and has spectacular powers or gadgets and who knows what's good, but is still flawed and conflicted. He has to work hard to defeat the bad guys, but comes out victorious in the end in a spectacular fashion. That's whom we'd like to save us. Perhaps that's why so many people reject the idea of a humble, meek man who claimed to be God and ended up dying on a Cross. That just doesn't fit with our idea of a hero these days. But Jesus did more than just die on the Cross. He also rose from the dead, and one day He is returning to completely defeat the bad guys in what will be the most spectacular display of power we'll ever see—with no special effects needed. You see the good news is we do have a Savior who has done everything possible to protect and save us. Just because He doesn't wear a cape doesn't make Him any less heroic or any less super.

June 10
The Dark Knight Before the Dawn

"See, darkness covers the earth and thick darkness is over the peoples, but the Lord rises upon you and his glory appears over you. Nations will come to your light, and kings to the brightness of your dawn"
(Isaiah 60:2-3).

THE DARK KNIGHT is a dark, bleak film . . . and it happens to be my favorite in Christopher Nolan's brilliant trilogy. The truth is, I think the dark mood of that film still reflects the mood of our culture even today. There doesn't seem to be a lot of hope these days. One of my favorite lines from that movie was spoken when it was acknowledged that things were worse than ever in Gotham, but "It's always darkest before the dawn." Some may feel that's exactly where we are now, but my question is: What exactly is the dawn we're looking for? Are we looking for a mere end to our problems? Are we hoping for better times to arrive so we can get on with life as it is? You can do that if that's all you want. As for me, I'm looking forward to an entirely different kind of dawn, a dawn of a new, eternal life, a dawn where evil is defeated and righteousness reigns, a dawn where I will continually dwell in the presence of God. I am looking forward to the dawn of Christ's return, and what a glorious dawn that will be. It may be true that it's always darkest before the dawn, and although I'm not sure we've yet reached that point, I do know the return of Jesus Christ is the only dawn that will truly banish the darkness around us. More than that, I know it's a dawn I can hope for and know I won't be disappointed.

June 11
Is Anything Truly Reliable?
**"Heaven and earth will pass away,
but my words will never pass away"
(Mark 13:31).**

'VE BEEN THINKING A LOT about absolutes recently, especially since we live in a society that seems determined to eliminate them. I've been reexamining what it is I can rely on, what's truly concrete in my life. When I look at this passage in Mark, I realize two things. One: Jesus must have been more than just a good teacher to say this. Only someone supremely arrogant and full of himself would say such a thing; or only someone who is truly divine and knew this statement was true. It's absolutely clear from statements like this that you can't say Jesus was a philosopher and a good moral teacher. He either was who He claimed to be, the Son of God, or the premiere egotist of His time. The second thing I notice is if Jesus is who He said He is and what He said is true, then His Word is something I can rely on, something absolute that will never change. Despite all attempts to eliminate or retranslate the true meaning of the Bible, no one has ever been successful in doing either. It's a miracle on our bookshelves. We all need a point of reference in life, an absolute to anchor onto. I think it's really good news to know God's Word can be that absolute in our lives.

June 12
I Can't Complain

"Do everything without complaining or arguing, so that you may become blameless and pure, children of God without fault in a crooked and depraved generation . . . "
(Philippians 2:14-15).

LOVE THE ENGLISH LANGUAGE. I especially love how we can use it to make something sound like something other than what that something really is. (That wasn't too confusing, was it?) For instance, we don't we complain, we're just *thinking out loud*, sharing our *concerns*, expressing an *honest opinion*, or we're just *venting*; but it's definitely not complaining. You know what? No matter what we call it or how we describe it, the fact is we all complain a lot. In fact, I'm a complainer. However, I always get this uneasy feeling when I catch myself complaining because of this verse in Philippians. In the movie *Saving Private Ryan*, Tom Hanks' character said that complaints are always supposed to go up. What a profound insight. God is the One we should complain to in our own private and secluded prayer life. When we complain to each other, those complaints aren't going up, they're going horizontally and they don't make us look much better than the world we're trying to change. Besides, God's really the only One who can actually do anything about our complaints, and He loves us so much He wants to comfort us in the midst of our complaints. That's good news and doesn't leave us with a whole lot to complain about.

June 13
Avoiding the Ticket

"My dear children, I write this to you so that you will not sin. But, if anybody does sin, we have one who speaks to the Father in our defense—Jesus Christ the righteous one"
(1 John 2:1).

AN ARTICLE I READ once had ten tips to help you avoid getting a speeding ticket. Interestingly enough, *not speeding* wasn't one of the tips. It did, however, have tips like be a courteous driver, blend in with a group, drive a nondescript car, and so forth. Sometimes, we treat sin the same way we do a speeding ticket. We all know we're going to sin (just like we apparently speed), so instead we try just to blend in, not stick out, and avoid being caught. Unfortunately for us, God isn't some divine cop with a "sin radar" that only picks out the really bad ones. We all have sinned, we all are caught, and we all need a Savior. We need a Savior because paying the price for sin isn't like paying a speeding ticket. In fact, it's a price we could never pay. That's why Jesus Christ died on the Cross and rose from the dead, to pay the price for our sin. The best way to avoid a speeding ticket is to *not speed*, and the only way to avoid a sin ticket is to be in Christ. Personally, I think it's good news to know there is such an option.

June 14

How to Hit the Mark . . . and Maybe Make Par

"But if we walk in the light, as he is in the light,
we have fellowship with one another, and the blood of Jesus,
his Son, purifies us from all sin"
(1 John 1:7).

ONE OF THE WAYS the Bible describes sin is missing the mark. Well, I confess that I sin an awful lot when I golf because I'm constantly missing the mark. In fact, I'm usually nowhere near the mark. Sometimes I'm so far off the mark I'm on the wrong fairway or up to my knees in scrub brush looking for my golf ball. I have a lot of trouble hitting the mark in golf, and one of the best ways to fix that is to take lessons from a pro. Well, life isn't all that different. Just like in golf, in my life I'm constantly missing the mark and find myself sinning. And just like in golf, what I need is some help from a pro, although here's where things get slightly different. You see the fact is I can never be good enough to hit the mark of perfection God has set for me in this life. That's why Christ stepped in to die on the Cross and rise from the dead; He hit the mark for me. My goal every day is to learn how to let Him take the shots for me. It's only when I try to do things on my own without His help and guidance that I end up missing the mark. A pro in golf can help me learn to be good enough to get the ball where I want it to go, but in life, I need to let the pro—Jesus Christ and His Holy Spirit—do the work for me and through me. The fact that there's hope for me to hit the mark more often in life is what I call good news.

June 15
What's the Difference?

*"What shall we say then? Shall we go on sinning
so that grace may increase? By no means?
We died to sin; how can we live in it any longer?"*
(Romans 6:1-2).

ACCORDING TO A SURVEY I read not long ago, when it comes to day-to-day life and daily activities, there's virtually no difference between Christians and non-Christians. The survey revealed that Christians are just as likely to gamble, visit a pornographic website, steal, consult a medium or psychic, physically fight or abuse someone, get drunk, use drugs, lie, gossip, get revenge, and covet other people's belongings as someone who isn't a Christian. I don't know about you, but I think that's sad. I also think it's wrong. Perhaps part of the problem is we've accepted that sin will always be a part of our lives, so we just let it stay there. We've lost our will to fight. Yet when I read the Bible, I'm encouraged about my war against sin because it says we are constantly being transformed into the image of Christ, and as that image increases in my life, sin decreases. It says we are dead to sin. It says we are free from sin and it no longer rules our lives. You see, the good news is Jesus Christ died on the Cross and rose from the dead not just to pay the price for sin, but to free us from sin. He gives us the strength and the freedom to choose not to sin. We won't always make the right choice, but at least we have the freedom in Christ to do so. It looks like it's time for us to start making that choice so we can show the hurting, hopeless people of this world that there is a better way to live.

June 16
The Challenge and Reward of the Puzzle

"It is the glory of God to conceal a matter; to search out a matter is the glory of kings"
(Proverbs 25:2).

I ENJOY SOLVING CROSSWORD PUZZLES. I like being able to decipher clues and fill in the words to solve the puzzle. It's challenging and rewarding. In many ways, I'm beginning to understand God's Word is fairly similar to a crossword puzzle. There are some things that are easily discovered and understood in the Bible, and then there are other things that are more difficult. One of the problems Christians face today is that we don't take the time or put in the effort to search out answers for the more difficult questions and clues. We seem to prefer to be spoon-fed answers from our vast multi-media options rather than searching them out for ourselves in thorough Bible study. I know I'm guilty of that. This needs to change in my life because the world needs people who have an expansive knowledge of the Bible that comes from in-depth, personal study. This world is directionless, hopeless, and desperate; it needs answers, answers provided by God's Word. The trick is we won't be able to provide those answers if we haven't taken the time to find them for ourselves. I don't always finish crossword puzzles; sometimes they're just too difficult. I don't always solve Biblical puzzles during my study for the same reason. But just like my crossword puzzle habit, I find that in-depth Bible study is challenging and rewarding. Don't let the challenge keep you from the reward of really studying and puzzling over just how amazing the good news of the Bible really is.

June 17
Going Beyond the Conversion

"Therefore go and make disciples of all nations, baptizing them in the name of Father and of the Son and of the Holy Spirit"
(Matthew 28:19).

WE'VE HEARD IT ALL BEFORE: Jesus called us to make disciples, not just converts. Well, if you're like me, you've heard that and thought, *Hmm. Good point,* and then moved on with your day. However, God's not letting it go at that with me, and recently He's been helping me understand just how important it is for us not to just get people saved, but to help them mature in their relationship with God and their understanding of the Bible. Think about this: among born-again believers under the age of forty, only 3 percent of them have a biblical worldview. That's not just astonishing, that's outright frightening. Only 3 percent of Christians under the age of forty filter their daily lives through the lens of what the Bible says. I'm convinced it's time for that to change, in my life and the lives of others. It's time for the good news to have an impact on us for life, not just for conversion. So what am I saying here? I'm saying don't just invite someone to church or some ministry event in the hopes they'll get saved (although that's good). Pray they get saved and then invest some time in helping them grow. Help them get plugged into a discipleship group, or a Bible study, or one-on-one time with a mentor. Whatever we do, let's make sure we don't just make conversions with the good news. Let's invest the time and effort in making disciples with the good news. It could radically change our world.

June 18
Real Life Home Alone

What do you think? If a man owns a hundred sheep, and one of them wanders away, will he not leave the ninety-nine on the hills and go to look for the one that wandered off?
And if he finds it, I tell you the truth, he is happier about that one sheep than about the ninety-nine that did not wander off.
In the same way your Father in heaven is not willing that any of these little ones should be lost.
(Matthew 18:12-14)

REMEMBER THE MOVIE *Home Alone*? Not that long ago, I read about a family traveling from Israel to Paris that pulled a "home alone" as their four-year-old daughter was left at the airport while the parents, their other four children, and their eighteen suitcases raced to make their flight. The family didn't realize they were one short until the pilot of their plane finally informed them in mid-flight. When someone gets left home alone in real life, it's much more scary than funny, especially for the parents. That's why God wants to make sure no one gets lost. He wants everyone to make it home with Him and doesn't want anyone to be left behind or miss the flight when Jesus returns. You see, like any loving parent, God loves His children—all of us, even the rebellious ones—and He's very patient, waiting as long as possible to make sure none of us are left home alone. However, eventually the time of departure will come, so let's help our heavenly Father and make sure no one misses the flight as we share the good news with them.

June 19
Random TV and Worship

I John, am the one who heard and saw these things.
And when I had heard and seen them, I fell down to worship at the feet of the angel who had been showing them to me.
But he said to me, "Do not do it! For I am a fellow servant with you and with your brothers the prophets and of all who keep the words of this book. Worship God!"
(Revelation 22:8-9)

HAVE YOU EVER turned on the TV and watched something you didn't really want to watch but you were too lazy to do anything else? No? Well, maybe that's just me. I don't know what it is, but sometimes I'll sit there and watch the stupidest things all because I'm too lazy to pick up the remote and change the channel. For example, I often end up watching random awards shows. Why? See above. Anyway, I remember one awards show that made me rather sad because there were thousands of young people giving unadulterated praise, adoration, and worship to some so-called stars. What was even more disturbing was many of these stars not only accepted the worship, but encouraged it as well. Anyone who thinks idolatry isn't a problem here in the West just needs to turn on the TV. It's a huge problem. Here's the deal: it's obvious that we were created to worship—we do it so naturally—the problem is we usually worship the wrong people. It's not our place to give or receive worship to or from anyone. Only God is worthy of worship, and when you stop to think about all He's done, from creating the universe to dying on the Cross and rising from the dead in order to pay the price for our sin, I think you'll realize why that's true and why it's good news.

June 20
Remember the Date

"Remember the former things, those of long ago; I am God, and there is no other; I am God, and there is none like me" (Isaiah 46:9).

WHEN YOU'RE IN A RELATIONSHIP with someone there are a lot of dates to remember. My wife and I recently celebrated our fourteenth wedding anniversary, which as any married guy will tell you, is a very important date to remember. Then there are several other dates to remember: the date of your first date, the date of the day you got engaged, the date of the first time you went out for pizza, and so forth. Relationships are filled with memorable dates we don't want to forget. Well, our relationship with God should be the same. Do you remember the day you fell in love with God? Do you remember the day you surrendered your life to Him? Do you remember the first time you heard the good news? Do you celebrate those dates as being something special like you do in other relationships? In our house we have a special little tradition called re-birthdays. We make a cake, put some candles in it, and celebrate the day we were reborn in Christ. It's just one way we show our children that our relationship with God is very special, just as our relationship with each other is special. The greatest romance we'll ever experience is in our relationship with God. I think that's good news worth celebrating.

June 21
The Winning Edge

"Be strong and very courageous. Be careful to obey all the law my servant Moses gave you; do not turn from it to the right or to the left, that you may be successful wherever you go"
(Joshua 1:7).

WHENEVER THE LATEST VERSION of the Madden NFL football video game comes out, I like to make sure I can play among the elite players of the world. So what do I do in order to achieve that moon-shot of a dream? I go out and get a strategy guide. Why? Because the guide shows me all the tips, techniques, and inside hints on how to succeed and win at Madden NFL. You know what's funny? God has given us a similar kind of strategy guide for life, a guide that provides tips, techniques, principles, and guidelines for success in life. And yet far too many of us (myself included) prefer to read something written by mere mortals rather than what God, the very author of life, wrote down for us. Picking up a strategy guide for my Madden football video game reminds me just how much I need helpful hints to succeed both in an online football video game and in life. That's why it's such good news to know that God loved us enough to provide just such a guide for our lives. It's called the Bible. All we have to do is take the time to pick it up and read it.

June 22
Who Says Change is Good?
"I the Lord do not change"
(Malachi 3:6).

THEY SAY CHANGE IS GOOD. They say variety is the spice of life. Well, I don't know who *they* are, but they don't know us very well, because truth be told, there aren't very many of us who like change. I sat at the same desk at my job for . . . well, since I started. If anyone wanted to know the exact date that was, they probably could have just measured the layers of dust on all of my toys I had sitting around. Eventually though, I had to change desks. Now I know that doesn't sound like such a big deal, and I didn't think it would be until the moment came. Suddenly, I was very reluctant to change because I was more comfortable with the way things were. It was then I realized whoever said that change was good probably didn't have a lot change in his life. The good news, however, is no matter how much things change in our lives, we can count on the fact that God will always remain the same. He will always be the same loving, reliable, forgiving, just, righteous, and compassionate God He has been since the beginning of time. The only constant we have in life is that very few things are ever constant and unchanging. That's why it's such a relief to people like me who don't handle change well to know God never changes.

June 23
The Almost Good-enough Haircut

"All of us have become like one who is unclean, and all our righteous acts are like filthy rags . . . "
(Isaiah 64:6).

IT'S JUST ONE OF THOSE THINGS every kid eventually does. And the night did indeed arrive when my daughter decided to cut her own hair. The funny thing was she actually did a pretty good job. For only being six years old at the time and not having gone to barber school, she did so well I didn't even notice. My wife did, however, and I felt pretty oblivious that my daughter was able to cut her own hair while I was home without my noticing. (I am an attentive parent, really!) Now, although my daughter did a fairly good job of cutting her hair, the problem was it wasn't quite good enough. It didn't meet my wife's standard for a good haircut, and it probably wouldn't meet most people's standard for a good haircut. (As a guy, it's less of a problem; we just put on a hat.) We face the same problem when it comes to righteousness.

You may be a pretty good person. In fact, you may be a great person. You may do just about everything in your life right, but when you measure that goodness and righteousness against a perfect and holy God, well, my friend, you don't quite measure up. In fact, none of us can even come close to meeting God's standard for goodness and righteousness. That's why Christ had to come and meet that standard for us. Through His death and Resurrection, we can now share in His perfection. Now when God looks at us, He sees the perfection of Christ instead of our own bad haircut. Isn't that good news?

June 24
Think About the Good

"Many, O Lord my God, are the wonders you have done.
The things you planned for us no one can recount to you; were
I to speak and tell of them, they would be too many to declare"
(Psalm 40:5).

HAVE YOU EVER NOTICED that we pay more attention to what goes wrong and what goes bad than what goes right or what's good? For instance, at work and school we usually hear more when we do something wrong than when we do something right. In the news, we usually hear more about all the bad goings on in the world than all the good. Even in our own memories, we have a tendency to remember the bad more than the good. When I came across this verse in Psalm 40, I realized I was guilty of that. However, when I took the time to stop and really think about all God has done for me, all the ways He has blessed me and cared for me and loved me and answered my prayers, I realized this Psalm was right. His wonders really were too many to declare. And you know what, that's good news that's worth thinking about all day long. Go ahead; give it a try. You might find it'll change your perspective on your day-to-day life.

***

June 25
Is it Really Real?

"Do not be anxious about anything, but in everything, by prayer and petition, with thanksgiving, present your requests to God. And the peace of God, which transcends all understanding, will guard your hearts and your minds in Christ Jesus" (Philippians 4:6-7).

DO YOU REALLY BELIEVE what you believe is really real? I mention this because I'm willing to bet most of us don't think much about this verse when things are going well, and when things suddenly go poorly we might look at it and say, "What's the deal? How come this isn't working?" Well, the question of what you believe is really put to the test in those moments when things seem to go awry. If you really believe what you believe is really real, if you truly believe God's Word really means that you don't need to be anxious, and instead can have peace in any situation when you go to God in prayer and thanksgiving, how might your life be different? Oh, I know we all believe God's Word is true, but do you believe it's *really real*? Do you believe it is reality? Do you believe this is how the universe works? I don't know about you, but as for me, it's time to start making God's Word really real in my life. Starting with this verse.

***

June 26
You're So Very Small, But So Very Loved
"What is man that you are mindful of him,
the son of man that you care for him?"
(Psalm 8:4).

DO YOU HAVE ANY IDEA how small you really are? No seriously, you, my friend, are a tiny speck on a wee dot floating through a huge cosmos. I don't know if you've seen any of them, but there are tons of videos out there (often on YouTube) that point out how our solar system is about the size of a quarter, if the North American continent were the size of our galaxy. And that's just our galaxy. That doesn't take into account our size in a universe filled with billions and billions of galaxies. Wow! We are really *so small*. Now I know that may be a blow to your ego, to your sense of self-importance, but what's really humbling is the fact that although we may be so very small, God still cares a great deal about us. In fact, God so loved us He sent His only Son to our tiny blue speck in the universe to live, die, and live again just to make a way for us to know God. To know His love, to know His mercy, to know His grace, and to know His face. You see, to God, even the universe can be measured in the span of His hand, but His love for us, well, that is absolutely immeasurable. That's why it's called good news.

June 27
Oysters, Pearls, and God's Love

"Again, the kingdom of heaven is like a merchant looking for fine pearls. When he found one of great value, he went away and sold everything he had and bought it"
(Matthew 13:45-46).

READ A STORY of a couple in Lebanon who were having oysters for lunch when they discovered one of the oysters had twenty-six pearls inside. Granted, some of the pearls were very small, but they had never seen an oyster with so many pearls inside. As you can imagine, that's one oyster they decided to keep rather than eat. I don't know if you've ever had a moment where you found something extremely rare, but I'm willing to bet when and if you do, you'll probably make every effort to keep that priceless thing. Well, it may surprise you to know that's the way God feels about us. We are a rare treasure to Him, and He gave everything He had to purchase us. He thought we were so valuable He was willing to die in our place for our sins to purchase our freedom and eternal life. We are a treasure that God doesn't want to lose. What an amazing, humbling love God has for us. It's a rare treasure we should make sure we cling to.

June 28
What Are You Addicted To?
*"Do not get drunk on wine, which leads to debauchery.
Instead, be filled with the Spirit"*
(Ephesians 5:18).

DON'T KNOW if you spend a lot of time thinking about addictions, but there are occasions where I do. Specifically, I think about the things I'm addicted to that keep me from fully experiencing God every day. I look at this verse in Ephesians and in the place of *wine* I substitute whatever it is I feel like I can't do without. I do that to remind myself the only thing I really can't do without is God. It says to me, "Do not get drunk on chocolate," or "Do not get drunk on video games." It says to me the only thing in life I can over-indulge in and not have any negative side effects from is the Holy Spirit. Unfortunately, that's often the one thing I under-indulge in. Isn't ironic how we try to find things that will meet the insatiable longing and desire we all have inside and none of those things we try really help? While we soak ourselves in our addiction of choice and wonder why we aren't satisfied in life, Jesus beckons us to come to Him because He came to give us the very thing we're seeking, the very thing we're longing for and desperately desire: a full and abundant life. We won't find it in any other addiction other than an addiction to Jesus. And you know what? I think that's good news. In fact, it's the good news I need to be reminded of every now and then.

June 29

Good and Simple News

"This is love: not that we loved God, but that he loved us and sent his Son as an atoning sacrifice for our sins"
(1 John 4:10).

I DON'T KNOW ABOUT YOU, but sometimes it's nice just to receive a random word of encouragement. To have someone tell you for no particular reason that you do a good job, that they like one of your characteristics, that they think you are valuable in what you do and how you serve God. Sometimes it's nice to be told that you're loved just for who you are. It really means a lot to me when I hear that. So to all of you who have the gift of encouragement, I thank you for sharing your gift and encourage you to be bold in doing so. A simple word of encouragement is a very valuable, very precious thing. And so along those lines, I wanted to share this simple encouragement with you: God loves you. Let us never forget that very simple, extremely precious truth. No matter who you are, God loves you. He doesn't wait for you to love Him first, but rather He loves you right now. You'd be surprised how much it means to people to hear that. So if nothing else, let's make sure we take the time to encourage each other with the simple truth—"Jesus loves me, this I know, for the Bible tells me so." That, my friends, is truly good news.

June 30
Dare to be Different

"While they were worshiping the Lord and fasting, the Holy Spirit said, "Set apart for me Barnabas and Saul for the work to which I have called them"
(Acts 13:2).

MOST OF US don't like to stand out in a crowd. We feel uncomfortable when we get singled out in a large group. For the most part, we just prefer to go unnoticed. However, I've been realizing lately that isn't what God intends for us. Just a glance at the Bible reveals God calls us to be set apart from the rest, to stand out from the crowd for Him, and to go against the flow. If you really stop to think about it, it's a very radical life God calls us to. It means we're going to be different, we're going to stand out from the world. In fact, that's just a part of normal Christianity. You see, the good news is God sets us all apart for a very special, very important purpose. However, if we want to fulfill that purpose, we need to leave the world completely behind and give ourselves solely to serving Christ. Radical? You bet. Worthwhile? I can't think of anything that's more worthwhile than living a life set apart for Christ.

July

For day and night
Your hand was heavy upon me;
My vitality was turned into the
drought of summer. Selah

Psalm 32:4

July 1
Somebody's Always Watching

"O Lord, you have searched me and you know me.
You know when I sit and when I rise; you perceive my thoughts
from afar. You discern my going out and my lying down;
you are familiar with all my ways"
(Psalm 139:1-3).

OCCASIONALLY I HAVE caught my kids doing something they knew they shouldn't be doing, but thought they could get away with because I wasn't watching. But this isn't about them; it's about you and me. This is about God's kids and how many times we do the exact same thing: we do something we know we shouldn't because we think no one is watching, including God. The Bible tells us God sees all that we do, but do we believe that's really real? Do we really believe God always sees what we're doing? If we did, how differently might we act when we're alone, knowing we aren't truly alone because God is there with us? How might temptation be less powerful if we really believe God was watching our struggle and the outcome? For some, the thought of a God who knows and sees everything we do is uncomfortable, but it shouldn't be. God loves us, and He watches over us in order to care for us and protect us, which I think is good news. Plus, if we really believe God really is watching us at all times, it's great way to stay out of trouble, even when we're all alone.

July 2
Paying the Debt

"This is love: not that we loved God, but that he loved us and sent his Son as an atoning sacrifice for our sins"
(1 John 4:10).

ONCE READ A STORY of a seventy-five-year-old blind woman in Massachusetts who was threatened with a lien against her home due to an unpaid amount on her sewer and water bill. The amount was exactly (are you ready for this?), one cent. Yep, just a penny. When the story broke, people all over the nation were calling in saying they were willing to pay the one penny so this woman could keep her home. Well, the good news is God has done something similar for us, although the stakes in our case were much higher. God was willing to pay the price for our sin so that we could keep our life, but it cost Him the life of His one and only son. What's more, God did this long before we ever knew Him, while we were still strangers to Him. Why? Because He loves us. People wanted to pay the penny for that woman in Massachusetts because they thought what was happening to her wasn't fair. God paid the price for our sin because He loves us so much He didn't want to see us die. It's good news that someone helped the woman pay her bill to get her out of trouble, but isn't it better news that God gave everything to save our lives? Isn't that a story worth sharing?

July 3

The Creepy Crawlies

"He will cover you with his feathers, and under his wings you will find refuge; his faithfulness will be your shield and rampart. You will not fear the terror of night, nor the arrow that flies by day"
(Psalm 91:4-5).

HAVE A DEATHLY FEAR OF SPIDERS; they give me the creepy crawlies like crazy. In fact, I remember one time when there was a spider by my desk at work, and because of that I didn't sit at my desk the rest of the day. In fact, I even had trouble trying to sit at my desk the following day. However, this fear of spiders is something that really frustrates me. Why? Because the Bible tells us not to be afraid, to take courage, and to fear not. Now I understand there are some very sound psychological reasons people have fears such as arachnophobia, but I also know that we serve a mighty God. You see, if we really believe what the Bible says is really real, then the good news is we can overcome our fears. God may heal us miraculously, or we may need a more methodical approach. Either way, God will give us the strength and the courage to overcome our fears, be they of spiders, of the current economic situation, or whatever. When I see the Bible telling me I don't need to be afraid, that's what I'm going to choose to believe . . . even if I see another spider . . . but hopefully I won't.

July 4
Celebrating the Truth of Freedom

"To the Jews who had believed him, Jesus said, 'If you hold to my teaching, you are really my disciples. Then you will know the truth, and the truth will set you free'"
(John 8:31-32).

TODAY IS THE FOURTH OF JULY, the day when we celebrate our freedom and independence by eating food that's bad for us and setting off mildly dangerous explosives. At least, that's what we're supposed to be celebrating, but I can't help but feel that a lot of this celebration is a farce. Why? Well, Jesus said that it's the *truth* that will set us free, and yet, we seem determined to eliminate truth from our nation. From the post-modern beliefs that are leaking into the Church which refuse to define truth, to a belief among Christians that there's really more than one way to define truth, we are quickly losing sight of what truth is. And if we lose the truth, we will lose our freedom. So this Fourth of July, as you celebrate your freedom I hope you'll also celebrate the truth of God's Word and the truth that Jesus Christ embodied while He was here on Earth. It's that truth which truly sets us free. That is why it's such good news.

July 5
Money Worries

"I was young and now I am old, yet I have never seen the righteous forsaken or their children begging bread. They are always generous and lend freely; their children will be blessed" (Psalm 37:25-26).

I HAVE A CONFESSION TO MAKE (in fact, it seems I make a lot of those when writing these little thoughts . . . oh well, I hope they help). I have trouble trusting God in one particular area of my life: money. Sure, I can trust God for redemption, forgiveness, and eternal life, but a few extra bucks to pay the bills this month, not so much. I don't know why, but I've always been insecure about money. However, I've been working to change that because the truth is I don't know what I've been worried about. No matter the situation, we've always had what we needed, and we've even had enough to share with others who really need some help. Plus, the Bible repeatedly says God can handle that aspect of our lives. What's really funny is when our nation faces any sort of economic crisis, I can honestly say I'm not worried. Oh, I'm concerned about making wise financial decisions, but I'm not worried that I suddenly won't be able to feed my children. Strange, isn't it? In those moments when the nation has been worried about money are often the times I'm learning not to worry because I'm investing and banking on God. The good news is you can do the same.

July 6
Aircraft to Tower; Hello?

"*He who watches over you will not slumber, indeed, he who watches over Israel will neither slumber or sleep*"
(Psalm 121:3-4).

THIS IS A TRUE STORY: a few years back two airplanes trying to land on one of the Greek Isles had to circle around for forty minutes before landing. Why? Because the air traffic controller was still asleep at home. Apparently, he just forgot to set his alarm and overslept, so there was no one in the tower to give the planes directions to land. Isn't it nice to know that the "air traffic controller" of our lives never has that problem? We never have to worry about calling in for directions from God and not getting an answer back because He overslept, doesn't feel well, or forgot to show up for work that day. God is always there, He's always aware of our needs, and He's always ready to help us. We can call to Him any time night or day for instructions and He'll be there to help us and guide us. Our lives don't have to be left in a holding pattern, circling around and around doing the same things over and over again. Sometimes it's easy to take for granted the fact that God hears and answers our prayers, but after reading about that sleepy air traffic controller, I was reminded of just how good it is to have a loving God who never tires or sleeps.

July 7

Letting Go of What's Holding Me Back

"Those who live according to the sinful nature have their minds set on what that nature desires; but those who live in accordance with the Spirit have their minds set on what the Spirit desires. The mind of sinful man is death, but the mind controlled by the Spirit is life and peace"
(Romans 8:5-6).

WHAT IS CONTROLLING YOUR LIFE? Because if it's anything other than the Spirit of God, you aren't truly free and you aren't truly set apart for God. This is something I've become more and more convinced of over the years. You see the fact is we all have areas of our lives that either we like to be in control of ourselves, or they're ruled by something else. We all have weakness, vices, little habits that aren't really beneficial, but aren't really harmful. To be honest, I've coddled my own addictive tendencies and have called them cute little quirks. However, I've become convinced since Jesus Christ died on the Cross and rose from the dead for my sins, He deserves all of me. The fact is there isn't anything or anyone else who was willing to or able to pay the price for my life. That being the case, I can't let anything hold me back from surrendering everything to Jesus. Besides, when I give up my life to Christ, wholly and completely, He says that's when I'll find true life, abundant life, and a free life. That sounds like good news to me, so now it's good-bye to anything and everything that controls any part of my life, no matter how small.

July 8
The "Joy" of Comfort Foods

"O God, you are my God, earnestly I seek you . . .
My soul will be satisfied as with the richest of foods;
with singing lips my mouth will praise you"
(Psalm 63:1, 5).

COMFORT FOODS. We all have them. We all have certain foods that just make us feel better when we eat them. Or to put it another way, we feel comforted. My comfort food is pizza. Yep, I'm pretty much like a Ninja Turtle. It's a good thing I got married because otherwise that would still be all I'd eat. I also find chocolate rather comforting. Now, I don't know what your comfort food is, but when I was reading Psalm 63 the whole concept of comfort food was suddenly a very uncomfortable one for me. The verse talks about seeking God and says, "My soul will be satisfied as with the richest of foods." In short, God should be our comfort food. When stressed or distressed, we shouldn't turn to something we consume, but to the One who consumes us in His love. I've noticed the comfort I get from my comfort foods never really lasts. Plus, that comfort always takes extra work to burn off later. Perhaps it's time I started making it God's job to comfort me, and perhaps I'll find it far more satisfying and lasting. That sounds like good news to me.

July 9
Sleeping Beauty and the Sword of Truth

"And there was war in heaven.
Michael and his angels fought against the dragon,
and the dragon and his angels fought back.
But he was not strong enough,
and they lost their place in heaven"
(Revelation 12:7-8).

SLEEPING BEAUTY, as odd as it may sound, is actually one of my favorite Disney films. There's a scene where Prince Phillip faces off against Maleficent, who takes the form of a dragon. Eventually the battle is won when Phillip tosses the sword of truth into the dragon's belly. Even as a kid, I found this imagery extremely powerful. From a very young age I was taught that God's Word, which is truth, is our sword, and it is how we can overcome all the powers of hell. (Interestingly, that's the very phrase used by Maleficent as she becomes a dragon.) The problem in today's world is we're trying to eliminate truth. But if we do that, how will we fight the dragon? The Bible tells us an all-too-real dragon has been flung to Earth, and its appetite for destruction is immense. If we are going to overcome it, we must, at all costs, cling to the truth of the good news and always have our sword at the ready. Best of all, if we do that, the Bible promises us our own fairy tale ending.

July 10
The Secret to Success

" . . . because the Lord was with Joseph and gave him success in whatever he did"
(Genesis 39:23).

WOULDN'T IT BE WEIRD if one day you were invited to the White House to solve a problem, and after you solved the problem the president put you in charge of the entire nation? He gave you power over everything and everyone but himself? That would truly be bizarre, wouldn't it? Not to mention farfetched. And yet, that's what happened to Joseph in the Old Testament. One of the traits I've always admired about Joseph was his diligence. No matter what situation he found himself, be it a slave, a prisoner, or a ruler, he went about his duties with diligence and faithfulness, making sure he gave his best to whatever his task was. God honored that, and the Bible says He gave Joseph *success in whatever he did*. That's a phrase I have always desired to be true about me. It's why I apply myself to do my best in any and every task because I want to be like Joseph. I may not ever be asked to rule a country, but if God notices my faithfulness and diligence like He did Joseph's, I would consider that very good news.

July 11
Why Salvation Isn't "Do-It-Yourself"

"For it is by grace you have been saved, through faith—
and this not from yourselves, it is a gift of God—
not by works, so that no one can boast"
(Ephesians 2:8-9).

'VE NEVER BEEN MUCH of a "do-it-yourselfer," but my dad has always loved doing those kinds of projects around the house. He helped me put in the tile on the front walkway of our house, and while my dad deserves most of the credit for how well it turned out, I have to admit, I was pretty proud of the little I was able to do. After spending a couple hours laying tile, mixing grout, and the rest, when I surveyed what I had accomplished, I felt really good about how it looked. I couldn't help thinking to myself, "Look at that. That looks good. I did some of that." We all have a propensity to admire and be proud of our own handiwork, which is why I think God had to do all the work for us when it came to salvation. If we were able to secure our own salvation in even the smallest way, we would never really acknowledge what God did for us because we'd be too proud and too busy admiring what we did for ourselves. God doesn't give us that option. He did all the work by dying on the Cross and rising from the dead for our sins. He paid the price and did the work we could never do on our own. We must rely completely and solely on what He did on our behalf out of His love for us. For "do-it-yourselfers," that isn't easy. But it's the only way to find eternal life, which is why it's such good news.

July 12

Good News! You're Rich!

"Then the King will say to those on his right, 'Come, you who are blessed by my Father, take your inheritance, the kingdom prepared for you since the creation of the world'"
(Matthew 25:34).

HAVE you ever received one of those emails that announce how rich you've suddenly become? You know, the ones that tell you about an overseas account or some lottery or even an inheritance from a distant rich relative you were never aware of, but now suddenly decided to leave everything they have to you. Obviously it's a scam, but still, deep inside of us we kind of wish it were true; that we could suddenly have great riches for free. Well, my friends, if you've ever seen those emails and felt that way, I definitely have good news for you. You can have great riches and you don't need to do anything to earn them, not even share your personal account information. Well, I take that back. There is one condition for you to inherit this fabulous wealth: you must become a child of the Most High God. How do you do that? Through Jesus Christ. What will you inherit? Well, you may not get lots of money here on Earth, but you will get something far more valuable. You will inherit the riches of the Kingdom of God. You will be a beneficiary of the King of Kings. You, my friend, will inherit eternal life and the glorious riches and majesty of the heavenly realm. You won't find this fantastic offer in any email, only in the Bible. And it is a limited time offer. It's only good as long as life lasts, and who knows how long that will be. So don't delay, respond today. It may cost you surrendering your life to God, but you'll gain far more than you give up.

July 13
Look-alikes

"And just as we have borne the likeness of the earthly man, so shall we bear the likeness of the man from heaven"
(1 Corinthians 15:49).

"DO YOU KNOW WHO YOU LOOK LIKE?" Have you ever had anyone say that to you? I am consistently told two things: I either remind people of Jim Carrey or I look like Dan Akroyd. I'm never quite sure how to respond to something like that. Do I thank the person? Do I try to emulate the person I look like even more? Do I pretend I've never heard this before? Do I wonder if I look so much like them, why don't I make as much money as they do? In any event, this whole "You look like" phenomenon got me thinking about who I should really look like which quite honestly is Jesus Christ. Now, when I asked my daughter (she was three at the time) how we could look more like Christ, she said we should grow beards. While that may help aesthetically, what I really want to happen is for my attitudes, my thoughts, the way I treat others, my compassion, and my love to closely resemble Christ's. So instead of people saying I look like Jim Carrey, they'll say there's something different about me, something they like and are drawn to. That something should be the good news of Jesus Christ on display in every aspect of my life.

July 14
The Power of Words

*"How can a young man keep his way pure?
By living according to your word. I seek you with all my heart;
do not let me stray from your commands. I have hidden your
word in my heart that I might not sin against you"*
(Psalm 119:9-11).

WORDS ARE POWERFUL. They're so powerful they can even control video games. Thanks to the power of things like the Xbox's Kinect, I can do things like tell my armies where to go and what to do just by speaking. I can unleash the massive destruction of powerful weapons with a simple, spoken command. Yep, words are powerful in the realm of video games, just as they are in real life. Do you realize it was just a simple word spoken by God that brought the universe into being? Think about that for a moment. God spoke, and BAM! It was there. I wonder what that looked like? If God's Word is powerful enough to bring into being all we behold, shouldn't we act as though His Word is powerful enough to change lives, powerful enough to fear, and powerful enough to be worthy of our obedience? Sometimes we wait for God to act, but all He really needs to do is speak. Why? Because when God speaks, you know something mighty is going to happen. The good news is, for those of us who are His children, for those of us who believe and trust in Him, those powerful words are often spoken lovingly on our behalf and for our benefit. No video game can ever top that.

* * *

July 15
Planning for Death . . . and After Death

" . . . This grace was given us in Christ Jesus before the beginning of time, but it has now been revealed through the appearing of our Savior, Christ Jesus, who has destroyed death and has brought life and immortality to light through the gospel"
(2 Timothy 1:9-10).

ARE YOU READY FOR DEATH? I know, that sounds like a morbid question, but there was a man in North Carolina who was definitely ready. How ready was he? He won a prize at the state fair for building his own coffin. Not only that, he already had his pallbearers lined up, and he had written his own eulogy. It's obvious he put a lot of thought into his eventual demise, to the point where he won a blue ribbon for his own coffin design. When I was reading that story, I couldn't help but wonder what his plans were for *after* death? I mean it's nice his custom coffin will be comfortable, and have a place for pictures of his family, and has his signature embedded in it, but what happens after he's in that coffin? You see, the good news is there's more to death than just death. In fact, for those who are in Christ, there's a whole lot more living to do after death. The unfortunate thing is if you don't plan for what happens after death . . . well, let's just say eternity is going to be very uncomfortable and rather hot. Look, death smiles at us all sooner or later, but the question isn't what do we want our funeral to be like, but what do we want our eternity to be like? May I simply suggest the alternative Jesus Christ gave us through His death and Resurrection is not only preferable, it's worth living for.

July 16
Here is God's Will for You

"Be joyful always; pray continually; give thanks in all circumstances, for this is God's will for you in Christ Jesus" (1 Thessalonians 5:16-18).

ONE OF THE MOST common things people want to know is, "What is God's will for my life?" Well, interestingly enough, I came across a verse in the Bible that actually reveals the will of God. In fact, it reveals what God's will is in every situation you may encounter. Isn't that amazing? We're often trying to figure out God's will for this or that situation, and the good news is the answer is right here in the Bible. The good news is you can really know the will of God for any circumstance or eventuality you may encounter. Consider what the Bible says is God's will for us: be joyful always—which isn't dependent on our circumstances like happiness is; pray continually—which is absolutely crucial in every situation we encounter, both good and bad; and give thanks in all circumstances—which is often neglected or taken for granted, but can have a huge impact on our outlook on life. Well, now we know what God's will is for us in every circumstance and situation, I guess the real question is: Are we carrying out that will in our lives, in our nation, in our communities, and in our world?

July 17
The True Sin of Sodom

"'Now this was the sin of your sister Sodom: She and her daughters were arrogant, overfed and unconcerned; they did not help the poor and needy'" (Ezekiel 16:49).

HONESTLY DON'T KNOW if this Scripture really needs much commentary. When I came across it, I couldn't get it out of my head. Look, I know there's a lot going on right now. There's always plenty happening in our world to cause stress, anxiety, and worry and it can cause us to look to our own well-being and self-interests. Well, this passage in Ezekiel is a reminder to me not to let distractions keep me from doing the things God has called us as the Church to do. To be loving, to pray even for people we don't agree with, to reach out and help those in need, and to be generous with what God has given us. Most of us think the sin of Sodom was simply homosexuality, but if this passage is true, then we may be guiltier of Sodom's real sin than we thought. In any event, we can do something about it. We serve a loving God who is gracious and forgiving, plus He's the source of our provision, our joy, and our abundance of grace. So you see, the good news is if God is taking care of us, then we have no reason to avoid helping and taking care of others. And we can avoid the true sin of Sodom.

July 18
Would You Like a Prayer Booth?

"But when you pray, go into your room, close the door and pray to your Father, who is unseen. Then your Father, who sees what is done in secret, will reward you"
(Matthew 6:6).

THERE WAS AN ARTIST in New York who created what he called "prayer booths." (Talk about literally going into your prayer closet.) They basically looked like telephone booths, except they said *prayer* instead of *telephone* and they had a flip-down kneeler. No really, this actually happened. They were even put on display in midtown Manhattan. The artist said the reason he created the booths was because he wanted to spark dialogue about prayer. That's all fine and good, but how about actually praying? Instead of talking about prayer, instead of discussing its pros and cons, and whether or not it's really effective, why not just do it and find out? You know the sad thing is having a prayer booth on a street corner might actually remind some of us to pray more often; I know it would help me. My point is whether you have an actual prayer closet or not, let's make sure we are people of prayer. No matter if we need direction, a little help, some comfort, healing, wisdom, provision, or just Someone to talk to who really cares about us, the good news is God is always there for just that reason.

July 19
Sharing is Good . . . Really

"Instruct them to do good, to be rich in good works, to be generous and ready to share . . ."
(1 Timothy 6:18, NASB).

HAVE TWO LITTLE GIRLS, and if there's one thing I've noticed about little girls, or about kids of any age it's that they have hard time sharing. No matter what it is—a Barbie or even a cardboard box—they may play together nicely for a while, but eventually that self-preservation gene of "everything is mine . . . or should be" kicks in and crying begins. I know you're snickering about this, adults, nodding your heads thinking, "It's so true." But I've seen plenty of adults acting the same way. The truth is, sharing doesn't come naturally, which is exactly why I think it's such big part of the Kingdom of God. God wants us to share and be generous because it stands out in contrast to the selfish nature of the world. When we give, especially when there's nothing in it for us, people want to know why. And when they want to know why, that's the perfect opportunity to share the good news of Jesus' love with them. So let's be a sharing, generous people, and in doing so, we just may find ourselves sharing the Kingdom of God with people who desperately need that more than anything else.

July 20

Who Says Girls Can't Play Baseball?

"But Moses said to God, 'Who am I, that I should go to Pharaoh and bring the Israelites out of Egypt?' And God said, 'I will be with you'"
(Exodus 3:11-12).

NOT LONG AGO a sixteen-year-old girl was added to the roster of a pro baseball team in Japan. She's the first female pro-baseball player there, although she isn't exactly playing for the Yankees. The team she joined is pretty far down the totem pole, but it's still the first time a woman has been a part of a pro team in Japan. You know, sometimes people get into the mindset of they can't join God's team for this, that, or some other reason. They'll say things like, "God can't use me because of what I did in the past," or "God can't use me because I'm too shy," or a host of other excuses. Well, the good news is, not only can God use you, He *wants* to use you for His purposes and plans. He has something very special in mind for you to do, and He knows you're the best person for the job. How does he know that? Because He made you. He knows exactly what you can and can't do. So the issue is really what will *you* do? Are you willing to be a part of a God's team and play whatever role He may have for you? Are you willing to believe God wants to use your abilities and skills for the glory of His Kingdom, His team? The truth is, if He can use someone like Moses, then He can use you. Women can play pro baseball, so there shouldn't be anything to keep you from playing on God's team.

July 21
Flying the Jet Pack of Faith
"Have faith in God," Jesus answered"
(Mark 11:22).

DID YOU KNOW a man wearing a jetpack once flew across a canyon in Colorado? It took him twenty-one seconds to fly across a 1,500-foot canyon, traveling at about seventy-five-miles-per-hour. Some would say that's daring. Some would say it's bold. Some would say that's stupid. (I know if it tried it that's what my mom would say.) Well, whatever you may think about someone flying across a canyon wearing a jet pack, God is essentially asking us to do the same. He's asking us to strap on the jet pack of faith and fly off into the unknown. However, He's not asking us to put on a blindfold as well. To be truthful, I don't really believe in "blind faith." Why? Because if nothing else, I know the character of God. Even if I can't see anything else, I can see God has always been faithful, always kept His promises, has always loved me, and will always be there for me. So even when everything else in life is foggy and uncertain, I can still strap on the jet pack of faith and fly confidently across any canyon of trial, challenge, or attack. I like to think of that as the power of the good news.

July 22
The Trouble With Anger

"In your anger do not sin. Do not let the sun go down while you are still angry, and do not give the devil a foothold"
(Ephesians 4:26-27).

TALK ABOUT YOUR INAPPROPRIATE ANGER ...I remember a story about an eight-year-old boy in Germany who stole his teacher's car after she expelled him from the classroom for being disruptive. What's worse is that he didn't make it very far before crashing into another car. Apparently, the little boy wanted to go home and complain to his mother about how his teacher kicked him out of class, and the best way he could think of for doing that was taking his teacher's car. The truth is, we all do stupid things when we get angry. I'm no exception. I remember one particularly frustrating moment where I got so annoyed about something I ended up spilling ice cold lemonade all over the inside of my car. What sticky mess that was. The good news is the Bible doesn't tell us not to get angry; that's bound to happen, but it's what we do with our anger that matters. When we're angry, we should bring it to God. We can vent and yell and express ourselves to Him, and then collapse into His loving, compassionate arms as He helps us let go of our anger. Considering the alternatives, I think that's good news. Although, sometimes I wish the Bible had said in our anger to not be stupid, but I guess sin amounts to the same thing.

July 23

The Day the Earth Really Stood Still

" . . . The sun stopped in the middle of the sky and delayed going down about a full day. There has never been a day like it before or since, a day when the Lord listened to a man" (Joshua 10:13-14).

IN 2008, moviegoers had a chance to see a remake of the sci-fi classic, *The Day the Earth Stood Still.* I actually have some pretty fond memories of the 1951 original. It's one of the few classic sci-fi films that really got me thinking. (Which I couldn't really say for the remake. Are remakes *ever* as good as the original?) More importantly, however, this is a story that's based on fact. The fact is the Earth really did stand still once. What's really fascinating is the Earth didn't stand still because of some weird UFO landing, or some god-like advanced technology an alien used to stop time. No, the Earth stood still simply because a man asked God to do it. Now, I don't think that means every time you're facing a final in school or are dreading going in to work you can ask God to stop time for you, but it does illustrate that God does listen to our requests. In fact, there's no telling what God might do on our behalf if we would just ask. After all, Jesus Christ came as a baby, lived, died, and lived again just so we could present our requests to God. Perhaps in the midst of our busy lives we need to ask Him to help *us* stand still for just a moment so we might remember when Jesus came as God in the flesh. That was good news that should still cause the Earth to stand still in awe.

July 24
I've Always Wanted to Fight Pirates
"The thief comes only to steal and kill and destroy; I have come that they may have life, and have it to the full"
(John 10:10).

NEVER THOUGHT I'd hear so much about pirates in the twenty-first century, but in recent years they have been a persistent and dangerous problem, particularly off the coast of Somalia. So much so, that the U.S. Navy even headed up an international fleet to fight pirates. You heard right, the U.S. Navy is in the business of battling pirates at sea. Kind of like the movie *Pirates of the Caribbean*, but with all kinds of high-tech, modern warships. All this talk of pirates got me thinking about another pirate that needs to be dealt with: Satan. Jesus said Satan comes to steal, kill, and destroy. Sounds like the MO of a pirate to me. The question is: What do we do about this pirate that's pillaging our culture, our youth, and even our neighbors? Well, I think we need to do something similar to what the U.S. Navy did. It's time to deploy a task force from the Church to fight this pirate. Who should be in that task force? You and me. We need to be willing to go out into the dangerous, pirate-filled waters of the world, and share the truth and the good news of God's love and grace. We need to share the good news that Jesus Christ brings life—a full, abundant, meaningful, everlasting life. If we don't, then our culture is truly sunk. So, are you ready to fight some pirates with the sword of truth? C'mon, it might be some swashbuckling fun!

July 25
Finders Keepers
"You will seek me and find me when you seek me with all your heart"
(Jeremiah 29:13).

IF I WERE TO TELL YOU there was a satchel with one hundred thousand dollars hidden somewhere in my backyard and the first person who came here and found it would get to keep it, how many of you would suddenly be very interested in knowing where I live and doing whatever it took to find that money? Now, don't go running to your cars or booking flights to Albuquerque because I don't have a hundred grand hidden anywhere; I'm just trying to make a point. When money is on the line, we're willing to do just about anything to get it. Right now you're thinking about all of the crazy things you would do for money. However, the Bible promises us if seek after God with all of hearts we will find Him, and yet how many of us put in as much effort into finding God as we would in getting free money? My point is when there's money involved, we're usually pretty motivated to get the cash into our pockets. But when it's the power and presence of God we're told to pursue, it's often a half-hearted effort at best because . . . what? We don't understand the benefit? The concept of "God's power and presence" is too vague? You know, if we would put in the same effort chasing God as we do money, just think how different our lives would be, think of how different our world would be. I guess it just comes down to a question of value. Sure, money is up for grabs in this world, but so is the presence and power of God. Which are you going to pursue?

July 26
One of Those "Well, Duh" Moments

"It is good to praise the Lord and make music to your name, O Most High, to proclaim your love in the morning and your faithfulness at night"
(Psalm 92:1-2).

DON'T YOU HATE IT when someone states the obvious? It's like you can't figure out for yourself that the sky is blue, the grass is green, and the Denver Broncos are going to win the Super Bowl (just tossed that one in to see if you were awake). I don't know about you, but when someone states the obvious to me, it makes me feel like they think I'm some sort of dunderhead because I couldn't figure that out myself. Well, the other day I was reading along in the Psalms, and suddenly I came to a passage where the Bible states the obvious, "It is good to praise the Lord," and naturally I responded, "Well, duuuuh." But then a thought occurred to me, "If it's so obvious, then why don't I do it?" Sure it may be obvious that praising the Lord is good, but if it is so good, then the question really is why don't we do it more? Why don't we praise Him on the good days . . . and praise Him on the bad days? Why don't we praise Him in the morning . . . and the evening? Look, maybe you do, but I just had to be honest with you and let you know it took a perfectly obvious Scripture, a slap upside the head, that said, "Hey dummy, you know this already," to remind me that praising the Lord, no matter our circumstances, is just plain good.

July 27

There's No Escape, but There is Hope

"To him who loves us and has freed us from our sins
by his blood, and has made us to be a kingdom and priests
to serve his God and Father—
to him be glory and power for ever and ever! Amen"
(Revelation 1:5-6).

DON'T KNOW IF YOU HEARD ABOUT THIS, but there was a financial manager who tried to fake his own death by parachuting out of a plane he was flying just before it crashed. He was later arrested in Florida. Why did this man try to fake his own death? Because he was trying to escape his past. Apparently he was going to be prosecuted for financial fraud. To be honest, I can completely identify with this guy. After all, how many of us would like to run away and try and hide rather than face the consequences of our sin? I can think of a few times where I wish I could have done that. However, as this guy found out, not even faking one's own death is enough to escape the consequences of sin. That being the case, you might wonder what hope is there? Well, the good news is even though we can never escape from sin, Jesus Christ died on the Cross and rose from the dead to pay the price for our sin. He faced the consequences for us, and then offered us forgiveness and freedom. Why? Because God loves us. He doesn't want to see sin catch up with us, He wants us to enjoy freedom from our sins, and to enjoy His love freely and unhindered. You can't fake a death to escape sin. You can only accept Jesus' death in your place.

July 28
Suffering for the Name

"The apostles left the Sanhedrin, rejoicing because they had been counted worthy of suffering disgrace for the Name" (Acts 5:41).

ALL OVER THE WORLD Christians are suffering for the name of Jesus. They are being imprisoned, beaten, ostracized, harried, and sometimes killed. Their lives are made miserable because of their faith in Christ. It's been like that since the day the Church started. However, I have a confession to make: I don't know if I could be like the disciples and rejoice because I was worthy of suffering for Christ. Maybe I'm a wimp, maybe I'm soft, maybe I'm a coward, but that's hard for me to think of—to rejoice because I'm worthy to suffer. Yet people all over the world are doing just that, and because of their courage lives are being changed for all eternity. The truth is I may not have the courage, but that courage can't come from myself anyway. It's God who gives us the courage and ability to stand for Him. It's God who gives us the means to withstand any challenge and any persecution. It's God who will change lives through our bold testimony. And it's God who will never leave us or forsake us. Sounds like good news to me. So maybe I am ready to be counted worth to suffer disgrace for the name. How about you?

July 29
Miracle on the Hudson
" . . . pray continually . . . "
(1 Thessalonians 5:17).

DO REMEMBER the "Miracle on the Hudson"? Man, what a crazy story that was. A commercial jet, US Airways flight 1549, hit a flock of geese six minutes after takeoff and was forced to land on the Hudson River. The reason it's remembered as a miracle is because all of the passengers, all 150 of them, survived; and there weren't even any major injuries. I remember watching the stories of the survivors on the news, and one thing struck me about what they all said: there was a lot of prayer on that plane as it was going down. It's safe to say those prayers were answered by the tremendous skill and quick thinking of the pilot, but it also left me wondering why we wait for a plane to crash before we offer up serious, passionate prayer. Yet, many times that's exactly what it takes to get us to pray fervently—some sort of tragedy, some sort of crisis, some sort of plane crash landing on the river. Look, God loves you, and He's there to answer your prayers all the time, even when there isn't a crisis. In fact, the more you pray when planes aren't crashing, the more you'll discover just how deep and amazing God's love for you really is and how that love can carry you through the

230

dark times of tragedy. Plus, I think you'll find prayer is powerful even when there isn't an emergency as you daily connect to the wisdom, peace, guidance, and kindness of God. Doesn't that sound like good news?

July 30
The Jaws and Bread of Life

"'For the bread of God is he who comes down from heaven and gives life to the world.' 'Sir,' they said, 'from now on give us this bread.' Then Jesus declared, 'I am the bread of life'"
(John 6:33-35).

SOMETIMES PEOPLE DO STRANGE THINGS. One time a small-town volunteer firehouse in Alabama was broken into and their Jaws of Life was stolen. The firefighters couldn't figure out why anyone would want to steal a piece of equipment that weighs over sixty pounds and is used to pry people out of tight spaces in order to save their lives. My guess is the thief was hoping that maybe the Jaws of Life would save his life someday. Well, I have good news for that thief, and for all you honest citizens as well. You don't need the Jaws of Life to save your life; all you need is Jesus Christ. He died on the Cross and rose from the dead for that very purpose: to save our lives. God loved us so much that He wanted to save us from death, which is the penalty for our sins. But the only way to do that was to have someone die in our place. So God sent His Son to pay a price with His life that we could never fully pay on own, and in doing so, He saved our lives. In a world that will do anything to avoid death, even to the point of stealing the Jaws of Life, we need to let people know that in order to truly experience life what they need isn't the Jaws of Life. It's the Bread of Life.

July 31
Free Stuff is Always Good News
"Thanks be to God for his indescribable gift!"
(2 Corinthians 9:15).

LOVE GETTING FREE TOYS WITH MY CEREAL. Sometimes those toys come in the cereal, or sometimes I can get a toy just because of the cereal I buy. I remember one time my cereal came with a coupon for a free Hot Wheels, which I took to a store and redeemed for a cool looking black Ferrari 250GT. That was great. You may think it strange for a grown man to get excited about a free toy, but I say, "Who says I've grown up?" Besides, we all enjoy free stuff. The strange thing is we can get excited about something like a free Hot Wheels, but when it comes to God's grace and eternal life being free, we often react almost nonchalantly. All it cost to get a free Hot Wheels was cutting a piece out of a cardboard cereal box. The forgiveness of sins, the grace of God, and eternal life cost God the life of His one and only precious Son. Jesus then offers His life as a coupon for eternity; all we have to do is accept it. That's the most amazing, incredible, fantastic free gift I can think of. It's the type of good news we shouldn't be able to contain. I mean if I can get excited about telling you about a free toy car, I shouldn't even be able to contain myself when it comes to telling you about free eternal life. So, how excited are you about the "*indescribable gift*" God has given? The fact is people always like to hear about free things, especially in this economy, so let's start sharing with them something that's eternally valuable and also completely free. More than that, let's get excited about doing so.

August

As snow in summer
and rain in harvest,
So honor is not fitting for a fool.
Proverbs 26:1

August 1
Prayer for the Common Cold

"Praise the Lord, O my soul, and forget not all his benefits—
who forgives all your sins and heals all your diseases . . . "
(Psalm 103:2-3).

T HERE ARE THOSE OCCASIONS when we get a cold bouncing all around our house. Not literally, of course, because that would be gross; but, you know, just moving from person to person. There are a lot of remedies for colds—from soup to vitamin C to myriads of drugs you can take to ease the symptoms. But there's one remedy we don't often indulge in: prayer. All of those other things are good and we should try them; however, at the same time we shouldn't neglect prayer. They say there's no cure for the common cold, but my Bible says God heals all of our diseases, so I'm assuming that includes even the common cold. And yet, we don't often pray for healing for simple things like that. Why? Are we afraid God isn't going to answer? Are we afraid He doesn't heal anymore? I recently heard a pastor say that he's always surprised when he prays for someone and they aren't healed. I like that. It shows a childlike expectation and it's surprising when it isn't fulfilled. The good news is our God still heals, including the common cold. So instead of prayer being a last resort, let's make it one of our first remedies.

August 2
The Musical Life

*"I will sing to the Lord all my life;
I will sing praise to my God as long as I live"*
(Psalm 104:33).

ONE OF MY FAVORITE MOVIES is the classic Disney film *Mary Poppins*. The last time I watched it, I decided something: life would be better if it were a musical. If people randomly broke into song and dance throughout the day at school, work, and at home, I think this world would be a much happier place. It's hard to be cynical, downcast, and otherwise unhappy when you're singing and dancing. In fact, the more I thought about it, the more I believe this is exactly the way we as Christians should live. Our daily lives should be filled with music. Okay, so maybe we don't need to disrupt our school or our work by singing and dancing on our desks (wouldn't that surprise some people?), but we should have a song of joy in our hearts. We can hum and whistle and otherwise let the music of praise saturate our daily lives. We have so much to praise God for, and we have more reason to be joyful than anyone else, including Mary Poppins. God loves you, He sent His Son to die for you, and Jesus Christ rose from the dead and lives today so you also might have life. If that isn't joyful news that fills your heart with song, I don't know what is. So by all means, Christian, be musical, fill your day with song. After all, He is worthy of our praise, and a little music expressed in joy to our Savior goes a long way in bringing light even into the bleakest of days.

August 3
Answering the Tough Questions

"But in your hearts set apart Christ as Lord.
Always be prepared to give an answer to everyone who asks
you to give the reason for the hope that you have"
(1 Peter 3:15).

KIDS HAVE A GIFT for asking tough questions, don't they? I remember one such question from my daughter. She asked, "Daddy, what's the Internet?" Well, I thought about it a moment, and then I realized I couldn't really explain it to her. I wasn't even sure if I could explain what the Internet was to myself. I've never really thought about it, let alone tried to figure out how to explain it to a six-year-old. I just use it on a daily basis; I don't think about how it works. That's often the case with our Christianity, isn't it? We just sort of do it, we don't really think about it and therefore when it comes time, we don't really know how to explain it. We don't know how to answer questions such as, "What is the Trinity?" "How did Jesus rise from the dead?" "Why is there evil?" "Where did the Bible come from?" Well, I don't know about you, but I want to do more than just use Christianity without understanding it, and the good news is we can learn answers to those questions. In fact, the Bible exhorts us to learn all we can so we'll always have answers. Not so we'll be super intelligent, but so we can lovingly and thoughtfully guide people to the truth of the good news by always being ready to give a reason for the hope that we have.

August 4
Getting Out of the Rut of Routine
"Be wise in the way you act toward outsiders; make the most of every opportunity"
(Colossians 4:5).

EVERY DAY IT'S THE SAME OLD ROUTINE: I get up, I read my Bible while eating my Cocoa Krispies, I brush my teeth, get dressed, go to work, do my work, come home, help make dinner, help clean up dinner, help the kids get to bed, get ready for bed, go to bed . . . that's pretty much my day, every day. Your day is probably fairly routine as well, and I'm willing to bet that routine is pretty comfortable. But what do you do when that routine is interrupted? What do you do when you're presented with something outside your routine, something extraordinary and unique, something that could change another person's life? I'll be honest and admit my routine is so mind-numbing I often miss those opportunities. I either just plain don't notice them or I'm so upset about my routine getting interrupted I choose to ignore them. I think the reason Jesus and Paul, the apostle, connected so well with people and were such effective ministers is because they didn't get lulled into a routine. They were alert and ready for the opportunities that were presented to them. The good news is we can be too. We can be ready 1), by not getting upset when our routine is interrupted, but rather excited at the adventure of something new; and 2), by making sure we don't let our senses get so dulled by a regular routine that we don't notice when opportunities present themselves. There are opportunities to change people's lives and to change the world around us every day at work, at school, at the movies, in the grocery store—everywhere we go. Are you ready to seize those moments and make the most of them?

August 5
Sacrifice is a Messy Business

"Unlike other high priests, he does not need to offer sacrifices day after day, first for his own sins, and then for the sins of the people. He sacrificed for their sins once for all when he offered himself"
(Hebrews 7:27).

WHEN I WAS IN COLLEGE, we lived overseas in Turkey. Every year, the people there would celebrate their holy festivals, and during one of them, they would all sacrifice goats. You might be walking down the street, and a family would be killing a goat for their sacrifice right in front of you. It was pretty nasty; I'm not going to lie. The gutters would run with blood, and with it being so hot, it was pretty smelly. Well, as I was reading through the requirements God made for sacrifices in the Old Testament, I was reminded of that experience. I don't know if you've read those requirements recently, but they involve a lot of blood, a lot of animal parts, and they require it on a regular basis. Sacrifices were a messy, nasty business; which I guess is only appropriate since sin is also a messy, nasty business. Anyway, thinking about that made me grateful that Christ has set us free. He gave His blood, He gave His body, He gave himself as a sacrifice for sin, and it covered all our sin for all time. No more sacrifices; just grace, mercy, and forgiveness for all who accept His one sacrifice. It was still messy and still nasty, but at least it only had to happen once. That makes Christ's sacrifice so special and such good news.

August 6
Experiencing Happiness
**"But may the righteous be glad and rejoice before God;
may they be happy and joyful"
(Psalm 68:3).**

WHEN IT COMES TO HAPPINESS, researchers have discovered that experiences provide more satisfaction than possessions. This is partly due to the fact that once you buy something you quickly get accustomed to seeing it every day, whereas experiences always seem to provide happy memories. What's interesting, however, is the fact that experiences can also provide happiness for others as well. I'm glad those researchers finally figured that out because I've known it to be true most of my life. One of the happiest experiences I've ever had was the day I met Jesus. And what's better, that's an experience I can enjoy on a daily basis, and it's an experience I can share with others. Which by the way, I've noticed has led to their happiness as well. Now that's not to say I'm happy all the time, but experiencing Jesus has led to an overall happier life for me. And I don't need researchers to verify that good news for me, but I'm glad they did.

August 7
Love That Lasts

"This is love: not that we loved God, but that he loved us and sent his Son as an atoning sacrifice for our sins"
(1 John 4:10).

SCIENCE IS ALWAYS FUN. Did you know that after conducting brain scans of various couples, scientists discovered that 10 percent of couples have the same level of passion for their spouse as they did twenty years ago? Previous research suggested that true love and romantic feelings inevitably fade within the first fifteen months, so how couples could still have the same chemical reaction in their brains in response to their romantic feelings for someone twenty years later left scientists scratching their heads. Now, I don't have the answer to that mystery, but I do think I understand how love can last. The fact is love doesn't rely on feelings. Sure feelings play a part of it, but true love is so much more than that. Love is a choice, and, in fact, the greatest demonstration of love was when Jesus Christ died on the Cross and rose from the dead. I know that's not typically the first thing we think of when we think of romance. But that was love on display as God died in our place to pay the price for our sin so we might be free and have eternal life. If we truly want to know love for a lifetime, we need to get to know the love God has displayed toward us, and then emulate that in our own lives. If we can do that, then we'll have some pretty crazy brain scans of our own as we learn to love like the God who *is* love. And then every year, on this day in particular (my wedding anniversary), that sounds like good news to me.

August 8
Do-It-Yourself Christianity

"For it is by grace you have been saved, through faith—
and this is not from yourselves, it is the gift of God—
not by works so that no one can boast"
(Ephesians 2:8-9).

WE ARE A DO-IT-YOURSELF, self-service, I-don't-need-any-help nation. Don't believe me; just go look at the *Dummies* section at the bookstore (you know, those books for dummies that teach you how to do your taxes, fix a shelf, learn computers, and so on). They even have a *Christianity for Dummies* book, which I find pretty interesting (especially since some think it's only dummies that would ever believe in Christianity). I've always been curious if that self-help *Christianity for Dummies* book explains that Christianity isn't something we can do for ourselves. There is no way for us to either become a Christian or successfully live as a Christian if we try to do it on our own. So then, you ask, what are we supposed to do? Two things: 1), accept the fact that you can't do it yourself, no matter how many self-help-for-dummies books you may read; and 2), ask God for help. Jesus Christ makes it possible for us to be a child of God because of His death and Resurrection, and the Holy Spirit provides all the help and guidance we need to live out our lives as believers. When it comes right down to it, the only book you need when it comes to the Christian life is the Bible, which personally I think is good news.

August 9
Serious Rest on the Sabbath

"For six days, work is to be done, but the seventh day is a Sabbath of rest, holy to the Lord. Whoever does any work on the Sabbath day must be put to death"
(Exodus 31:15).

IT'S USUALLY RIGHT AROUND THURSDAY, or as I like to call it, Friday Eve, when I really start looking forward to the weekend. Personally, I really enjoy doing a whole lot of nothing on the weekend, but I know that's not the case with everyone. Some of you probably have a bunch of projects that need to be done. Some of you probably try to finish all the work you don't finish during the week. But how often do we think about how to set apart an entire day for the Lord on the weekend? I have to be honest; I've recently started thinking about weekends a bit differently since once again I've been reading through the Old Testament. I was especially struck by how seriously God took the Sabbath day of rest. He took it so seriously He said anyone who didn't honor it was to be put to death. Sure that may sound kind of harsh, but this was important to God. More than that, this day was holy to God. The good news is He doesn't kill us for not honoring that day, especially seeing as there probably wouldn't be very many of us left if He did, but perhaps we should be taking this concept of Sabbath rest a bit more seriously. Perhaps we really should include the Lord in our weekend plans. I think He'd really like that.

***

August 10
Economic Stimulus From a Fish

"But so that we may not offend them, go to the lake and throw out your line. Take the first fish you catch; open its mouth and you will find a four-drachma coin. Take it and give it to them for my tax and yours"
(Matthew 17:27).

THE ECONOMY has dominated the headlines quite a bit in the past few years. There seemed to be an almost constant stream of bad news, along with news about government stimulus packages and Washington bailouts. In fact, I think in the past five years I've heard people talk more about money than ever before. You know Jesus talked about money quite a bit as well, but He usually talked about it by encouraging us not to worry about it so we could talk and think about more important things. Repeatedly, we are told God knows our needs, and He will be faithful to meet them. I love the story about the temple tax because not only does it show just how unconcerned Jesus was about money, but also how God sometimes provides in very bizarre ways. (After all, when's the last time you looked for a stimulus check in the mouth of a fish?) Look, the economic crisis has been big, but our God is bigger. Isn't that good news? We need to be wise, we need to be prudent, and we need to be smart with our money, but we also need to leave our money worries with the Lord and trust that His economy can do just fine even when the world's isn't.

August 11
Are All Laws Really That Important?
**"Oh, how I love your law! I meditate on it all day long"
(Psalm 119:97).**

HERE IN ALBUQUERQUE, New Mexico, our city tried a little experiment. It tried to make certain intersections safer by installing cameras that would record speeders and those who ran lights and then send them a ticket. Well, I realized something profound sitting at a red light: we don't think certain laws are all that important. Think about it, if we all valued laws such as speed limits and red lights, would there be any need for traffic cameras at intersections? What's even more fascinating is the funding for that system (at least here in Albuquerque) comes from the fines paid by people caught breaking those "minor laws" on camera. So in essence, the government assumes we'll break those laws so we'll have to pay the fines that fund the cameras that catch us breaking the law. If we all obeyed the law, there'd be no money for the cameras. Now compare that attitude to the attitude the Psalmist displays toward God's Law in Psalm 119. I get the impression that someone who loves the law won't treat some of those laws as minor, unimportant, or as laws that can be bent every now and then. And yet, once again, how many of us do just that? How many of us use little white lies, or steal just a little bit, and then reason at least we're not murdering or committing adultery. No, if we truly love God, we'll love His commands, and if we love His commands we'll obey them—all the time. After all, His traffic cameras are on us all the time and it's not like we can get away with anything. So why try? Why not just honor and obey His Law? I think in doing so we'll discover some really good news.

August 12
God Made You Good at Something
" . . . See, the Lord has chosen Bezalel son of Uri, the son of Hur, of the tribe of Judah, and he has filled him with the Spirit of God, with skill, ability, and knowledge in all kinds of crafts . . . "
(Exodus 35:30-31).

WHAT ARE YOU GOOD AT? Now I know some of you right now are saying "nothing," but that's not true. Seriously, take some time to think about it: What are you good at? What are you skilled at? What are you talented in doing? Why am I asking this? Well, so many people want to know how God can use them. Sometimes we get the impression the only people God uses, the only people that are specially gifted to serve our heavenly Father, are missionaries, preachers, evangelists, and other full-time people. Well, my friends, I have good news. I'm here to tell you that's not true. When God gave Moses instructions on how to build the Tabernacle and the Ark of the Covenant, He told Moses His Holy Spirit had gifted artists and weavers and people who were good at fashioning gold and had set them apart to help make the Ark and all of the holy implements. God needed their talents, just like He needs yours. God gave them their talents to serve Him, just like He has given you yours. So, again I ask: What are you good at? Because whatever it is, God gave you those skills and talents for a purpose—to bring glory to Him as you use them to serve and expand His Kingdom.

August 13
No Cussing Allowed

"Do not let any unwholesome talk come out of your mouths, but only what is helpful for building others up according to their needs, that it may benefit those who listen"
(Ephesians 4:29).

A FEW years ago, a tenth-grader in Los Angeles helped create the very first "no-cussing" week in L.A. County. That's right; for an entire week there was no cussing allowed in Los Angeles. Now if you're wondering how they enforced that, the answer is they didn't. However, this tenth-grader said the main point of a no-cussing week was to draw attention to how we treat and speak to people. This teenager believed if we could learn to be more civil to each other, we'd work together better in facing the big problems of the world. I think that no-cussing week is a great idea. The fact is, we really don't know how to speak or treat other people with proper respect, or at least not as much as we used to. The funny thing is the Bible exhorts us to do just that: to speak kindly and courteously to each other. It's one of those exhortations in the Bible that's often overlooked or regarded as minor, but I don't think it is. The way to speak to each other and the way we speak to people in general, says volumes about how real to us the love of Christ is. It's hard to change our speech from being self-centered to others-centered, but if we can, we won't just be able to enjoy a no-cussing week— we'll also be able to better share the good news.

August 14
God's Not in; Leave a Message

Therefore, brothers, since we have confidence to enter the Most Holy Place by the blood of Jesus, by a new and living way opened for us through the curtain, that is, his body, and since we have a great priest over the house of God, let us draw near to God with a sincere heart in full assurance of faith, having our hearts sprinkled to cleanse us from a guilty conscience and having our bodies washed with pure water.
(Hebrews 10:19-22)

A DUTCH ARTIST set up an answering machine for God. No really, you could call God and leave a message. (And why are artists always the ones doing these strange sorts of things?) The artist said the reason he did this was to help people contemplate life, because according to him leaving a message helps you organize your thoughts. It's an interesting idea, but why leave a message when you can actually speak to God directly? Instead of just leaving a message and hope He gets back to you, isn't it nice for Him to listen to you and answer right away? The good news is that's exactly what we can do, thanks to Jesus Christ. When Jesus died on the Cross and rose from the dead, He cleared the lines of communication for us. We no longer have to leave a message; we could approach God ourselves and present our requests, our petitions, our praise, and our pain to Him in person. Better yet, if we're willing to linger there in His presence, we can receive comfort and guidance and assurance and peace as we fellowship with Him. It's a wonderful thing, this thing called prayer. It's a much better option for contemplating our lives than just leaving a message.

August 15
Suffering Isn't Always Pointless
"I will show him how much he must suffer for my name"
(Acts 9:16).

HAVE LEARNED something very important. If you have bad allergies and it's windy outside, don't go out. Yet far too often, despite suffering from allergies, I just can't resist going outside in the gusty wind and playing basketball or playing with my kids in the backyard. Which, of course, makes things worse for me. I don't know about you, but I don't like suffering. That's why I've always thought it was kind of depressing when Jesus said He was going to show Paul how much he had to suffer for His name. I mean, that doesn't sound like a compelling reason to follow Christ, does it? The truth is, the Bible talks a lot about how we will suffer as Christians (which generally are the parts we don't like to read). When you suffer from allergies, you suffer for no really good reason; there's seemingly no point to it. However, when we suffer for Christ, the Bible tells us it builds character and perseverance, and that we suffer with hope. Better yet, suffering helps us draw nearer to Christ and identify even closer with Him. In short, the Bible tells us suffering is good news. Now I may have a hard time understanding that with my allergies raging the way they do just about every year, but considering how much Paul accomplished for the gospel, maybe suffering for Christ isn't such a bad thing after all.

August 16
Won't You Be My Neighbor?

*"'Which of these three do you think was a neighbor
to the man who fell into the hands of robbers?' The expert in
the law replied, 'The one who had mercy on him.'
Jesus told him, 'Go and do likewise'"*
(Luke 10:36-37).

REMEMBER MR. ROGERS, that kindly fellow who was always asking you to be his neighbor? (If not, go look him up on YouTube.) I always thought he would be the greatest guy to be my neighbor because he had one of the coolest train sets around. However, when Jesus was asked the question, "Who is my neighbor?" He didn't answer by giving a checklist to use to determine who our neighbors are. Instead, He told a story that illustrated what it meant to be a good neighbor and then told us to do the same. In essence, He didn't tell us who our neighbors *are*, but rather how to *be* a neighbor. Far too often we wait for the right people to come along to be neighborly with, yet Christ told us that we are the ones who should show mercy, kindness, consideration, generosity, and even love to anyone we come across who may need it. When it comes to this idea of being neighborly, I recently realized I shouldn't be looking for someone like Mr. Rogers with a really cool train set to be neighbors with; rather I should *be* Mr. Rogers. When I do that, I'll have many more chances to share the good news.

August 17
Helping the Needy; All of Them
**"For he will deliver the needy who cry out,
the afflicted who have no one to help"
(Psalm 72:12).**

D ID YOU KNOW that about one out of every fifty American children is homeless, and about 42 percent of homeless children are younger than six years old? Those are startling statistics and I don't think any of us would have any trouble recognizing those children are certainly needy. However, recently I've been thinking about our responsibility as Christians to help the needy, and I've realized the needy include more than just the extreme segments of society. There are others we don't often see as needy: the outcasts, the lonely, the left out, the mocked and ridiculed, the ostracized. These people are also in need, and they're also the ones who are heard by God when they cry out. In fact, there may be needy people in your school—those kids whom no one wants to talk to or sit with. There may be needy people in your work place—a person everyone gossips about, but won't talk directly to. There may be needy people in your church—single mothers, divorcees, homeless—all people who are often left out. The point is this: the needy are more than just statistics, they are people who are hurting and are often unnoticed or ignored. But God sees their hurt, and He wants us to help. Before we can help however, before we can share the good news of God's love, we first have to open our eyes so we can see the needy ones around us. Then we must learn to have a compassionate heart, like our heavenly Father's heart, in order to show the care, love, and help that can help rescue the needy.

August 18
A Not So Hidden Message
"... since what may be known about God is plain to them, because God has made it plain to them"
(Romans 1:19).

NOT LONG AGO, The National Museum of American History discovered a secret inscription on the inside of a gold watch that was owned by Abraham Lincoln. The inscription records the day the Civil War started. Apparently, a watchmaker was repairing Lincoln's watch and heard the first shots of the war being fired at Fort Sumter, so he unscrewed the dial of the watch and recorded that historic day with an inscription Lincoln was never aware of. Sometimes people treat God like that watchmaker. We think God is trying to send us a message, but it's a secret message that He's hidden away someplace we'll never think of looking. However, that isn't the case at all. God hasn't made His message of grace and salvation a secret; in fact, He's done everything possible to make that good news very plain. The truth is if God's message of love to humanity is hidden, it's only because you and I are hiding it. Maybe we should start doing what that popular Sunday School song told us to do when we were children: "This little light of mine, I'm going to let it shine."

August 19
Just Don't Do It

"If we deliberately keep on sinning after we have received the knowledge of the truth, no sacrifice for sin is left, but only a fearful expectation of judgment . . . "
(Hebrews 10:26).

BERNARD MADOFF pled guilty to eleven criminal counts after swindling investors of billions of dollars—in some cases, taking their entire life savings. He ended up going to jail. I have to say, when he got around to doing it, I found his confession and apology a little confusing. Madoff claimed he was ashamed of what he had done and he always knew that one day he would be caught and would be judged. Yet, he *kept on doing what he was doing.* That's the part I don't get. If he knew it was wrong and he knew eventually he would be caught, tried, and punished, why not just stop before it happened? That's a question we all need to face, regardless of the sin. We all know that sin is wrong, we all know we're going to get caught, and we all know that one day we'll be judged for our sins. If you don't know that, you're only fooling yourself. The question is, if we know sin is wrong and God one day is going to judge us for it, why keep doing it? And saying *we just can't help it* isn't going to be enough. I think it's time we admit something: sin is a choice, which means we can choose *not* to. Madoff had a choice, but he enjoyed money a bit too much. Granted, sin can be enjoyable for a time, but is it really worth the price in the end? I'm not saying we'll always make the right choice, but isn't it good news to know Jesus Christ gives us the option, and that He'll be at our side when judgment finally comes? Will He be at your side?

August 20
Making Good Spiritual Investments

*"'For I know the plans I have for you', declares the Lord,
'Plans to prosper you and not to harm you,
plans to give you a hope and a future'"*
(Jeremiah 29:11).

THE RECENT BAD ECONOMY hasn't been bad for everyone; in fact there are a few businesses that actually grew. One of them is psychics. During all the ups and downs, people have turned more and more to psychics for comfort and guidance. One person pointed out that people are looking for a sense of control in these uncertain times, and another said if times aren't normal, why not turn to the paranormal? That's all fine and good, but may I suggest you turn to a spiritual source that has never been wrong in any of its predictions, that's always been wise in its advice given, and has never steered anyone wrong with its guidance? May I suggest you turn to an all-knowing, all-powerful God who just so happens to love you so much that He wants to help you and give you guidance in these uncertain times? However, let me warn you that He isn't as interested in your current investments as He is in your eternal investments. That's not to say He isn't concerned about your financial status, but rather He has plans for you that extend beyond just surviving a recession. So if you want advice, if you want comfort, if you want a direction to go in, turn to God in Christ Jesus. It's an investment you'll be glad you made. Plus, He doesn't charge by the hour.

August 21
The Secret of the Book of Acts
"Do not get drunk on wine, which leads to debauchery.
Instead, be filled with the Spirit"
(Ephesians 5:18).

WHENEVER I read through the Book of Acts, one of the things that strikes me is how every time the disciples did something, the Holy Spirit was involved. When they performed miracles, Acts says they were filled with the Holy Spirit. When they spoke boldly about the gospel, they were filled with the Holy Spirit.

When they needed guidance and direction, they were filled with the Holy Spirit. I'm starting to pick up on a pattern here—we need to be filled with the Holy Spirit. I often hear Christians complain about the lack of power and miracles in their lives. Again, perhaps we need to be filled with the Holy Spirit. After all, God never changes, His Spirit never changes, and His power never changes. So if we want power and faith to do miracles, if we want boldness and courage in proclaiming the truth of the Bible, if we want guidance and direction to help us in uncertain times, we need to be filled with the same Holy Spirit that filled the apostles. Doesn't that sound like good news?

* * *

August 22
Celebrating the End of Division

*"Surely the arm of the Lord is not too short to save,
nor his ear too dull to hear. But your iniquities have separated
you from your God: your sins have hidden his face
from you so that he will not hear"*
(Isaiah 59:1-2).

TO COMMEMORATE the twentieth anniversary of the tearing down of the Berlin wall, the people of that city celebrated in a unique way. They set up a two-kilometer-long set of eight-foot dominos and then toppled them over. Not only does that sound like a lot of fun—because who wouldn't want to set up and then knock down a bunch of giant dominos?—but I think it's also something we should do as Christians. We were once divided from God by a wall of sin, but Jesus Christ tore down that wall by dying on the Cross and rising from the dead, an event we celebrate every year on Easter. My family enjoys celebrating something we call re-birthdays: the day we were born again in Christ. We have cake and ice cream and candles and the whole works (no presents, though, because we already got our present—grace) as we remember that precious day when the wall of sin that divided us from God was torn down by Christ. That may not be quite as spectacular as knocking over two kilometers of giant dominos, but the point is our reuniting with a Holy God through Jesus Christ is good news worth celebrating. Besides, your celebration just might attract the attention of others who will want to join in.

August 23
Beware of Imposters

"At that time if anyone says to you, 'Look, here is the Christ!' or, 'Look, there he is!' do not believe it. For false Christs and false prophets will appear and perform signs and miracles to deceive the elect—if that were possible.
So be on your guard . . . "
(Mark 13:21-23).

WHEN ROBERT SCHULLER, the founder of "The Hour of Power" and pastor of the famous Crystal Cathedral, tried to set up his own Twitter account, he learned something very interesting; somebody already had done so under his name. An imposter was using images and popular sayings from Schuller to send out Tweets, and in just two weeks after setting up the account this imposter gathered over a thousand followers on Twitter. This all brings up a very important question: How do you tell the genuine article from a fake in today's technology driven world? To be honest, I'm not sure what the answer is aside from making sure you do your research, but I do know this: we better get in the habit of testing for fakes, because the Bible says we'll be faced with a lot more of them as we move further into the end times. We also need to make sure we are very familiar with the real Christ and the truth of God's Word, because if we know it well, it will be that much harder for us to be deceived. I'm sure it was shocking for Pastor Schuller to see how easily people could be tricked into following an imposter, and we as Christians need to make sure we aren't tricked into following a fake Christ. If we can learn to see through the deceptions in order to remain faithful to the one, true Christ, well, that can only be called good news.

August 24
Is This Okay?

"When Jesus landed and saw a large crowd, he had compassion on them, because they were like a sheep without a shepherd"
(Mark 6:34).

WE USED TO GET INTERESTING EMAILS at the radio station where I worked, and I remember one in particular that asked an interesting question. Somebody wanted to know if it was okay for people to show compassion for outsiders and to care for those nobody else cares about. I was really touched by this question, and yet saddened at the same time. I was touched by the fact someone was moved with compassion for people that others would dismiss or even show disdain for. I was saddened, however, that someone would even have to ask the question. What are we doing as a Church that would make Christians unsure of whether or not it's okay to show godly compassion to the ungodly, to share care and kindness with those no one else cares about? This should not even *be* a question. In fact, it should be at the core of everything we do, because it was at the core of everything Christ did. It was His compassion that moved Him to heal people, it was His compassion that moved Him to show kindness and tenderness to the hurting, it was His compassion that moved Him to welcome the unacceptable, and to forgive those who were considered unforgivable. Indeed, it was His compassion for you and me that moved Him to die on the Cross for our sins and to rise again from the dead. This is the essence of the good news: to show care, kindness, love, forgiveness, and compassion to the outcast, the downtrodden, the left out, and those in need. Are you ready to share that good news? Go ahead. You don't even have to ask for permission first.

August 25

God Likes Legos

"For we are God's fellow workers;
you are God's field, God's building"
(1 Corinthians 3:9).

LOVE LEGOS, and I have since I was a kid. There's just something very satisfying about building cool vehicles and buildings that I've never stopped enjoying. Plus now they have Star Wars, Indiana Jones, Batman

Legos and even Teenage Mutant Ninja Legos! I think God likes Legos, too. Why? Because He seems to like building things. After all, He created everything we see; built it, put it together, made it run, and said it was good. Also, He's constantly building our lives, making additions, tearing down other parts, and in general helping us to look more and more like Him. When you start building with Legos, you start out with a bunch of pieces, but as you follow the instructions, something really great begins to take shape. So it is with God in our lives. He's building something step by step in us with the power of the Holy Spirit, and only He knows what that final result will be. However, you can be sure of this: it's going to be something brand new that will glorify Him; and that's good news. So, go ahead, let God play with the Legos of your life. I think you'll like what He builds.

August 26
A Little Help Here

"I lift up my eyes to the hills—where does my help come from? My help comes from the Lord, the Maker of heaven and earth" **(Psalm 121:1-2).**

THERE ARE DAYS when it just feels like I could use a little extra help. You know the days I'm talking about? Those days where everything seems overwhelming, where obstacles seem insurmountable, where your strength and energy don't seem like they'll be enough to carry you through. As I was thinking about this the other day, a day that I felt like I just wouldn't be able to make it through, I started to wonder where I could get some help. It was then I realized, much to my shame, that the one source I could always count on for help was often the last source I turned to. Why do we use God and His help as a last resort? He should be our *first* resort. He loves us, He wants to help us, He's even given us a Helper called the Holy Spirit to provide us with all we need to face each and every day. God asks us to present our requests and worries to Him, He promises us strength and wisdom in return, and best of all, He's always there to comfort and calm us on those overwhelming, insurmountable days. I need help on a daily basis, and I can get that help from the Maker of Heaven and Earth. That's good news.

August 27
Trouble With "Stretching" Days

"Father, if you are willing, take this cup from me; yet not my will, but yours be done"
(Luke 22:42).

LOVE THE WAY KIDS PRAY. I remember one evening when our family was praying and my daughter thanked God for helping us through a "stretching" day. Now, I'm fairly sure she meant to say a "stressful" day, but I think her way of phrasing it was much more accurate. The truth is, none of us enjoy being stretched, and that most often happens when things are most stressful and life is its most difficult. Few things indicate just how human Jesus was as much as His prayer right before He was arrested. Knowing He was about to face a brutally stressful day, even Jesus prayed there might be some way out of it. However, what sets Him apart from most of us, including me, is that He didn't leave it at that. Although He would have preferred not to suffer and die, what He wanted most was to do the will of His Father because that would ultimately bring about the most good. And so it is with our "stretching" days. I know I would much rather avoid those days, but I also know those are often the days I rely most on the Holy Spirit and when I grow the most in my walk with God. Just like Jesus, my prayer should always be to do my Father's will, especially on the stretching days. Because when I do, that's when I'll discover some truly precious good news.

August 28
Dead Isn't Always Dead

"Jesus said to her, 'I am the resurrection and the life. He who believes in me will live, even though he dies; and whoever lives and believes in me will never die. Do you believe this?'"
(John 11:25-26).

ONE OF MY ALL-TIME FAVORITE TV shows was *Lost*. I remember toward the end of the series some pretty strange things happened, like people-coming-back-from-the-dead strange. Some of the characters had a hard time accepting the fact that someone they thought had died could somehow come back to life. I thought that was rather ironic. Considering all of the amazing, mystical, magical, and even miraculous things they had seen happen on the strange island where they were isolated, the one thing they couldn't believe was the idea of someone coming back from the dead. As one character put it, "Dead is dead." Well, the truth is there are exceptions to every rule. Did you know the Resurrection of Jesus Christ is one of the most well-documented events in history? Did you know that in the ancient world no one debated the fact that Jesus' tomb was empty? Did you know there are eye-witness accounts of the Resurrection? Jesus' Resurrection is a fact of history, and it is the only exception to the rule "Dead is dead." However, the good news is when we believe Jesus was who He said He was—God in the flesh—and He has the power to bring the dead to life, well, then you and I can become exceptions to the "Dead is dead" rule as well. So, let me repeat Jesus' question: *"Do you believe this?"*

August 29
Sticking With It 'til the End
**"When he had received the drink, Jesus said, 'It is finished.'
With that, he bowed his head and gave up his spirit"
(John 19:30).**

WHEN YOU BEGIN SOMETHING, how willing are you to see it through to the end? If things start to get tough, or there are distractions, or things just aren't working out the way you thought they would, how quickly do you give up? This is an important question for us to answer, not just in our work, not just in putting together a puzzle, not just in writing a novel, not just in learning how our smart phone works, but in how we live our lives. The truth is, far too many people who call themselves Christians give up on Christ when the going gets tough. I'm glad

Christ wasn't like that. I'm glad He never gave up. I'm especially glad that He stuck with His mission and saw it through to the finish, even though that finish meant His death. Had He given up, you and I would be lost. We would have no forgiveness, no life, and no hope. The question we all face is how are we going to finish? Are we willing to see this Christian life through to the end, no matter what? Or, once it becomes uncomfortable and inconvenient, will we abandon it? Our Savior was willing to die for us in order to finish God's plan to save us. The least we can do is to be willing to do the same.

August 30
Loving the Law

"Because I love your commands more than gold, more than pure gold . . . "
(Psalm 119:127).

UNLESS YOU'RE A LAWYER, law isn't probably something you love. In fact, the law is probably something you only think about when you get caught breaking it. However, I've been thinking about that attitude toward law and I don't think it's the right one to have toward God's Law. In fact, if you look through Psalm 119, you see repeated over and over and over again a passionate love for the Law and commands of the Lord. It's so radically different from how the world feels about the law, especially God's Law. The world looks at God's commands and sees something to disdain and ignore because they're restrictive, they're offensive, and they ruin our fun. Yet that's not why God gave us His laws and commands. He gave them to us so we might have the freedom to enjoy life without the unfortunate consequence that comes from living apart from law. He gave them to us to keep us safe and protect us from harm, and in truth, to really enjoy and have fun in life without getting hurt. The world may think that *rules are for fools*, but I would much rather be foolish and say I love God's Word and His commands more than pure gold than to try and foolishly live without them.

August 31
Pursue Something Worthwhile
"Wisdom is supreme; therefore get wisdom.
Though it cost all you have, get understanding"
(Proverbs 4:7).

THINK IT WAS OS GUINNESS who stated that we're living in one of the most anti-intellectual periods in Church history. Deep, theological, doctrinal, and apologetic study of the Bible and Christianity has given way to the ease of spoon-fed, three-point sermons, ten-step Bible studies, and fill-in-the-blank Bible trivia. If it takes too much effort, if it's difficult to understand, or requires time to study, our culture would rather skip it for whatever is easier. I always think about that when I read this Proverb. You know, most people today probably wouldn't think that wisdom and understanding are the primary goals we should pursue. In fact, most would probably say we should pursue success. But Proverbs tells us to pursue understanding and wisdom even if it costs everything. That indicates to me that it won't be easy, but it will definitely be worth it. Sounds like good news to me. So let's pursue wisdom and understanding, and then what Jesus said of the Church will be true of us when He said, " . . . *even the gates of Hades will not prevail against it.*"

September

"The harvest is past,
The summer is ended,
And we are not saved!"

Jeremiah 8:20

September 1

Chewing Gum and Brain Power

"Do not let this Book of the Law depart from your mouth;
meditate on it day and night, so that you may be careful
to do everything written in it.
Then you will be prosperous and successful"
(Joshua 1:8).

ACCORDING TO A STUDY funded by the Wrigley Science Institute, chewing gum may be good for your brain. This study discovered that students who chew gum during homework actually had a 3 percent increase in their academic performance. Fascinating, isn't it? I have a confession to make. I have a real hard time memorizing Bible verses. I know I need them, I know that having God's Word in my heart and mind ready for instant recall is a valuable tool, but I just have a hard time memorizing God's Word. However, the truth is I don't think chewing gum would help, although it probably wouldn't hurt. No, memorizing God's Word is one of those things we just have to be self-disciplined about. There's no easy way, no magic formula. It's something where the best advice is to "just do it." The Bible repeatedly encourages us to hide God's Word in our hearts and lists the many benefits of doing so. So no more excuses for me; it's time to get serious about integrating the Bible into my mind, heart, and daily routine. After all, people need its truth now more than ever, so we should all be ready at any moment to share that truth. Even if it means talking while chewing gum.

September 2
Is Christianity Ending in America?
"We must pay more careful attention, therefore, to what we have heard, so that we do not drift away"
(Hebrews 2:1).

D ID YOU KNOW that over half of Americans will change their religion at some point during their lives? This, along with some other statistics, has some saying that we're seeing the end of Christian America. It does seem like everywhere we look there are signs of the Church eroding. What's happening? Well, there are a lot of factors, almost too numerous to go into, but I think most of it boils down to exactly what we read in Hebrews today: we aren't paying close attention to what we've heard. We aren't paying close attention to what we've heard about God, His truth, His Son, and His love. We aren't paying close attention to what we've heard the Bible say about our lives, God's promises, how to face the challenges of a post-modern society, and how to stand firm in our faith. Is this the end of Christian America? Is religion something you change like your socks, finding something to match your mood? Or is it the bedrock foundation of life upon which we can build with confidence and assurance knowing that when we stand on Christ, the solid rock, all other ground is sinking sand? Well, the good news is, when we pay attention to what God has to say, we can be sure we won't drift away. And that this world will continue to have *truth* boldly proclaimed and *light* lovingly displayed by the children of God. Are you up to the challenge?

September 3
Finding True Superpower

**"Do not envy a violent man, or choose any of his ways.
For the Lord detests a perverse man,
but takes the upright in his confidence"
(Proverbs 3:31-32).**

WHEN WOLVERINE'S first solo movie, *X-Men Origins: Wolverine*, debuted back in 2009, it had no problem clawing its way to the top of the box office. For whatever reason, people have always been fascinated with the character who is the best at what he does. Now don't get me wrong; I remember a time when I thought Wolverine was super cool as well, but eventually I realized he really isn't all that powerful. The truth is that anger and violence may feel powerful, but all we'll find in trying to emulate that in real life is pain and regret. We may think the brooding anti-hero is compelling, but living life that way only leaves you isolated and empty. You see, God has given us a better way to live. He's given us a truly powerful way to live. He's given us a way to live that is full of peace and joy. Heroes like Wolverine and Batman may seem powerful in how their anger and rage give them strength, but the truth is nothing is as powerful as God's love. So if we really want to be heroic, following in the angry, violent footsteps of some superheroes isn't the answer. If we really want to be heroic, we need to choose to follow in the footsteps of Christ.

September 4
Stealing to Get to Church on Sunday

"Live such good lives among the pagans that, though they accuse you of doing wrong, they may see your good deeds and glorify God on the day he visits us"
(1 Peter 2:12).

A FEW YEARS AGO in Connecticut, a man accused of stealing cars was arrested at church after one of the cars he had stolen was spotted in the church parking lot. Apparently, every time this man needed gas, he would just steal a new car. As to why he was at church when he was arrested, who can say? Maybe he felt guilty. Or maybe that's just where he went to church. I know it seems odd that a guy who stole cars would go to church, but the truth is we're all probably guilty of doing something similar. We're all probably guilty of harboring some sort of sin during the week and then going to church on Sunday while pretending everything's fine. I know I've done that. However, that's not what the world needs to see. The world sees plenty of dishonesty, inconsistency, and hypocrisy. They certainly don't need to see someone who goes to church in a stolen car. So let's make the effort to live the same way we do on Sunday all throughout the week. The truth is, if we're really following Christ, it shouldn't be all that difficult. Plus, a life lived for Christ seven days a week is one of the best ways to testify to the good news of the gospel.

September 5
School is Cool?

"Let the wise listen and add to their learning, and let the discerning get guidance . . . "
(Proverbs 1:5).

IT'S GENERALLY AROUND THIS TIME OF YEAR, back to school time, that I think back on my own time in school and how I thought it would never end. In elementary school I had middle school to look forward to, in middle school I had high school to look forward to, in high school it was college that was next, from college there was graduate school . . . it just seemed to go on forever. The problem was I wasn't very good at school, so I really had a difficult time all those years knowing that no matter how much I did, there was always more school to come. Here's the funny thing I discovered after I finished school: you never really stop learning, or at least you shouldn't. Especially as Christians, we always have more to learn because there's always more to God and more in His Word to discover. More importantly, today there are more and more false teachings and deceptive philosophies showing up trying to lure us away. Well, here's the good news—not only is there always more to learn, but that it's actually quite exciting and fascinating to apply one's self to the study of God's Word and disciplines like apologetics. In fact, if I had known learning was actually a fun part of life (and not just a necessity only for when you're in school), I might have done much better. Maybe.

September 6

Boldly Go . . .

**"Have I not commanded you? Be strong and courageous.
Do not be terrified, do not be discouraged,
for the Lord your God will be with you wherever you go"
(Joshua 1:9).**

"TO BOLDLY GO where no one has gone before." Those immortal words have become a part of our cultural cannon in the past several decades as a show—*Star Trek*—that was described as "a *Wagon Train* in space" continued to live on even after the show itself was cancelled. There was just something compelling about the idea of an intrepid crew of explorers traveling to the deep reaches of space and discovering what had never been seen before. I think deep inside all of us is a desire to do just that: to explore, to discover, to boldly go where no one has gone before. Unfortunately, our fear holds us back. The fear of the unknown, the fear of the *what ifs*, the fear of change. Joshua 1:9 is one of my favorite verses because it almost sounds like God's version of the *Star Trek* motto, with a slight difference. God calls us to boldly go where no one has gone before, but He assures us that we don't have to go alone. He is always there with us, and therefore, we have nothing to fear. Isn't that good news? Life is full of new civilizations and new lives for us to seek out. It is our final frontier and God is calling us to explore it as we walk with Him. Let's go.

September 7

Good News; You're Not Soup

"So God created man in his own image, in the image of God He created him; male and female he created them"
(Genesis 1:27).

AS YOU PROBABLY KNOW, genetic information for all life is contained in DNA, but that particular molecule is far too complicated to have just suddenly appeared. Many scientists believe that RNA, a single strand molecule that helps make proteins and can contain genetic information in viruses, may have come first. Well, some scientists think they have figured out the process by which RNA came first from a "seething soup of simple chemicals." You know, call me crazy, but I fail to see the appeal of believing we came from soup. All these discoveries are labeled as great moments of enlightenment, but to discover I came from soup seems like it would be supremely depressing. After all, what is the point of soup? To be eaten with some crackers, right? Is that our lot in life? Is that all we're good for, to be consumed with some crackers? No, we were meant for so much more. My friend, you and I were created by a loving God who designed each and every one of us specifically for a purpose: to know Him and make Him known. You are not soup; you are the image of the living God who gives our lives purpose and meaning. Now that's a discovery I consider good news.

September 8
Afraid of Success

"I tell you the truth, anyone who has faith in me will do what I have been doing. He will do even greater things than these because I am going to the Father"
(John 14:12).

JESUS WAS A MAN OF COMPASSION. He saw the needs of the blind, the sick, the lame, and the demon possessed and He prayed for them and healed them. I am a man of cowardice. I see those same needs around me today and I look the other away and try to pretend I didn't see them. Why? Well, odd as it may sound, I'm afraid if I do pray for their needs and they are healed, more and more people will come seeking the same thing. Worse, I might get caught it up in the midst of some debate and controversy as people try to prove that what happened was real or unreal. Yes, odd as it may sound, I'm afraid that what God said *will* work. I'm afraid of success, I'm afraid of the miraculous. However, that's a silly thing to be concerned about, and it reveals the fact that I have far too much self-consciousness. Everything I'm afraid of happened to Jesus, and yet He continued to have compassion for people and continued to pray for their needs. He's called you and me to continue that same miraculous work, and He's called us to do even greater things in His name. People are in need now more than ever. It's time to take courage, time to set ourselves aside, and time to step out in compassion and faith and meet those needs. Some may not like what happens when we do that, but others will have their lives changed forever by the good news of Jesus Christ. I don't want to be afraid of that. I want to be a part of it.

September 9
How You Are Like Spock

"So I say live by the Spirit, and you will not gratify the desires of the sinful nature. For the sinful nature desires what is contrary to the Spirit and the Spirit what is contrary to the sinful nature. They are in conflict with each other, so that you do not do what you want"
(Galatians 5:16-17).

YOU AND I ARE A LOT MORE LIKE SPOCK, the famous Vulcan from *Star Trek*, then we realize. Spock is a fascinating character because he struggles with two sides of his nature: his logical, emotionally controlled Vulcan side and his passionate, emotionally expressive human side. Spock eventually found a happy medium between the two where he was able to draw on the strengths of both sides. Such an option, however, is not open to us when it comes to the two sides of our nature. We also struggle with two extremes: our godly inclinations led by the Holy Spirit and our worldly inclinations led by our flesh. Both are emotional, but like Spock, one is controlled and tempered while the other is reckless and self-indulgent. These two natures war within us, but they do not rule us. Early in his life Spock made a conscious decision to embrace his logical side, and we, too, are left with a choice. We can be ruled by our passions, or we can rule over them with the help of the Holy Spirit. However, keep in mind that unlike Spock, there can never be any compromise between the two. We must choose one or the other. We must choose to embrace our Christ-like nature or our sinful nature. There is no middle ground. So choose wisely.

September 10
The Terminator Lacks a Savior
**"But our citizenship is in heaven.
And we eagerly await a Savior from there, the Lord Jesus Christ, who, by the power that enables him to bring everything under his control, will transform our lowly bodies so they will be like his glorious body"
(Philippians 3:20-21).**

ONE OF THE THINGS I really enjoyed in the film *Terminator Salvation*, starring Christian "I'm Batman" Bale, was the fact that it was filmed right here in New Mexico. In fact, there are several recognizable areas of our state highlighted in the movie. However, I have to admit I think the name of the film is somewhat of a misnomer, because the movie really doesn't have as much to do with salvation or a savior as it does with finding redemption. The good news for us, though, is that in our own never-ending battle with sin, there most definitely is a Savior for us to turn to. One who has already defeated the enemy forces, and who offers us life and victory. He has done more than any other hero in history to provide salvation for those who would follow Him. So if you're looking for salvation, if you're looking for a savior, don't turn to the movies, even if there is one called *Terminator Salvation*. Turn to the pages of your Bible. It's there you'll discover what a Savior and salvation really are.

September 11
Always Remember

"I will remember the deeds of the Lord; yes, I will remember your miracles of long ago. I will meditate on all your works and consider all your mighty deeds"
(Psalm 77:11-12).

SEPTEMBER 11 is a day most of us will never forget, and some of us wish we didn't have to remember. It was a day of tremendous tragedy and heartbreak, a day of grief, fear, and loss. It was truly a day that reshaped the world, and none of us have been the same since. All these years later, the pain for some has started to fade, as has the memory for others. Yet this is day we must never forget, not because of how tragic it was, but because of all the little miracles that took place throughout that day. People who were supposed to be on one of those planes, but weren't. Workers who were unexpectedly late to work. People trapped with no way out who suddenly found a way to escape. When we remember 9/11 we must remember two things: 1), God grieved with us that day over the horror and the loss. Those were people He loved who died; people He desperately wanted to know Him, so they would know eternal life, and He felt the loss as much as any of us. And 2), we must remember all the little miracles that took place that day.

We must remember even in the midst of tragedy, God was at work. He was granting courage to rescue workers, strength to citizens as they helped each other, fortitude to leaders, and even peace to those who never saw a loved one ever again. The Bible is replete with calls to remember the things of the past. This day is no exception.

September 12
Set Your Mind Above

"No eye has seen, no ear has heard, no mind has conceived what God has prepared for those who love him"
(1 Corinthians 2:9).

"IT IS A FAR, FAR BETTER REST that I go to than I have ever known"—that's one of the more well- known lines from *A Tale of Two* *Cities*. It was even quoted in *Star Trek II* and *The Dark Knight Rises*. However, I've often felt it's a quote that should represent how all Christians feel about Heaven. The truth is, I don't always give Heaven a whole lot of thought. In fact, most of the time I'm too preoccupied with the here and now to dwell on eternity. And yet considering how often this world can make me feel tired, discouraged, and hopeless, I have to wonder why I don't keep Heaven more in mind. After all, few things motivate us better than the promise of a reward. It's why teams give all they have in the playoffs, it's why it's why we work hard in school and at our jobs, it's why we like to play games. Rewards such as good grades, better pay and promotion, and, of course, trophies and cash prizes are motivating. Heaven is the ultimate reward, and it's promised to all who follow Jesus Christ. The good news is the more heavenly minded we are, the more earthly good we will be.

September 13
Growing Up is Hard to Do

"Come to me all you who are weary and burdened and I will give you rest. Take my yoke upon you and learn from me, for I am gentle and humble in heart, and you will find rest for your souls. For my yoke is easy and my burden is light" (Matthew 11:28-30).

RESPONSIBILITY CAN BE A HEAVY BURDEN. I wish someone had told me that as a kid, because I probably would have taken off to Never Never Land had I known. As a kid, you just don't realize how heavy the burdens of bills, jobs, families, ministry, and the rest of life can be. Maybe you've been feeling weighed down, maybe you've been feeling like those burdens of responsibility are just too big to carry any more. Well, I have good news for you. I know Someone who wants to help. Jesus Christ calls all of us who are weary and overloaded to come to Him and to take up yet another burden. However, this one's different. This one is easy and light. This one makes it possible for us to live up to our responsibilities without feeling like they're too heavy or wearying. Jesus Christ gives us a chance to live life like a child again as a child of God. So in a way, it is like going to Never Never Land. True, our responsibilities will never go away as adults. We must continue to be wise and prudent about them, but with Jesus' help, those unbearable burdens become light and easy as we let Him bear the load while we simply take up our cross and follow Him.

September 14
Battling the Tyranny of the Immediate
"He has made everything beautiful in its time"
(Ecclesiastes 3:11).

'VE OFTEN STRUGGLED with the tyranny of the immediate. Maybe you're familiar with that struggle. It's when everything that has to happen has to happen right now. The problem with the tyranny of the immediate is it often causes us to put off what's important. The important things in life are rarely the things that need to be done immediately, but they are the things that must be done if we are to truly enjoy a high quality of life. So the question becomes, how do we break free from the tyranny of the immediate and make room for what's important? One thing that helps me is to remember is that God is never a slave to the immediate, but rather He makes sure everything takes place in its appointed time. You've probably noticed you can never force God to do something immediately, but He's always there to help us with what's important. As one author put it, we need to trade the rhythm of our lives, which is often so quickly paced, for the rhythm of God's heart, which is steady, calm, and peaceful. Granted it isn't always easy because the immediate is always beckoning to us. But when we're willing to make sure that what's important has just as much priority in our lives as what's immediate, I think you'll find life isn't quite so harried. Wouldn't that be good news?

<hr />

September 15
How to Carpe Diem

**"The thief only comes to steal and kill and destroy;
I have come that they may have life, and have it to the full"
(John 10:10).**

IN PIXAR'S CLASSIC MOVIE *UP*, the main character Carl Fredricksen discovers what it means to have a full, adventurous life—and it wasn't quite what he expected. The truth is, many of us are like Carl Fredricksen. We're constantly putting off living a full life for some distant point in the future when we can finally get around to it. In the meantime, the everyday monotony of life continues to get in the way and keeps us from living our lives to the full . . . or so we think. My friend, you don't have to wait to experience a life lived to the full; you can experience it right now. Jesus Christ himself said that He came to give us life to the full, and He also said that this is life, to know the only true God and Jesus Christ whom He has sent. You don't need to travel to distant lands like the jungles of South America to experience a full, adventurous life. And that's exactly what Mr. Fredricksen discovers. The truth is that mundane, everyday life you're going through can be a life lived to the full, a life filled with excitement, joy, love, and adventure. All you need is the right partner: Jesus Christ. So go on, start living life to the full with Jesus Christ. As the movie *Up* points out, "Adventure is out there." It's time we started experiencing it and invited others to experience it with us.

September 16
To Tell the Truth
"Kings take pleasure in honest lips;
they value a man who speaks the truth"
(Proverbs 16:13).

DID YOU KNOW that 80 percent of people have admitted to lying, or at least to telling half-truths? The other 20 percent were most likely lying about not lying because, because, quite frankly, it's something we all have in common. Whether we admit it or not, we all lie. There are lots of reasons why we lie—to shift blame, to get what we want, to avoid conflict and so on—but instead of focusing on all the reasons and rationales we have for lying, I've found it's helpful to avoid lying by focusing on reasons to tell the truth. What are those, you ask? Well, our verse in Proverbs presents some pretty good ones. Kings take pleasure in the truth, and I'm sure that's true for the King of Kings as well. Wouldn't you like the King of your life to take pleasure in you? Tell the truth and He will. Another compelling reason is when we lie, we aren't speaking the language of Christ, but the language of Satan. Jesus himself said that lies are the native language of the devil. I don't know about you, but as a child of God, I certainly don't want to do anything that identifies me with the enemy. Look, we all lie, but that's because we choose to lie. The truth is lying isn't the easy way out, it usually only leads to more trouble. So let's start choosing truth, you and I, and maybe we can be the 20 percent in a survey who actually don't lie. Just think of the impact that would have on our society.

September 17
Making the Right Choice
"In your struggle against sin, you have not yet resisted to the point of shedding your blood"
(Hebrews 12:4).

I'M HERE to do a little myth busting today (because I just love that show *Mythbusters*). Today's myth I'm going to bust is the myth of your not having a choice. This is something we often encounter when we face sin and temptation. Something comes up we know is wrong, but honestly, we really want to do it and we may feel like we have no choice because the temptation is too powerful and we just can't help ourselves. I've felt that way many times, and because of it, I've made many mistakes. Well, I'm here to share with you some good news: you always have a choice. No matter what the situation is, there's nothing that can ever *make* you do anything—the choice is yours. Look, I know temptation is powerful and sin is alluring, but Jesus Christ died on the Cross and rose from the dead to set us free from that power. He gives us the power to make the choice not to sin. He gives us the strength to resist any temptation. I'm not saying it's always going to be easy and I'm not saying you're *never* going to sin, but I am saying you can make a choice to sin less. You always have a choice. Make the right one.

September 18
Surprised by Mercy

*"Praise be to the God and Father of our Lord Jesus Christ!
In his great mercy he has given us new birth into a living hope
through the resurrection of Jesus Christ from the dead"*
(1 Peter 1:3).

A MAN WALKED into a New York store with the intent of robbing it. However, the storeowner pulled out a rifle, and that's when the would-be robber broke down. He started sobbing, saying he was just trying to feed his hungry family. The storeowner, taken by surprise at this, decided to show mercy and gave the man bread and forty dollars. It's an interesting story because we just don't hear of that kind of mercy much these days. The good news is God has shown us far more mercy. We, too, were caught in the act and were guilty because of our sin. God, however, did more than just let us go. He took our place, paid our price, and then gave us new life through Jesus Christ. He didn't have to do it. You and I are guilty of sin, there's no arguing that. But because of His great love for us God showed us mercy and did more than just excuse our sin, He completely took it away. He didn't just give a little help to get by. He invited us to be His children, He provides all that we need, and He allows us to constantly be in His holy presence. That is good news.

September 19

Enjoying the Storms

"He replied, 'You of little faith, why are you so afraid?'
Then he got up and rebuked the winds and the waves,
and it was completely calm"
(Matthew 8:26).

YOU KNOW WHAT, I enjoy stormy weather. We don't get a lot of it in New Mexico, but when a good storm does show up, when the thunder rolls and the lightning flashes, I like to cuddle up with my wife and listen to the wind and the rain and just enjoy the storm. I even find it a bit relaxing. Weird, I know. The reason I say it's weird is because when storms roll into my life, I don't just sit back and enjoy them, I get stressed and freaked out. I worry and I fret and I wonder when the storm will be over and why I ever had to go through it the first place. Well, the good news is when we realize our Lord and Savior Jesus Christ is going through those storms with us, He's there to take care of us, and ultimately to help us grow through those storms of life, then we can be excited rather than frightened by them. Just like those occasional thunderstorms I find exciting to listen to from the safety of my home and the comfort of my wife's arms, we can find the storms of life exciting as we reside safely and comfortably in the arms of our loving Savior Jesus Christ. It's not always easy, but if I truly trust Jesus, then perhaps it's time I changed my perspective on the storms of life.

September 20

The Joy of Movie Watching

*"As the deer pants for streams of water,
so my soul pants for you, O God"*
(Psalm 42:1).

MY TWO DAUGHTERS know how to get the most out of a movie. When they watch a Blu-Ray at home, they not only watch the feature, they also watch all the previews, all the music videos, they look at all the games, they'll watch the extras multiple times, even the ones that bore them. They just keep watching and watching and watching. I think I'm the only parent who has to tell kids to turn off a movie after it's over, because if I didn't, they'd just keep sitting there watching anything and everything over and over again just so long as the movie doesn't end. I hope I can instill in them that same zeal and ravenous appetite for God's Word. I hope I can show them that's exactly the type of attitude we should have toward the Bible. And the good news is when we approach the Bible with that kind of passion, we'll find answers, guidance, insight, advice, comfort, peace, joy, and blessings. In other words, we'll find so much more than just previews of coming attractions. I never thought I'd learn anything about Bible study habits from the way my girls watch movies on Blu-Ray, but now that I have I hope it's a lesson I'll never forget.

September 21

Dreaming About Hell (Scary, Right?)

*"Do not be afraid of those who kill the body
but cannot kill the soul. Rather, be afraid of the One
who can destroy both soul and body in hell"*
(Matthew 10:28).

ONE WEEK NOT LONG AGO I had a dream about hell three out of the five nights. Odd, right? Well, here's the interesting part. Instead of these dreams making me afraid (and they were a little scary), more than anything I woke up feeling sad. Why? Because so many people are heading to hell and they may not even realize it. Every day I walk through the world full of people oblivious to their fate apart from Christ. Now that's scary, but more than anything it's sad. It's sad because I know how to keep them from going to hell. I know how to prevent hell from being their fate by the death and Resurrection of Jesus Christ. That is the good news. That is the really good news. The sad thing is that good news doesn't seem to be getting out nearly enough. These dreams I've had have me thinking about all the ways I could do a better job of sharing this good news with neighbors, friends, strangers, people at the store, and anywhere else I may go. What about you? How do you feel about the people around you possibly going to hell? Are you willing to do anything about it?

September 22
Don't Forget to Share the News

"Preach the Word; be prepared in season and out of season; correct, rebuke and encourage—with great patience and careful instruction"
(2 Timothy 4:2).

TO HELP SHOW SOLIDARITY with employees during tough economic times and to help cut costs in order to save jobs, a British Airways CEO announced he would work without pay for an entire month. There was just one problem with his plan: he forgot to tell his wife. She read about it in the newspapers after the decision was made. It's never a good idea to let your family learn about bad news by reading it in the paper instead of hearing it from you. The funny thing is, we as Christians are guilty of something similar. Far too often, we're absent-minded and forget to tell people around us the good news. We go about our day and never make the most of the opportunities we have to share with people the wonderful news that Jesus died for their sins and rose from the grave so they could have eternal life. One day, everyone will know about that good news, but for many it will be too late to do anything about it. I wonder how many of them will be upset and ask, "How come no one said anything to me?" You know what? Let's make sure that doesn't happen. Let's make sure people aren't reading about the Rapture in the paper after it already happened. Let's make every effort to share the good news with them here, now, today. After all, it's one thing to forget to mention that you're not going to get paid for a month, but how in the world can we possibly forget to mention the amazing grace of Jesus Christ?

September 23

How to be Like Batman . . . and Jesus

"And we, who with unveiled faces all reflect the Lord's glory, are being transformed into his likeness with ever-increasing glory, which comes from the Lord, who is the Spirit"
(2 Corinthians 3:18).

A FRIEND OF MINE gave me *The Batman Handbook: The Ultimate Training Manual,* one of my favorite gifts. At first I thought it was cool because it was about Batman, but then I started reading it and I realized it wasn't just about Batman, it was telling me how I could *become* Batman. Seriously, this book tells you everything you need to know to be just like Batman, from bullet-proofing your own Batmobile to making a utility belt to learning how to do a back flip. It's all there in this handy, dandy manual. Well, as terrific as it would be to be like Batman, a far better option is to learn how to be like Christ. That's where the handy training manual known as the Bible comes into play. This nifty little guide will tell you everything you need to know to live a righteous, successful life as you follow Jesus Christ. In fact, if you follow the words of this book, you will become more and more like Christ. And considering how He changed the world, having a bunch of people like Him could only turn this world upside down. And that, my friends, would be good news. So take the time to read your training manual daily, and then put it into practice.

September 24
The Days I Sin the Most

"This righteousness from God comes through faith in Jesus Christ to all who believe. There is no difference, for all have sinned and fall short of the glory of God, and are justified freely by his grace through the redemption that came by Christ Jesus"
(Romans 3:22-24).

YOU KNOW WHEN I do the most sinning? It's whenever I play golf. And it's not because I'm swearing and cursing and breaking things, it's because I miss the mark all day long. In fact, I don't even come close to getting that little ball in the hole. The real problem with sin, however, is that no matter how good you are you can never really hit the mark anyway. Phil Mickelson would probably, *probably* do a better job of hitting the mark on the golf course than I. But if we were both teeing off for a hole on the moon, he might get closer, but we'd both fall way short—just as we both fall short of the mark when it comes to being holy like God. Fortunately for us, God provided a solution. He didn't move the mark any closer or make it any easier for us to hit it, which apparently is what I need to happen in golf. But rather God hit the mark for us through the death and Resurrection of Jesus Christ. Jesus did the work, and then offers us the result if we'll just choose to let Him run our lives. It'd be like me letting Phil

Mickelson play for me on the golf course and then give me his score as my own at the end of the day. Of course, the penalty for sin is far more severe in life than not hitting the mark on the golf course. The fact that Jesus hit the mark for us is definitely good news.

September 25
The Dine and Dash Costs
"But if you fail to do this, you will be sinning against the Lord; and you may be sure that your sin will find you out"
(Numbers 32:23).

A FEW YEARS AGO in Detroit Michigan, four women enjoyed a nice early breakfast at a local IHOP. However, once they finished, they decided they didn't want to pay for their nice breakfast. So they ran out of the restaurant without paying. Unfortunately, as they tried to make their getaway, the woman driving lost control of the car and ended up driving through a wall *into* the IHOP. Needless to say, they ended up paying for their breakfast, and a lot more. The fact of the matter is there's no escaping the cost of sin. Sooner or later, it will catch up with us and we will have to pay the price for our sin. The good news, however, is God has already paid it for us. When Jesus Christ died on the Cross and rose from the dead, He paid the price for our sin and then offered us freedom from sin in Him. We don't have to dine and dash, we can enjoy ourselves knowing the bill has already been paid. That's good news we should share everywhere we go in order to help others from crashing while trying to avoid the cost of sin.

September 26
The Wisdom of Gandalf is Still Relevant
"If you falter in times of trouble, how small is your strength?"
(Proverbs 24:10).

"ALL WE CAN CHOOSE is what to do with the time that we are given." I love watching *The Lord of the Rings* movies, and every time I do it feels like that line from Gandalf is more relevant now then when the films first premiered. It's easy to look around at what's going on in the world today and wish we hadn't been around for times such as these, for they are indeed dark times. I especially feel that way whenever I receive bad news, which no one really enjoys. It makes me want to say, "Why have I lived to see these dark times just keep getting darker?" And yet, Gandalf's words keep coming back to me, and in them I hear wisdom similar to that of Solomon's. The fact of the matter is dark or not, these are the times God has chosen for us to live in—and that was no accident. Times may be tough, but our God is tougher still and He will provide the strength, the wisdom, the insight, the tenacity, and the courage to not only face dark times, but overcome them. He wants you and me to shine a bright light in the darkness, but we must choose to do so. We must choose to let His strength shine through us in times of trouble. That sounds like good news to me, so that is what I will choose to do. And in doing so, I know I will not falter in times of trouble.

September 27
Why is There Hope?
**"Therefore we do not lose heart. Though outwardly we are
wasting away, yet inwardly we are being renewed day by day"
(2 Corinthians 4:16).**

WHY DO WE HAVE HOPE? Have you ever stopped to consider that? Why do we cling to hope in a world so full of hopelessness? I think the only answer is to ask, "What are you hoping in?" There are a lot of things in this world we can put our hope in, but they will ultimately disappoint us. We've already seen that we can't hope in financial institutions, or that corporations will always be around. And we all know that hope placed in people is bound to let us down. As I pondered the question of why can we have hope, I could only come up with one answer: because of God. We can have hope because there is a living God who loves us. We can have hope because there is a God who sent is Son to die on the Cross and rise from the dead to free us from sin and give us new life. We can have hope because there is a God who is never-changing and is eternal. I think the fact that we cling to hope even in the darkest of times is evidence that we all innately know there is a God. Hope exists because God exists, and that's good news because we desperately need both.

September 28
Does the Meaning of a Word Matter?
"Like a muddied spring or a polluted well is a righteous man who gives way to the wicked"
(Proverbs 25:26).

AS A WRITER, I have some pretty strong opinions on a topic you may think is rather trivial. Do we concede the meaning of a word, or do we refuse to give in to our culture's definition of it? It may seem like a trivial thing, the definition of a word, but as I read today's Proverb, I realized it's not all that trivial at all. If we as Christians are truly going to make a difference in our culture, we must make a stand on the big issues, and we must make a stand on the little issues. For instance, the word *religion* used to be used almost interchangeably with *Christianity*. They were practically one in the same. Today, however, Christians are afraid to use the word religion because it has an entirely different meaning and connotation now than it did in the 18th and 19th centuries. The truth is we've conceded far too much to our culture and we've compromised on far too many issues. Enough is enough, I say. The line must be drawn, and if it starts by drawing the line on the definition of a word, then so be it. Our world is dark and hostile, this is true, but it is also desperate for hope and longing for truth. I know it may not always seem that way. I know it may seem the world is out to destroy those very things needed most, but we must not draw back. Instead, we must shine the light of truth, we must make our stand in Christ, and we must not concede anymore. It's time to say we will not give way anymore, even in how we define a word. Fellow Christians, it's time to go forward and share the good news.

***

September 29
The Problem With Sequels
"You too, be patient and stand firm, because the Lord's coming is near"
(James 5:8).

IT'S ALWAYS TOUGH to make a sequel to a successful movie. People always want the second one to be bigger and better than the first. *Transformers: Revenge of the Fallen,* is a prime example of a movie that tried to do that, but failed. It's so bad, I pretend it doesn't even exist. It took all the good of the first movie and made it even better, true, but it also took all the bad and made it even worse. Well, there is one sequel I know for sure won't be a disappointment. When Jesus Christ came to this Earth the first time, He came to die on a Cross for our sins and to rise from the dead to give us new life. It was the most amazing, loving act in all of history—and a tough one to improve upon. However, when Jesus comes a second time, it will be one of the rare times when the sequel is truly better than the original. While Jesus secured us a place in Heaven the first time He was here, He'll come to actually take us there the second time. While Jesus set us free from sin the first time He was here, He'll annihilate it once and for all the second time. In short, Jesus' Second Coming will be a sequel you don't want to miss, but the only way you can see it is through Jesus Christ. You don't have to purchase a ticket, just accept that Jesus already purchased the ticket for you. And that, my friends, is good news and a sequel we should be telling people about. It will be one we won't forget, as opposed to one we wish we couldn't remember.

September 30
The Know-it-all

"It is for freedom that Christ has set us free. Stand firm, then, and do not let yourselves be burdened again by a yoke of slavery"
(Galatians 5:1).

HAVE YOU EVER MET A KNOW-IT-ALL? Sometimes I feel like I live with a know-it-all. Kids are often like that. When my daughter was seven, she already knew just about everything. No matter what I said or talked about, odds were she'd respond, "I know." When we see that in a child it's easy to think it's funny or cute, but for me it's was a warning. Why? Because now that I'm older, now that I'm grown-up, I can fall into that comfortable place where I feel like I know all I need to know about the Christian life and have nothing new to learn. And since that's the case, I therefore have the right to tell everyone else what they're doing wrong because obviously everyone doesn't know as much as the know-it-all: me. That, my friends, leads to exactly what Paul is talking about in today's verse: it leads back to a burden and yoke of slavery. Instead of being a know-it-all, I should be a want-to-know-more. I should always be open to being taught, corrected, and discipled. In fact, Christ set us free so we could do just that—constantly learn more about Him and how we can apply that knowledge to our daily walk. I have so much more to learn, and every time I hear a kid who says, "I know," I'm reminded of that truth.

October

They are clouds without water,
carried about by the winds;
late autumn trees without fruit,
twice dead, pulled up by the roots;

Jude 1:12b

October 1

Homecoming is Depressing

"For by the grace given me I say to every one of you: Do not think of yourself more highly than you ought, but rather think of yourself with sober judgment, in accordance with the measure of faith God has given you"
(Romans 12:3).

FIND THIS TIME OF YEAR kind of depressing. Why? It's about the time you start seeing high schools put up their homecoming banners. That depresses me because it reminds me that when I was in high school I was never voted homecoming king. Let's be honest, when I was in high school, my classmates didn't even know I was in the same class. I look back at high school and wonder how I could have been more popular and important. Of course, I often look at my life now and wonder the same thing. Come on, admit it; we've all wanted to feel more popular or important at some point in our lives. We like feeling important. Yet, whenever that mood strikes me, I remember what Paul says in Romans, that I should be careful not to think of myself more highly than I ought. Elsewhere the Bible tells me to think of others more highly than myself. That's good advice. It keeps the ego in check and keeps my head from swelling. Better yet, the good news is when I remember I'm a child of God, a royal prince in the Kingdom of Christ, I realize I don't need to feel any more important because I'm important to God. Not even being homecoming king can compete with that.

October 2
The Tragedy of Death and Hell
"Just as man is destined to die once,
and after that to face judgment . . . "
(Hebrews 9:27).

ICHAEL JACKSON unexpectedly died at the age of fifty in 2009. There was a lot of talk about just how tragic his death was because of how and when it happened. But I think the real tragedy was the possibility that Michael Jackson, despite all of his fame, talent, and riches, may now be spending an eternity in hell. When he died, the King of Pop stood before the King of Kings, and if Jesus Christ wasn't his Lord and Savior, then it didn't matter who Michael Jackson was in life. He would still spend the rest of eternity in death. I know that sounds bleak, and it may even seem morbid and callous to speak that way about the deceased, but I want you to understand it was a tragedy that could have been averted. It's no secret that Michael Jackson wanted to be loved, yet as far as I know he never found the love of God. Maybe nobody told him about it, maybe he didn't believe it was true. Well, friends, the good news is it is true. God does love us and He wants us to enjoy eternal life through Christ. But if you and I don't tell people that, many people will suffer the same tragedy as Michael Jackson. It's a heartbreaking tragedy to die without Christ, and it's one we can prevent if we'll only be bold enough. We must care enough everything possible to make sure no one has to suffer eternal death in hell.

October 3
Your Identity in a Drink

"I have been crucified with Christ and I no longer live, but Christ lives in me. The life I live in the body, I live by faith in the Son of God, who loved me and gave himself for me" (Galatians 2:20).

TALL, FIVE-PUMP HOT CHOCOLATE. I find it interesting that we have reduced the summation of who we are to a list of attributes for a morning beverage. Tall, five-pump ot chocolate. Grande, caramel macchiato, extra hot. Tall, extra my cappuccino. These few words signify our identity in morning, and they give us a sense of security, confidence, feeling of being in control. It's a good way to start the . Well, my friends, I want to be known for more than of beverage I drink in the morning. I want to be known ave Christ in my life. In fact, I want my identity to be ly wrapped up in Christ that people don't even see see Christ. I want people to see me and say, "Tall, f Christ." That is what I want my identity to be, good one.

October 4

The Life, Death, and Life of Superheroes

"But Christ has indeed been raised from the dead,
the firstfruits of those who have fallen asleep.
For since death came through a man, the resurrection
of the dead comes also through a man"
(1 Corinthians 15:20-21).

DO YOU REMEMBER back when Captain America died? It was in 2007 and it was a rather shocking development for many comic book fans. Of course, the nice thing about comic books is you never have to shed too many tears over the loss of a favorite hero because odds are they'll make a return somehow, and that's no less true of Captain America. Just two years later, Steve Rogers made his unsurprising return from the grave. The fact that we can dependably count on dead comic book characters to return to life one way or another got me thinking; isn't the same true of us? Doesn't the Bible tell us that all who die will one day rise again to stand before God? Yes, yes it does. Jesus was the first to do this, but one day you and I will follow in His footsteps and we will be resurrected as well. It's kind of cool, when you think about it. It almost makes us comic book characters. We may die one day, but through Christ we will be resurrected and return to life, just like Superman, Captain America, and just about every other superhero in the history of comics. So if you know someone who would like to be a comic book hero and live forever, be sure to tell him about the good news of the resurrection through Christ Jesus.

October 5

Look, Up in the Sky

*They were looking intently up into the sky as he was going,
when suddenly two men dressed in white stood beside them.
"Men of Galilee," they said, "why do you stand here looking into
the sky? This same Jesus, who has been taken from you into
heaven, will come back in the same way you have seen him go."*
(Acts 1:10-11)

I'VE SAID IT ONCE and I'll say it again: Balloon Fiesta is my favorite time of year. I love driving into work while I stare into the sky watching those colorful balloons float gently and majestically over Albuquerque, New Mexico. Of course, then I realize while I was watching them I have inadvertently driven across five neighborhood lawns and now have a garden gnome sitting on the hood of my car. But that's not my point. During Balloon Fiesta, it's just fun to look up into the sky, which often for me is just a reminder of where I should be looking for Christ's return. I think it would be amazing someday to be watching the Balloon Fiesta only to see Christ descending through the clouds and the balloons to take us home. Well, it would only be amazing if we're looking forward to His return, and the truth is there are a lot of people who aren't . . . yet. As much as I enjoy looking into the sky, it's good sometimes to look around and see who isn't looking into the sky, and then gently share the good news with them. Then they, too, can gaze into the sky with anticipation.

October 6

It's Good to be King

"Do nothing out of selfish ambition or vain conceit, but in humility consider others better than yourselves"
(Philippians 2:3).

EVERY NOW AND THEN, we like to play "castle" at my house. I, naturally, am the king of the castle, one of my daughters is the princess, and one of them ends up as the servant. The problem is, no one really wants to be the servant. Everyone prefers being royalty over being subservient to each other. It's an interesting study in human nature. We all readily accept the concept of serving other people, but we usually accept it in the context of others serving us. When we actually have to do some serving of our own, then things are suddenly uncomfortable and unfair. Well, friends, if we're truly going to spread the good news as we fulfill this verse, we're just going have to get used to the idea that it applies to us as much as it does to others. You and I need to consider others better than ourselves, you and I need to be humble and subservient, and you and I must not be selfish and vain. Even when it's just pretend, no one wants to be a servant, but that's what Jesus has called us to do. And if He was willing to serve others, shouldn't we be willing to do the same?

October 7
How Much is a Soul Worth?

"And they sang a new song: 'You are worthy to take the scroll and to open its seals, because you were slain, and with your blood you purchased men for God from every tribe and language and people and nation.'"
(Revelation 5:9).

IN THE EUROPEAN NATION OF LATVIA the economy got so bad that one company offered loans in return for people's immortal souls. They promised that if someone failed to repay the loan, they wouldn't be visited by debt collectors trying to collect that soul, but that person would simply no longer have one as per the conditions of the loan agreement. Seriously, this happened. It was a sad sign, not only of the economic times when people were willing to sell their souls for a loan, but it also showed a lack of understanding when it comes to the value of a soul. How much is your soul worth? Well, to put it into perspective, Jesus Christ had to be beaten, humiliated, tortured, and killed, and then He had to overcome death when He rose from the grave—all just to pay the price for your soul. In fact, God thinks your soul is the most valuable thing in the entire universe, and that's why in His great love He was willing to sacrifice His Son for you. I think we forget the value of our souls far too easily. The good news is that God hasn't.

October 8
Bumper Sticker Philosophy

"A fool gives full vent to his anger, but a wise man keeps himself under control."
(Proverbs 29:11).

LOVE BUMPER STICKERS. I especially love the ones that make some sort of strong spiritual or political statement. It's almost as if those drivers are hoping you'll change your mind on an issue just by reading their bumper sticker. Suddenly you'll gasp and say, "I've never thought of it that way. I'm going to completely change what I believe. Thanks, mister bumper sticker!" The really fun cars are the ones with a lot of bumper stickers on them. They're like cars that are yelling at you. You almost want to tell them to calm down and take a few deep, cleansing breaths. Bumper stickers also remind me that as Christians we won't sway people with trite little sayings or by venting our righteous emotions on various subjects. No, if we want to bring people to Christ they need to get to know us. They need to see Christ in us. It's important for us as Christians to stand for what's right, but there's a better way to do that than bumper stickers, both in the real and allegorical sense. Let's live out the good news in our daily lives for all the world to see.

October 9
When Faith "Fails"

Without weakening his faith, he faced the fact that his body was as good as dead—since he was about a hundred years old—and that Sarah's womb was also dead. Yet he did not waver through unbelief regarding the promise of God, but was strengthened in his faith and gave glory to God.
(Romans 4:19-20)

STILL REMEMBER when I found out my little niece—she was a dear, spirited little girl all of three years old at the time—had cystic fibrosis. I can't tell how much I prayed while we were waiting for those test results to come back. I prayed fervently and desperately that either the tests would be wrong or that she would be miraculously healed. But the tests weren't wrong, and she wasn't healed, and I was left with wondering why and what to do next. What do you do when your faith seems fruitless, when your prayers seem to go unanswered, and God's promise seems to go unfilled? For some reason, I've never thought about the fact that Abraham faced that exact same situation. This verse reminds me that not only did he face that circumstance, he also refused to waver, refused to give in to unbelief, refused to give up on God, and refused to lose faith. In fact, it says his faith grew and he gave glory to God. I don't know why all of this has happened to my sister and my sweet little niece, but I do know this: our God is an awesome God, and I will trust in Him. My niece may not be healed . . . yet. But who knows what plans God has in store?

October 10

Making Like a Bunny

"In the same way, let your light shine before men, that they may see your good deeds and praise your Father in heaven" (Matthew 5:16).

AS I WROTE EARLIER, every morning when I walked into work I saw a bunch of bunnies eating the grass in front of our studio. As I walked by, some ran away, but others just bunched up really tight, got as low to the ground as possible, and sat really still. I guess they were hoping I wouldn't see them—even though they were two feet away and I could see them as plain as day. There have been plenty of times in my Christian walk where I've acted just like those bunnies. I've hunkered down and hoped no one would notice me. In fact, that's often the easiest thing for us to do as Christians. We can rationalize it by saying this world is so dark that we can't really do anything about it, so we'll just lay low and try to survive until Christ gets here and rescues us. However, that's not what Jesus wants us to do. He wants us to be noticed. He wants us to stand out. He wants us to shine our light in the darkness. And the truth is, just like those bunnies I see every morning, it's not like we're really hiding any way. The world is watching those of us who claim to follow Christ, so instead of showing them timid bunnies who are trying to avoid being noticed, let's show them bold, faithful, obedient, radiant, and attractive beacons of light.

October 11

Watch Where You're Going

"Therefore do not worry about tomorrow, for tomorrow will worry about itself. Each day has enough trouble of its own" (Matthew 6:34).

READ A STORY once about a teen in New York who fell into a manhole while texting on her phone. Granted, there probably should have been some barriers set up around an open manhole, but nevertheless, I can't help but wonder if this girl could have avoided this slightly painful, somewhat embarrassing, and very stinky accident if she had just watched where she was going. Actually, I'm surprised it doesn't happen more often, considering how often I see people walking around while looking down at their phones. The truth is, we often have the same problem with the future. We get so consumed with the problems we *might* face in our uncertain future that we forget to pay attention to what's going on now. I understand that in this troublesome world there's plenty to worry about when it comes to the future. But if that's all we focus on, we're going to find ourselves plummeting through a manhole of present problems. The good news is we serve a God who's big enough to handle our current problems—and our future ones. Even better, He loves us so much that He *wants* to help us. So let Him worry about the future, and let Him help you here in the present. Then you and I will both avoid those unexpected open manholes.

October 12

Is There One for Me?

*"Jesus said, 'Let the little children come to me,
and do not hinder them, for the kingdom of heaven
belongs to such as these'"*
(Matthew 19:14).

AT A GENERAL STOCK HOLDER'S MEETING not long ago, the makers of the Blackberry smart phone were stumped by a kid in the audience who asked whether or not they were going to make a phone for kids so his mom will let him have one. (Why that kid was at a stockholder's meeting and not at school is beyond me; maybe it was field trip.) The top executives at Blackberry seemed uncomfortable with the question, and they didn't really have an answer. The good news is that God does. Well, not about phones, but He does have answer for both kids and adults. In fact, no matter who you are or how old you are, God always welcomes your questions, He's always willing to answer your questions, and more importantly, He's always willing to hold you in His arms. So often the world can make us feel left out and unfulfilled because there's no right phone for us or no one seems to want us around, but that's never the case with God. He will always provide exactly what we need, and He will always love us. When you consider the fact that the God of the universe is more accommodating to the needs of young and old alike than executives of a smart phone company, it kind makes you wonder why everyone is so desperate to have the right phone instead of the right God . . .

October 13
Heaven and the Supreme Court

*"Know that a man is not justified by observing the law,
but by faith in Jesus Christ. So we, too, have put our faith
in Christ Jesus that we may be justified
by faith in Christ and not by observing the law,
because by observing the law no one will be justified"*
(Galatians 2:16).

I'VE LEARNED many interesting lessons in my life, and one of them is this: it's easier to get into Heaven than it is to get on the Supreme Court. Now, I don't know this because I've ever actually tried to get on the Court (I'm not *that* smart), but I've seen the approval process on those few occasions when someone new is appointed. Apparently, if you want to be on the Supreme Court you have to answer questions about your judgment, your background, your conduct, and so on and so forth. It's pretty intense stuff. Now, the traditional view of Heaven is that we'll all face a similar situation before going through the Pearly Gates. According to tradition, Peter or someone else will meet us at the Pearly Gates, look through the history of our lives, and ask questions about all the good and bad stuff we've done. If we've done more good than bad and if we answer all the questions correctly, we get into Heaven. Well, the good news is getting into Heaven isn't at all like getting on the Supreme Court. You won't face a panel of questioners, you won't be asked all about your past and your background, instead it will all boil down to one simple question: Do you know Jesus? It may seem a little unfair that it's easier to get into Heaven then on the Supreme Court, but considering the fact that if it weren't for Jesus Christ standing in our place, none of us could ever get into Heaven. None of us could ever measure up, be good enough, or answer enough questions correctly. I'm glad God provided an easier option for us. Oh, and I'm glad I won't ever have to worry about being appointed to the Supreme Court.

October 14
Getting a Ticket to Ride

"Now this is eternal life: that they may know you the only true God, and Jesus Christ, whom you have sent"
(John 17:3).

FOR OUR TENTH WEDDING ANNIVERSARY, my wife and I did something we always dreamed of: we went on a Disney cruise in the Caribbean. When we got the tickets for our cruise in the mail, it suddenly made our dream vacation a very real vacation. In fact, I got so excited about having those tickets I started calling my family to share the good news with them. Some people think the good news of the Bible is that we just get a ticket to Heaven. In fact, many Christians are content with the fact they have their ticket and they never really explore everything else that Christianity has to offer. They're content to wait until Heaven gets here and, in the meantime, miss everything God has in store for them now. When we went on the cruise, it didn't start until we were on the boat. The good news of eternal life begins the moment you receive Christ—it doesn't start when you die and go to Heaven, it starts right now. You can experience eternity right now, you can experience peace and joy and comfort and the love of God right now. You can experience the things that make Heaven wonderful right now. So don't miss out on what you can experience of eternal life right now, and don't just be content with getting your ticket to Heaven. After all, that would be like my being content with getting a ticket to go on a cruise and not going for another seventy-five years!

October 15
Slow Down, Lives Depend On It
"Be still, and know that I am God; I will be exalted among the nations, I will be exalted in the earth"
(Psalm 46:10).

SAW A SIGN driving into work one day that said, "Slow Down Albuquerque, Lives May Depend On It." It was at that point I glanced at my speedometer and realized . . . well, let's just say my speed wasn't exactly legal. The advice to slow down isn't just good advice for when we're driving, it's good advice for our daily walk with God. It's so easy to be consumed with the *next* thing that we never take the time to be still and know that He is God. The other tragedy of not slowing down is that we miss opportunities to help others. We don't like to have our tightly scheduled lives interrupted, but it is in those interruptions when some of the most meaningful ministry can be done. The truth is that lives, eternal lives, may truly depend on us learning how to slow down.

The good news is when we slow down and are just still, God will meet us in those moments and minister to us and refresh us. Better yet, when we take the time to slow down and notice the needs of others, God will use us to minister to those needs. Isn't that why we are here? To know God and help others know Him as well? If so, then it's time we all slowed down.

***

October 16

When One Giant Leap Isn't Enough

*"If as one people speaking the same language
they have begun to do this, then nothing they plan to do
will be impossible for them"*
(Genesis 11:6).

WHEN APOLLO 11 first landed on the moon, Neil Armstrong said, "One small step for man, one giant leap for mankind." It was a moment many hailed as a testimony of what humanity could do when people worked together in a common effort. Of course, that kind of achievement always carries with it an inherent danger, the same danger that was a part of the building of the Tower of Babel. The danger is that eventually we'll achieve so much that we'll start thinking we don't need God any more, or worse, that we're better than God. That's a danger for humanity as a whole and for each of us individually. The good news is you can never achieve enough or ever be successful enough to not need God. Why is that good news? Because it's a reminder that God loves us enough to do what we couldn't do on our own. We may never be able to achieve Heaven on our own, but God loved us so much He sent His Son to die on the Cross and rise from the dead so we could have Heaven anyway. It's humbling to think there are some things we just can't do, even if we did go to the moon. But it's also comforting to know there's a God who loves us so much He wanted to help us do that which we could never do on our own—no matter how giant a leap we may take.

October 17
Keeping the Main Thing the Main Thing

"I am not ashamed of the gospel, because it is the power of God for the salvation of everyone who believes . . . "
(Romans 1:16).

OUR ANNUAL FALL TRADITION in my family is to go to a place called McCall's Pumpkin Patch. It's a place for hayrides, corn mazes, games, food, activities, and a whole lot more. However, during the hayride out to the pumpkin patch, a cowboy with a microphone tells us what the pumpkin patch is all about. All the other rides and games and food and animals are just added fluff. All of those other things are fun, but going out to the pumpkin patch to pick your own pumpkin is what the pumpkin patch is really all about. That always grabs my attention because sometimes we need to be reminded of that same fact about the gospel. The Gospel of Jesus Christ is the main thing; it's what Christianity is all about. All of the other issues—baptism, spiritual gifts, pre-trib/post-trib, and the minor issues of buying Christian CDs, movies, and books while sipping Christian lattes—all of that stuff is just extra fluff. Don't get me wrong, it's important, but it's not the main thing. Sometimes, it's easy to get so distracted by all of the extras that we forget what Christianity is all about. That's especially true as we get ready to head into the typically busy holiday season. My annual trip to the pumpkin patch is always a good reminder that as a Christian, I should never forget the whole purpose of Christianity is to share the good news of Jesus Christ. We need to keep the main thing the main thing, and not get distracted by the extras—like a giant inflatable pumpkin bouncy room.

October 18
A Little Camel's Milk?
"But even if we or an angel from heaven should preach a gospel other than the one we preached to you, let him be eternally condemned"
(Galatians 1:8).

LOVE CHOCOLATE, but chocolate made with camel's milk (which apparently is a real thing) . . . well, I'm not so sure. Apparently camel's milk has more vitamin C, less fat, and less lactose than cow's milk, and I'm sure it makes chocolate that tastes just fine. But I've been around camels, and I just can't see myself eating chocolate made with anything other than good ol' cow's milk. The truth is I'm pretty finicky about the ingredients that go into my chocolate, and we need to be just as finicky about the ingredients that go into the doctrine of the Bible. Just recently I've read stories about people who have found new ways to experience spirituality and have established new worldviews based on a new gospel. Well, my friends, those are ingredients we don't need in our gospel. God's Gospel and the original ingredients never need to be changed to make it better. The gospel is as good as it will ever get, and it's far better than we deserve. Any alteration of it is an inferior imitation. So be finicky about the ingredients of the gospel, be discerning about what some try to pass off as truth. I'm not sure about camel's milk in chocolate, but I am sure there's nothing that ever needs to be added to the good news of the gospel.

October 19
God Loves a Good Party

Moses and Aaron, Nadab and Abihu, and the seventy elders of Israel went up and saw the God of Israel. Under his feet was something like pavement made of sapphire, clear as the sky itself. But God did not raise his hand against these leaders of the Israelites; they saw God, and they ate and drank.
(Exodus 24:9-11)

CHRISTIANITY OFTEN GETS A BAD RAP as not being any fun. With all of our rules and regulations dictating proper Christian behavior, the common misconception is that it squeezes all the fun out of life. I say that's rubbish. I say it depends on what you define *fun* as. Personally, self-destructive behavior that has emotionally and physically damaging consequences never sounded like all that much fun to me. On the other hand, I came across this unusual passage in Exodus and I thought, "Huh, looks like God enjoys a good party." It just struck me as such a strange statement—these leaders of Israel saw God and their response was to have a good time eating and fellowshiping with each other and Him. The holiday season may seem far off now, but it'll be here before you know it, and that got me thinking about all the parties we go to. It made me realize that 1), God doesn't mind a good party, and 2), I want to make sure He's a part of all the fellowship and fun of Thanksgiving and Christmas. Yes, Christians can have fun and enjoy a good party. After all, God did so with the leaders of Israel, and I'm sure He's still more than willing to do so with us.

October 20
God's Social Media

"I revealed myself to those who did not ask for me;
I was found by those who did not seek me. To a nation that did
not call on my name, I said, 'Here am I, here am I"
(Isaiah 65:1).

WITH SITES LIKE TWITTER AND FACEBOOK, you can know what just about anyone is up to at any time of the day, anywhere in the world. It's amazing the things people will share on Twitter and Facebook. I've seen everything from baby announcements to declarations that a person is hungry (why that needs to be posted on the Internet, I'm not entirely sure—just go eat). Still, it is interesting and sometimes useful just how much you can learn about people from their postings. In fact, it's so easy one might wonder why God doesn't use something like Twitter or Facebook to help people get to know Him. Well, to be honest, I don't know if that's really necessary. After all, what could he tell us in 140 characters on Twitter that He hasn't already told us in the Bible? What could He update on Facebook that He hasn't already done in the Bible? The issue isn't why God doesn't update us via all these new social networking sites, the issue is why don't we care enough to know God by reading all He's told us in the Bible? It's all there, it's easily accessed, you can read it in short spurts like any other update. You can even find Bibles on the Internet, or get verses of the day, or daily devotions from Scripture, and more. God has so much good news to share with us in His Word, and it's far better than anything anyone else will tell you on Twitter and Facebook. If we're willing to read all the pointless updates from those people, why wouldn't we be willing to read God's good news?

October 21
A Little Help for Your Choices

This day I call heaven and earth as witnesses against you that I have set before you life and death, blessings and curses. Now choose life, so that you and your children may live and that you may love the Lord your God, listen to his voice, and hold fast to him. For the Lord is your life, and he will give you many years in the land he swore to give to your fathers, Abraham, Isaac and Jacob.
(Deuteronomy 30:19-20)

WE FACE TOUGH CHOICES EVERY DAY. From what we eat to where we go to what we do. Every choice has different outcomes, and all those outcomes have different consequences. I don't know about you, but it would be nice to have someone tell me the results of all of those choices—kind of like looking up the answers to math problems in a junior high textbook. Well, there is one choice in life we've been given the answer to, and despite it seeming like an obvious choice, God still went out of His way to tell us what to do. We all have a choice between life and death—life in Christ or death in sin. By default we've all chosen sin because we're born into sin. However, God loves us so much He gave us another option when Jesus Christ died on the Cross and rose from the dead to pay the price for our sin and to give us new life through Him. We may not have the answers to all our choices in life, but the most important one God has helped us out with. He suggests we choose life.

October 22
The Gift of Mercy

"And the Lord said, 'I will cause all my goodness to pass in front of you, and I will proclaim my name, the Lord, in your presence. I will have mercy on whom I will have mercy, and I will have compassion on whom I will have compassion'" (Exodus 33:19).

YOU KNOW, mercy and judgment are funny things. When we see someone else speeding down the road, we want judgment. We want them to get pulled over and ticketed. However, when we're speeding down the road and we get caught, we want mercy. We want to get let off with a warning. Basically, we want judgment for other people and mercy for ourselves. Isn't it interesting though, that God told Moses that He's the one who chooses whom He will have mercy on? It isn't up to us to decide when others deserve judgment and when we deserve mercy. The fact is we all deserve judgment, but instead God has shown us mercy through Jesus Christ. That's the good news we need to share with this world; everyone can have mercy from a loving and merciful God. So let's not worry about whether or not anyone gets what they deserve. Let's start showing the same mercy God has shown us.

October 23

I Can See Clearly Now

"Once more Jesus put his hands on the man's eyes.
Then his eyes were opened, his sight was restored,
and he saw everything clearly"
(Mark 8:25).

ALWAYS FIND EYE APPOINTMENTS rather amusing, especially when the doctor has you look at a chart with random letters and then starts flipping lenses in front of your eyes as he asks, "Is this better, or this? A or B? One or Two?" Usually I get confused as to whether A is the same One and if B is the same as Two, or if they're all the same ... then I forget to focus on what I'm looking at. However, that flipping of lenses reminds me of how we all use a lens to see the world around us. It's called our worldview. In fact, some people try many lenses to help the world look just the way they want. They'll try this and that and the other thing in order to get a *true* picture of the world. Well, fortunately, when it comes to our worldview, the good news is it's far simpler than choosing the right lenses for your glasses. The truth is there's only one lens we can view the world through that will show us the truth, and that's through Jesus Christ. Through Him we can see the world as it really is, and we can see our need for a Savior, and we'll see that God loved us enough to provide us a Savior in Jesus Christ. So don't bother switching around from A to B or One to Two. When it comes to the lenses you use to view the world, just let Jesus help you see clearly.

October 24
A Whale of a Tale

"But you are a chosen people, a royal priesthood, a holy nation, a people belonging to God, that you may declare the praises of him who called you out of darkness into his wonderful light"
(1 Peter 2:9).

A FEW YEARS AGO in northeastern China, a Beluga whale helped save a young woman from drowning. Apparently the woman's legs cramped up so badly she couldn't swim, but a Beluga whale helped push her to the surface and saved her life. Often we hear a story like that and we marvel at how amazing it is. But when you tell people that God sent His Son to die on a Cross and rise from the dead to save our lives, people scoff. That has me scratching my head. I don't understand why we're willing to believe stories about whales capable of saving people in trouble but a loving and Almighty God who wants to save people, well, that's just silly. Truth be told, I believe the only reason a whale has the instinct to save someone's life is because it's merely reflecting the character of its Creator. We are all drowning in sin, but the good news is Jesus Christ sacrificed His life in order to lift us to the surface of righteousness so we might be saved. If we like sharing stories about whales saving people from certain death, we ought to be willing to share the story of the God who saves people from eternal death. That's good news!

October 25

We All Wear Masks

**"The lamp of the Lord searches the spirit of man;
it searches out his inmost being"
(Proverbs 20:27).**

I'M SURE YOU'VE NOTICED all the costumes in stores this time of year. Yes, it's once again time to dress up and pretend to be something you aren't. However, if we were all to be really honest with ourselves—brutally honest with ourselves—we'd have to admit we're all wearing a costume or mask of some sort most of the time. We're all trying to hide who we really are from the people around us. We're all trying to be better than we really are or just trying to be someone different from whom we really are. It doesn't matter what you believe about dressing up on Halloween, most of us are doing that in some form during the rest of the year. It's been that way ever since the Fall in the Garden of Eden; we are no longer capable of being truly transparent. Well, the good news is no matter what costume you may wear, be it one for Halloween or a more metaphorical one, God sees through it and knows who you really are. That may not sound like good news, in fact that may sound frightening. But it's good news because God loves you for who you are. He knows you and loves you. He sees through the masks and costumes and says to us, "Come be who I made you to be—a child of the King." He invites us to clothe ourselves in Christ, and that sounds like the best thing to put on no matter what time of year it is.

October 26
Fixing the Crash and Burn

"May the Lord answer you when you are in distress; may the name of the God of Jacob protect you. May he send you help from the sanctuary and grant you support from Zion"
(Psalm 20:1-2).

HAS YOUR COMPUTER EVER CRASHED? (I know, all you Mac users are saying, "Of course not!") It's a rather frustrating experience when I'm humming along, happily minding my own business, and all of sudden things start to go schizophrenic. I'm never really sure what happens exactly—maybe a virus, maybe the hard drive crashed, maybe something worse—but I do know that when it happens I need to get it fixed. The best way to do that is to take it to someone who knows and understands how computers work. Well, when the virus of sin messes things up in our lives or when life in this fallen, broken world suddenly causes everything to crash all around us, we need to do the same thing. We need to go for repairs to the One who understands us, the One who knows how we work, the very One who made us. I'm not asking my kids to fix the computer (although kids do seem to innately understand how these things work), and I'm not asking the world to fix my life when things go wrong. There really is no one else to turn to who can help us better than God. In fact Jesus Christ died on the Cross and rose from the dead to solve our biggest problem—sin—and then gives us access directly to God for the rest of our needs. In that sense, fixing a life that's crashed is easier than fixing a computer.

October 27

Carrying Another's Burden

"Brothers, if someone is caught in a sin, you who are spiritual should restore him gently. But watch yourself, or you also may be tempted. Carry each other's burdens, and in this way you will fulfill the law of Christ"
(Galatians 6:1-2).

WHEN I MARRIED MY WIFE, we became one. For me, that meant I had to learn how to deal with abortion, because that was something in my wife's past which was now a part of my life. However, because of my love for my wife, I was willing to help shoulder that burden. In fact, I was even able to do so joyfully. You know, it's no easy thing to do what the Bible asks when it comes to carrying each other's burdens. The truth is, sometimes those burdens may seem too heavy or too dirty and we may choose to just ignore them instead of offering our help. But we must always remember that Jesus was willing to carry our burden of sin to the Cross where He died. That's how much

He loved us, and while we can't die for each other's sins, we can show that same kind of love in helping the people around us find forgiveness and healing from their sins. We can help them carry the burden to the Cross where the blood of Christ will set them free. It's no easy task to help carry someone's burden, but then no one said the Christian life was easy. But it is definitely worthwhile.

October 28

Kids Are Expensive . . . But Worth It

"For God so loved the world the he gave his one and only Son,
that whoever believes in him shall not perish
but have eternal life"
(John 3:16).

ACCORDING TO the Agriculture Department (and why they keep track of this, I have no idea), the average cost of raising a child to the age of eighteen is $291,570. If I had known that raising kids was so expensive, I would have tried to win the lottery before having kids. The breakdown of that money has a third of it going toward housing, 16 percent going toward food, and another 16 percent for childcare and education. However, despite the cost, I read one report that suggested it's the little things like a loving hug from your kids when they're older, a playful kiss from your young daughter, or a smiling baby when it hears your voice are the things that make it all well worth the price. If anyone understands the tremendous cost it takes to have kids, it's God. It cost Him the life of His only Son Jesus to pay for the expense of our sin and to make us His children. However, I have a feeling that every time we worship Him, every time we praise Him, every time we read His Word and just spend time with Him, every time we tell Him we love Him, I'm sure His loving heart feels it was well worth the cost. We may want to share that good news with someone we know, especially if they're still suffering from sticker shock over the price of having a kid.

October 29

Is There Paradise on Earth?

"He who has an ear, let him hear what the Spirit says to the churches. To him who overcomes, I will give the right to eat from the tree of life, which is in the paradise of God"
(Revelation 2:7).

SOMETIMES PARADISE isn't all it's cracked up to be. When my wife and I visited the Bahamas for our tenth anniversary, it was supposed to be our dream vacation in paradise, but it didn't quite work out that way. On our cruise, my wife got seasick, which sort of put a damper on any fun we could have. When we got to the Bahamas, we discovered it was hot, really hot, and the humidity was so thick you could cut it with a knife. That made walking around and even hanging out on the beach a bit uncomfortable. Those and a few other little glitches made our trip to paradise a little less than ideal. I've often heard the term "paradise on Earth," but more and more I'm convinced there's really no such thing. The only way we'll ever truly know what paradise is supposed to be is when we reach Heaven and are in the presence of our God. When we finally roam the streets of gold, when we finally kneel before the throne of God, when we finally join the heavenly chorus of angelic beings and people from every nation in singing praises to our God, then and only then will we know what paradise truly is. And the good news is, there won't be anything about it that will disappoint us. I'm looking forward to that.

October 30

Appreciating a Great Pastor

"The elders who direct the affairs of the church well are worthy of double honor, especially those whose work is preaching and teaching"
(1 Timothy 5:17).

AMONG OTHER THINGS, October is Pastor Appreciation Month, so today I want to tell you about the greatest pastor I have ever known. I know the month is almost over, but as they say, I've saved the best for last. The greatest preacher I ever heard is a man who dedicated most of his adult life to the ministry. He preached in churches from Canada to Colorado, and then he joined the Air Force as a chaplain and preached around the world. He went to Desert Storm and assured troops facing their own mortality that there is more to life in Jesus Christ after we die. He was at the Pentagon after 9/11 and assured people that yes, there is a God who cares about what happened and who was grieving with us on that day. In all the decades he served in the pulpit, I rarely heard him share the same message, same illustration, same joke, or same material twice. As he once explained to me, there was always something new to discover in God's Word. Perhaps more remarkable was the way he lived out what he preached. I had the rare opportunity to see this great preacher behind the scenes at home, and more often than not, he lived what he preached. Now, in recent years he's facing his greatest challenge as he fights Parkinson's disease, yet even that ravaging disease hasn't quelled his desire to share insights, encouragement, and his knowledge from God's Word. My only regret is that more of you haven't had the privilege of hearing this great preacher preach. He is my father, and I am proud to be the son of the greatest pastor and the greatest preacher I have ever known.

October 31
What to do With Halloween

**"Dear friend, do not imitate what is evil but what is good.
Anyone who does what is good is from God.
Anyone who does what is evil has not seen God"
(3 John 11).**

T HE BIG QUESTION this time of year for many Christians is what we should do with Halloween. One the one hand, the Bible is very explicit in its exhortations not to imitate anything that's evil or conform to the world in any way, form, or fashion. On the other hand, in order to completely avoid evil and the influences of the world, we'd have to move to Pluto and live in a cave sealed off with Saran Wrap. So what are we to do? I'm sorry to say I don't have an answer for you, but I do have some good news. The good news is if we fix our eyes on Jesus, dealing with these types of issues will be a lot easier. Instead of looking for how much we can do on Halloween and still be Christian, let's look for how much we can do for Christ each and every day of the year, even if it is Halloween. Often, a simple shift in focus can dramatically change our perspective. So no matter what you do this Halloween, let me encourage you to keep your eyes on Jesus, look full in His wonderful face, and the things of Earth will grow strangely dim in the light of His glory and grace. That's definitely good news.

November

Then He said to them,
"The harvest truly is great, but the
laborers are few; therefore pray
the Lord of the harvest to send out
laborers into His harvest."

Luke 10:2

November 1

Check Your Local Retailer for the Time

"Now learn this lesson from the fig tree: As soon as its twigs get tender and its leaves come out, you know that summer is near. Even so, when you see all these things, you know it is near, right at the door"
(Matthew 24:32-33).

LOVE THIS TIME OF YEAR. The weather is getting cooler, the leaves are beginning to change, the Christmas decorations are in the stores . . . yes, this is a great time of year. I often wonder how we would know Christmas was coming if it weren't for retailers. If they didn't start putting out Christmas decorations right after Labor Day, how would we ever know Christmas is kind of near? If they didn't remove Halloween decorations overnight and replace them all with more Christmas decorations without even acknowledging Thanksgiving, how would we know it was time to start hinting to everyone what we want for Christmas? Yes, thanks to the stores, I always know what time of year it is . . . or at least when it's getting close to Christmas. Too bad they can't do the same thing for us when Jesus is coming back. The good news is there are lots of signs we can look for that will give us hints as to when we will be going home. We just need to look for them in places other than where we shop. Jesus told us all about them. If you're wondering what they are, check out the printed edition of the Good News: your local Bible.

November 2
Tweeting God

*"For you did not receive a spirit that makes you a
slave again to fear, but you received the Spirit of sonship.
And by him we cry 'Abba, Father'"*
(Romans 8:15).

IF YOU'D LIKE TO TALK TO GOD, you can do so
via Twitter. No really, there's a Twitter site that
promises to take the prayers sent to it and put
them in the Western Wall in Jerusalem, which some people
believe helps provide a direct line to God. While I appreciate the
sentiment, this all strikes me as a bit odd. After all, why would
you want to send a Tweet to God when you could just talk to
Him yourself? And why would you want your prayers rolled up in
a little piece of paper and shoved in a crumbling brick wall when
you can present those prayers to God yourself? Look, Jesus
Christ died and rose from the dead so we could not only have a
direct line to God, but so we could also call him Daddy. The fact
that people want to send Tweets to God merely indicates that
people all over the world have a thirst for God and desperately
want to talk to Him. Let's share with them how they can do that
through Christ.

November 3

Who Are the People in Your Neighborhood?

*"Each of us should please his neighbor for his good
to build him up"*
(Romans 15:2).

DON'T KNOW WHY, but for some reason one morning I woke up with a song from Mr. Rogers stuck in my head: "Oh, who are the people in your neighborhood? They're the people that you meet each day." As I worked to get that song out of my head (again, don't ask me why it was there in the first place), I thought about what it was saying and realized that the concept of neighbors and neighborhoods is something that's becoming extinct in our world. To be honest, I don't know that much about the people who live next to me. I don't know much about the local barista who gives me my hot chocolate with extra chocolate. I'm ashamed to say I don't know my neighbors all that well. This is tragic because in not taking the time to get to know our neighbors, I'm not fulfilling one of the greatest commandments: *Love your neighbor as yourself.* Who are our neighbors? They're the people we meet each day. So let's start taking the time to get to know these people. Let's learn about their hurts and needs and show them how Christ can help heal those hurts and meet those needs. It's one of the best ways we can share the good news of Jesus Christ—by knowing the people in our neighborhood.

November 4
Sweetness That Lasts

"If you find honey, eat just enough—
too much of it, and you will vomit"
(Proverbs 25:16).

IF YOU'RE LIKE ME, you probably enjoy sweets. In fact, I don't enjoy sweets so much as I enjoy chocolate. Sometimes, I enjoy chocolate too much. I remember one Christmas when I ate just about everything in my stocking before we went to church—and we were going to an early service. By lunchtime, I felt super sick, and betrayed. I felt betrayed because I couldn't understand how something so sweet and wonderful like chocolate could make me feel so bad. So it is with just about everything that's sweet in life. Indulge too much in it and it will make you sick. There is one exception, however, and that's a sweet relationship with Jesus Christ. It's one of the sweetest things we'll ever experience, and the good news is we can never have too much of it. Just about everyone I know is looking for something sweet in life, and they're often disappointed when those sweet things turn out so sour. Perhaps it's time you and I start sharing the one sweet that will never make us feel like vomiting, no matter how much of it we have.

November 5

The Search for Truth

"For the word of the Lord is right and true;
he is faithful in all he does"
(Psalm 33:4).

WHAT IS TRUTH? That's what Pilate asked Jesus, and it's a question that our culture is still asking today. People have a great thirst and a desperate desire to know what truth is. Many answers have been provided through the centuries to tell people what truth is, and yet people keep searching. Why? Because none of the answers they've been given truly satisfies. What fascinates me is that philosophers have been searching for truth for centuries, and yet Jesus Christ himself said the whole reason He came was to testify to the truth. You see the answer to "What is truth," isn't some complex, ethereal, philosophical concept. No, truth is actually quite simple: it's Jesus Christ. I'll leave it to you to explore all the reasons why that is, but it's my hope that just knowing that finding truth is actually quite simple. And it will be good news that you'll want to share.

November 6

Replacements Just Aren't the Same

"Or suppose a woman has ten silver coins and loses one.
Does she not light a lamp, sweep the house and
search carefully until she finds it? . . .
In the same way, I tell you, there is rejoicing in the presence
of the angels of God over one sinner who repents"
(Luke 15: 8, 10).

DID YOU HEAR THE STORY of the man in New Zealand who found his wedding ring at the bottom of the harbor more than a year after it slipped off his finger? The man had only been married three months when he lost the ring, and despite offers from his new bride to buy him a new one, he continued his search until he found his ring. I remember when my wife lost her wedding ring less than a year after our marriage. I also offered to buy her a new one, but through the tears she said it just wouldn't be same, and after many prayers and lot of searches the missing ring turned up. Both of these incidents remind me of how God feels about us. He loved us so much He wasn't willing to give up on us and let us stay lost and apart from Him. Sure He could have just gone and started over and created some new people to love Him, but that wouldn't have been the same to Him. He wanted you and me. He never gave up on us. He sent His Son Jesus to die on the Cross and rise from the dead so you and I might be found and be lost to sin no more. God loves people too much to ever give up on finding the lost ones. That's good news we need to share.

November 7

Praying for Your Non-Friends/ Non-Enemies

"But I tell you: Love your enemies and pray for those who persecute you . . . "
(Matthew 5:44).

IT'S NICE HAVING KIDS. They keep you honest. They keep you humble. They help make you aware of things about yourself you might not otherwise notice. For instance, one time my daughter prayed a very sweet prayer for some people that I didn't particularly like. These people weren't ones I would consider enemies exactly, but they weren't exactly friends either. They kind of fell in that gray area of people whom I'm indifferent to and generally just don't give a lot of thought to. I have better things to think of. Well, as I listened to my daughter pray, I realized my attitude was dumb. If Jesus can ask us to pray for our enemies, then certainly we should pray for the people we just don't happen to like. The funny thing is, that's probably harder to do. It's easy to pray for the people we love, and it's easy to pray for our enemies, but for those we don't think about much due to indifference, well, that can be a challenge. And yet these are the people I need to pray for perhaps more than any others. Not because of how it will affect their needs, but because of how it will affect my heart and the way I think of and treat them. I need to share the good news and I need to show the good news to friends, enemies, and those people who are somewhere in between, in that gray are of indifference and dislike. A good way to start doing that is simply by praying for them. I learned my lesson, and it only took a seven-year-old to teach me.

November 8
Death and Long Life

" . . . This grace was given us in Christ Jesus before the beginning of time, but it has now been revealed through the appearing of our Savior, Christ Jesus, who has destroyed death and brought life and immortality to light through the gospel"
(2 Timothy 1:9-10).

LOVE SOME OF THE HEADLINES you find surfing the web. I saw one once that proclaimed, "New Website Predicts When You Will Die; Plus, Ten Ways to Live Longer." I thought that pretty well summed up our culture's view on life and death. Our culture fears death and yet is fascinated by it, but it also worships youth and is desperate to find ways to stay young and live long. We're curious to know when we might die, but then we want tips on how we can live longer. Well, the good news is Jesus Christ holds the keys to life and death and the answers to both of those issues. For those who fear death, Jesus has conquered it by dying on the Cross and therefore, there is nothing left to fear. For those who want to live forever, Jesus Christ rose from the dead eternal and immortal and He offers the gift of life to all those who follow Him. So while it may satisfy some morbid curiosity to use the "death calculator" to try and predict when we might die, I think our time is far better spent telling people that death has been conquered. And there's really only one tip we need for living longer: follow Jesus Christ.

The Climb is Worth the View

"Consider it pure joy, my brothers, whenever you face trials of many kinds, because you know that the testing of your faith develops perseverance"
(James 1:2-3).

HAVE A CONFESSION TO MAKE, and it's not easy for me . . . I have watched *Hannah Montana: The Movie*. Not only did I watch it, I kind of liked it. Not only did I kind of like it, but I even learned something from it. One of the characters in the movie said, "Life's a climb, but the view is great." Not only is that a good way to approach life in general, but there's some biblical truth in that statement as well. The Bible tells us very plainly that life is hard, that we will have to climb over hardships, challenges, and trials, and sometimes that climb will be extremely difficult. However, the Bible also promises two other things. 1), that Jesus Christ will always be there to help us with our climb, and 2), not only will the view look great from overcoming those hard times in life, but when this life is over and we're at the very top of the mountain of eternity, the view from Heaven will be absolutely spectacular. Not only is that good news to help motivate us to keep climbing, it's good news that can help others who may feel like the climb is just way too hard.

November 10
How Would This Impress?

"Those who know your name will trust in you, for you, Lord, have never forsaken those who seek you"
(Psalm 9:10).

THIS IS A TRUE STORY. A man in New York tried to impress his girlfriend by calling her and telling her that his fishing boat had capsized. (Why he thought this would impress her, I have no idea, but love makes us do some crazy and dumb things.) However, since this woman had affectionate feelings for this man, she was understandably concerned and immediately called 911. When the police and fire department arrived where the incident was supposed to have taken place, they discovered the man had made up the entire story. I'm guessing something else was capsized though, like his relationship with his girlfriend. Relationships take trust—I'm sure you've noticed that—and that's the good news about having a relationship with God. He is trustworthy. God will never make up stories, He will never leave us or forsake, He is always there for us in times of need, and He will never betray our trust. In fact, when we use Him as a model for what a relationship should be, we will find ourselves modeling that same kind of trustworthiness, and that can help bring people to Christ. Best of all, you won't have to pretend to be an incompetent fisherman to impress anyone.

November 11
It's Good to be Family

"We always thank God, the Father of our Lord Jesus Christ, when we pray for you because we have heard of your faith in Christ Jesus and of the love you have for all the saints . . . "
(Colossians 1:3-4).

I'VE BEEN THINKING a lot about family recently. Not just about my mom and my dad or my brothers or sisters, although those are great. I was blessed to be raised in a home with a family that actually liked each other. True, we had our moments of disagreements and fights, but overall I remember growing up with parents and siblings that enjoyed each other and gained strength from one another. However, recently I've been dwelling on a bigger family: God's family. Because my dad was in the Air Force, I've had the privilege to travel the world, and in doing so I discovered just how big God's family is. I've met people who I could barely talk with, but the camaraderie and love we shared because we both belonged to God was more than enough to unite us. So, I just want to encourage you to appreciate your family, your Christian family. Be thankful for them, encourage them, love them, share with them, and enjoy being with them. The truth is when the rest of the world sees what a wonderful family we have in Christ, they'll naturally be drawn to it and want to be a part of it, too . . . and that's good news.

November 12

Can Dust Have Significance?

*When I consider your heavens, the work of your fingers,
the moon and the stars, which you have set in place, what is
man that you are mindful of him, the son of man that you care
for him? You have made him a little lower than the heavenly
beings and crowned him with glory and honor.*
(Psalm 8:3-5)

'VE ENJOYED more than a few lessons in humility. Well, I guess *enjoyed* isn't the right word . . . *endured* is probably a better one. In any event, those are times when I think about my proper place in the grand scheme of things, and guess what? It isn't all that significant. It's so easy for us to start thinking more of ourselves than we really should, to think that we're really "all that," to have puffed-up egos, and overarching pride. But who are we really? We are dust—mud from the ground. However, we are dust that's been made in the image of God and filled with the living breath of God. If we have any significance at all, if we have anything truly special about us, that is it: we are made in the image of God, filled with His life, and used for His purposes. Nothing I could ever achieve on my own will ever compare with the significance of the fact that I'm dust—dust loved by God, and dust God wants to use for the glory of His eternal purposes. If I ever act like there's anything more important or significant in life than that good news, you have my permission to smack me upside the head.

November 13

Letting the Scorpions Live

"My dear children, I write this to you so that you will not sin. But if anybody does sin, we have one who speaks to the Father in our defense—Jesus Christ, the Righteous One. He is the atoning sacrifice for our sins, and not only for ours but also for the sins of the whole world"
(1 John 2:1-2).

I CAN UNDERSTAND the need to try and make up for past sins, but I've never considered doing anything like one man from Thailand. After spending several years cooking scorpions to sell as food, something quite common in Thailand, this man changed his ways and let 4,600 scorpions live in the bottom floor of his two-story house. The man said that although he made good money cooking scorpions, it made him feel bad inside and he was afraid he was committing a sin. To make up for it, he now breeds living scorpions in his house. It's a good thing to feel guilt about sin, and it's a good thing repent from sin and to want to change our ways. However, we can never really do enough to make up for our sins or pay enough back to cover our sins. That's why it's good news that Jesus Christ died on the Cross and rose from the dead. His death and Resurrection more than paid enough to cover the price for our sins, so instead of spending our lives trying to repay a debt we can never repay, we can enjoy freedom from sin and the love of God. That's really good news since I could never share my home with a bunch of arachnids, no matter how much I sinned.

November 14

The Talk

*"The LORD would speak to Moses face to face,
as a man speaks with his friend"*
(Exodus 33:11).

IT'S EASY TO THINK sometimes that it would be easier to communicate with God if we could just see him face to face. Well, I'm here to tell you that just isn't so. How do I know? My wife and I have been married for fourteen years. Fourteen years now we've had the opportunity to communicate face to face, and yet we still regularly have the occasional string of miscommunications. Despite being together for fourteen years we still have times where we just don't understand each other. Why? Because she's a woman, and sometimes I just don't understand women. (Actually, a lot times I don't understand women.) Well, if the differences between men and women can cause trouble in communication, imagine what the difference between people and God would do when it comes to communication problems. It wouldn't matter if we could talk face to face, there would still be communication problems. The good news is Jesus Christ entered the picture to help us with those problems. Through Him we can approach the throne of God with confidence, through Him we can present our requests to God, and in His name we have the privilege to talk directly to God. Honestly, sometimes I think the problem isn't so much that people need to talk to God face to face, but they just need to talk to Him, period.

November 15
You Can Know the Future

*I say to you that many will come from the east and the west,
and will take their places at the feast with Abraham, Isaac
and Jacob in the kingdom of heaven. But the subjects of the
kingdom will be thrown outside, into the darkness, where
there will be weeping and gnashing of teeth.*
(Matthew 8:11-12)

MY WIFE AND I watched the *Back to the Future* trilogy recently. Do you remember those movies? I noticed a couple things while watching them: the eighties weren't quite as cool as we all thought they were at the time, and it's funny that in 1985, the year 2015 seemed so far away and so futuristic. Now we're almost there and I *still* don't have a flying car. I also noticed that they talk a lot about how no one should know too much about their own future. Well, I'm here to tell you that the Bible disagrees with that particular sentiment. In fact, the Bible reveals quite a lot about our future. It reveals that we have two choices: Heaven or hell. It also reveals that Jesus Christ died on the Cross and rose from the dead to make it possible for us to enjoy our future in Heaven—if we choose to trust and follow Him here in our present. Granted, the Bible doesn't reveal every detail about what will happen to us in the future, and in that sense perhaps it's true we're better off not knowing too much. But the Bible does tell us plenty about what really matters in our future, which is where we will spend eternity. I think the fact that it does so is good news. Oh, it's also good news that you won't need a time-traveling, flying DeLorean to get there.

November 16

Relationship With a Cardboard Cutout

"You will seek me and find me when you seek me with all your heart"
(Jeremiah 29:13).

IN ORDER TO FEEL CLOSER to her boyfriend who was deployed overseas with the military, a Florida woman decided to take a cardboard cutout of him everywhere she went. The cardboard replacement boyfriend went to the movies, to the beach, on vacation—and the real boyfriend only got to see pictures of it all. As you can imagine, this woman had more than a few people look at her like she was crazy. That got me thinking of just how crazy we are as Christians. We don't even have a cardboard cutout of God to take everywhere with us, yet we say God is indeed with us wherever we go and He hears whenever we speak to Him. However, the good news is that our "invisible God" is very real, and just because we don't see Him doesn't change that. Just because a woman carries around a cardboard cutout of her boyfriend doesn't mean her boyfriend isn't real, and the same is true for us as Christians. So don't worry if people think you're crazy because you talk to your *imaginary friend*, God. The fact is, the more time we spend talking to Him and reading His letters in the Bible, the more we'll understand just how real, powerful, and loving He truly is.

353

November 17

Rock in a Bog

*"He lifted me out of the slimy pit, out of the mud and mire;
he set my feet on a rock and gave me a firm place to stand"*
(Psalm 40:2).

THE DICTIONARY defines a bog as spongy, wet ground with soil composed mostly of decayed vegetable matter. I think that's also a good definition of life sometimes. In fact, far too often it does seem that life is nothing more than a bog of uncertainty. It is spongy, wet ground composed of our decaying dreams and hopes, and it's ground we have trouble traversing. And sometimes we just plain get stuck in it. Well, as I was reading this Psalm, I was struck by the power of its imagery. I could almost see God in His loving care reaching out to us as we wallow, caught in the miry bog of life's uncertainty. I see His hand grasping ours and pulling us up out of the muck, and then placing on us the solid rock of Jesus Christ. What good news to know we can go through life on solid, certain ground when we have Jesus in our lives. It's not that life becomes trouble-free with Him, but through Him we have a rock upon which to rest in the uncertain bogs of life. Right now a lot of people would like to hear that good news. So let's make sure we're inviting them to also climb up on the rock.

November 18
The Right and Wrong of Right and Wrong

*"Yet the Lord longs to be gracious to you; he rises
to show you compassion. For the Lord is a God of justice.
Blessed are all who wait for him!"*
(Isaiah 30:18).

WAS WATCHING A SITCOM not long ago in which a character made a very interesting comment. He said, "I decide what's right and wrong, so either I'm God, or right and wrong is relative." It's an interesting statement, and one that's reflective of our culture today. In the show, it was interesting when that kind of thinking was used on him, suddenly things were "wrong" and not fair. Therein lies the problem with moral relativism. Who decides what's fair, and how can there ever be justice when everyone has the option to decide that they're in the right? Quite frankly, there's no room for justice in a morally relative society, which is a huge problem because we all have an innate desire for fairness and justice. That's why it's good news that morals aren't relative, that we don't decide what's fair, and it's not up to us to decide what is just. God decides what's right and wrong, He decides what is just, and He's the only one truly qualified to be fair. The really good news is He is also a loving, gracious, and forgiving God, and through the death and Resurrection of Jesus Christ, God doesn't treat us *fairly*; He treats us *favorably*. We can pretend that right and wrong is relative, but that will only leave us dissatisfied. Or we can trust in a just God who also loves us dearly. That, personally, seems the better option.

November 19

Darkness and Dawn

"Then your light will break forth like the dawn, and your healing will quickly appear; then your righteousness will go before you, and the glory of the LORD will be your rear guard"
(Isaiah 58:8).

THE ENGLISH THEOLOGIAN and historian Thomas Fuller said back in 1650, "It is always darkest just before the day dawneth." So no, Harvey Dent was not the first to coin that phrase in the film *The Dark Knight*. Still, it's a popular saying, and the other day I was trying to figure out how exactly one would know they had reached the darkest point. After all, that seems to be pretty important because if you know when things are darkest, you'll also know when things will improve. There have been times in my own life when I've had trouble determining what that point was. No matter how dark things were, they just seemed to get worse. But then I realized I was focusing on the wrong thing. When we're constantly looking at how dark the darkness is, we aren't paying any attention to the promise of the dawn. The issue isn't when the dawn will come, but the simple fact that it *will* come. As Christians we can place a great amount of trust in this because God has never let the darkness win, nor will He in the future. So regardless of how dark the days may be, take confidence the light of dawn is coming—no doubt about it. That's good news, don't you think?

November 20

When Bitterness is Good

*"Get rid of all bitterness, rage and anger,
brawling and slander, along with every form of malice.
Be kind and compassionate to one another,
forgiving each other, just as in Christ God forgave you"*
(Ephesians 4:31-32).

SOMETIMES A LITTLE BITTERNESS is a good thing, like in dark chocolate. It gives the flavor a little extra kick. Of course, in just about every other area of life, bitterness is a bad thing. The question is how do we avoid becoming bitter when so often it seems as though daily life conspires to do everything possible to make us feel that way? The real problem is that while a little bitterness in chocolate might make it good, a little bitterness in our heart will go a long way to not only separating us from people, but also from God. The answer to this problem is quite simple, but it isn't always easy: forgiveness. In order to avoid being bitter people, we need to be forgiving people. But do you know what the good news is about that? When we're willing to be forgiving people, we'll also be free people. That's something we just can't be when we hang on to bitterness. So remember: bitterness in chocolate is good; bitterness in our hearts and minds is bad.

November 21
Gum Under the Table

"You know my folly, O God; my guilt is not hidden from you"
(Psalm 69:5).

'M CURIOUS at what point it became acceptable for people to dispose of gum by sticking it under a table or a desk. I don't know if you've taken the time to notice, but under just about any desk or table in America you'll at least find one or two pieces of gum stuck there. I suppose it goes back to the idea of being out of sight, out of mind. It's under the table, no one can see it, therefore it's like it's not there and that's just as good as throwing it away. The problem is we sometimes have the same attitude about our sin. We put it someplace where it's out of sight, where we think no one can see it, and no one will know about it, and we think that's just as good as getting rid of it completely. However, Jesus didn't die on the Cross and rise from the dead just for us to stick our sin away somewhere on the underside of our lives where no one can see it. He died for our sins so they would be completely washed away and He rose again so we could live free of sin. You see, the trouble with gum under a table or desk is sooner or later someone's going have to flip that desk over and then all that gum is exposed. The same is true with our sin. That's why it's such good news that through Jesus Christ we don't just hide sin—it can be removed completely and we can live as free, forgiven people.

November 22
Playing to the Crowd

"Whatever you do, work at it with all your heart, as working for the Lord, not for men, since you know that you will receive an inheritance from the Lord as a reward.
It is the Lord Christ you are serving"
(Colossians 3:23-24).

WOULD NEVER make it as professional football player, or a professional in any sport for that matter. I just don't think I could handle constantly trying to live up to everyone's expectations. From coaches to owners to fans to teammates, the constant pressure to perform, to excel, and to win would drive me crazy. To have every little thing I do scrutinized to see if I've "still got it" would just be plain wearying. To be honest, there are times when I still feel that way despite not being a professional athlete, where it seems that no matter how hard I try it's never good enough to please or impress those around me. That's when it's good to be reminded that I don't work for people and I'm not here to impress any man or woman with my work. I work for God. I excel and do my best because I know God is watching and I want Him to be pleased with what I do. To be honest, the approval of people is fickle at best, but the approval of God is something that will last for eternity. That's good news and worth working and doing my best for.

November 23

Do You Trust?

*"In God, whose word I praise, in the Lord,
whose word I praise—in God I trust; I will not be afraid . . . "*
(Psalm 56:10-11).

DICTIONARY.COM defines trust as "Reliance on the integrity, strength, ability, surety, etc. of a person or thing; confidence." So here's my question for you today: Do you trust God? No, seriously, do you really trust Him? I know it's a good thing for us to say that, but when you're standing on the edge of disaster, when it feels like life has thrown you off a cliff, when everything around you seems to crumble, then do you really trust God? Do you rely on His strength, His integrity, His ability? Are you confident in Him? To be honest, I've struggled with trust. There have been circumstances around me, which seemed to dictate there really wasn't anything to trust in. However, that's when I realized that trust is a choice. True, trust is earned by those who are trustworthy, but nevertheless we must choose to trust. When I read through the Bible, when I take the time to reflect on my own life, I realize I have no reason *not* to trust God. His strength never wanes, His abilities are all-powerful, He always keeps His word. In short, He's shown time and again that I can have confidence in Him. He has always proven himself trustworthy even when circumstances didn't look that way. Like the Psalmist, no matter what may take place in life, I will always say, "In God I trust, I will not be afraid." That sounds like good news to me.

November 24
Shopping for Eternity

"Jesus answered, "I am the way and the truth and the life. No one comes to the Father except through me" (John 14:6).

AFTER THANKSGIVING IS OVER, lots of people are out looking for bargains. On Black Friday, there are people who line up before dawn in order to be the first to find great deals at retail stores all over the country. Sadly, people often treat eternity the same way. They shop for the best deal in various religions trying to find the one they can get the most out of without having to put much in return. Well, spirituality just doesn't work that way. I'm afraid you can't shop around to find the best deal for the afterlife. The simple fact is you can either get Heaven for free through Jesus Christ (which when you think about it, is a pretty good deal), or you can seal you fate in hell by trying to find a better deal (which by the way, you won't). So on Black Friday and all the other shopping days leading up to Christmas, as everyone shops and tries to find the best deals, let's make the most of these opportunities to remind people they can't prepare for eternity with the same attitude. However, the good news is they can always find eternal life in the free gift of grace that's given to us by God. Which is really what this special season is all about anyway.

November 25
Happily Ever After

For the Lord himself will come down from heaven, with a loud command, with the voice of the archangel and with the trumpet call of God, and the dead in Christ will rise first. After that, we who are still alive and are left will be caught up together with them in the clouds to meet the Lord in the air. And so we will be with the Lord forever.
(1 Thessalonians 4:16-17)

IT SEEMS LIKE EVERY DECADE OR SO, a new edition of Disney's movie *Snow White* is released in a new exclusive set attached to some sort of precious material: the gold, diamond, or platinum edition. I'm betting the next one will be the unobtanium (the perfect, unobtainable metal) edition. In any event, as I was watching the most recent version with my daughters, one of the scenes in particular caught my attention. At the end of the film, Prince Charming comes along, awakens Snow White from her sleeping death with a kiss, puts her on a white horse and carries her off to a shining, golden city in the clouds. Call me crazy, but does that sound familiar to anyone? Doesn't the Bible say when Jesus Christ returns to this Earth that He'll show up riding on a white horse? Doesn't the Bible say that Jesus will awaken the dead to a new life through the power of His Resurrection? Doesn't the Bible say those who are in Christ will go to live with Him in the New Jerusalem, a city with gold streets, precious stones, and jeweled walls? Yeah, it does, so I guess maybe that song

Snow White sings is more accurate than we realize. Someday our Prince *will* come, and what a glorious day that will be. I just never thought I'd be reminded of that good news by watching a kids' movie.

November 26
Hitting All the Green Lights

"For no matter how many promises God has made, they are 'Yes' in Christ. And so through him the 'Amen' is spoken by us to the glory of God"
(2 Corinthians 1:20).

EVERY NOW AND THEN I make it to work in record time. No, not because I was speeding. It happens on those rare days where I happen to hit every light just right, when it's nothing but green from my house to work. I barely have to touch the brakes on those days, and I get to work so early, I even have time for an extra cup of hot chocolate. Don't you just love it when that happens? Don't you love getting all green lights? I've realized that the times in my life when I had the most green lights were when I was setting aside my will for God's. Everything just seems to flow so smoothly when I do that, it's like having nothing but green lights down the avenue of life. However, when I start trying to pursue my own desires, that's when I start slowing down with yellow lights or stopping completely at red lights. A wise man once said we should love God with all of our hearts and then do whatever we want. That's good advice. When we love God with all of our hearts, our desires will be His desires and we will want what He wants. That will lead to lots of green lights, and that's definitely good news.

November 27

Be Thankful for What You Have

"When the dew was gone, thin flakes like frost on the ground appeared on the desert floor. When the Israelites saw it, they said to each other "What is it?" For they did not know what it was"
(Exodus 16:14-15).

DON'T KNOW IF YOU'VE NOTICED THIS, but kids struggle with contentment. They wake up in the middle of the night and want a drink. When you bring them one, they ask, "What is this? Just water?" Of course, the truth is grown-ups often still display that childish attitude of discontentment. Take the Israelites, for example. They're in the middle of nowhere, they're hungry, they want food, God provides food for them, and what do they call it? Do they call it "Miraculous bread from Heaven"? Do they call it "Sweet sustenance from a loving provider"? No, they call it manna, or literally "What is it?" They actually have the gall to ask God for food and when He provides it miraculously, they say, "What's this? Just bread?" Friends, we need to overcome our childish attitude of discontentment. God said He would provide for our every need, He didn't say He'd provide for our every want. Instead of being upset when God doesn't do things our way, let's learn to praise Him when He provides for us according to His will. The fact that He's willing to do so is good news, don't you think?

November 28

Finding True Love

**"Daughters of Jerusalem, I charge you by the gazelles
and by the does of the field: Do not arouse or
awaken love until it so desires"
(Song of Songs 3:5).**

RIENDS, I BELIEVE IN LOVE. I believe in the kind of love that lives happily ever after, that's full of passion and zeal, that's filled with adventure and joy. Why do I believe in that kind of love? Because that's the kind of love I have experienced the last fourteen years with my wife. Why am I telling you this, because I want you to know that love is worth waiting for. We live in a culture that has cheapened love, turned it into a biological act of necessity, and as far as I'm concerned has removed any semblance of honor and romance from the concept. Love has become a selfish, self-fulfilling pursuit people rush into because of their demand for instant gratification. That saddens me, because so many people are missing out on true love, on the joy, the satisfaction, the contentment, the excitement, and the fun of real love. You might say I just got lucky by finding the right person (and you'd be right . . . to an extent), but no, to be honest I started experiencing that love long before I met my wife. I encountered that love when I met Jesus, and it's only because of Him that it's so freely expressed now in my marriage. So do you want to find true, storybook romance, and passionate, joy-filled love? Don't rush around to a variety of people trying to find it. Look for it in Christ, and He in turn will help you find it with someone else who's also in love with Him. Trust me, that's definitely good news.

November 29
One-and-Done
"Just as man is destined to die once,
and after that to face judgment . . . "
(Hebrews 9:27).

I'M probably going to make a lot of baseball fans upset right now, but I'm not a fan of the idea of "the series." The idea of playing the best out of five or the best of seven just to determine the winner seems like an excuse just to stretch things out. I'm sure advertisers love it, but personally I think it's more exciting when you get just one chance to win, and if you don't, then that's it. It's over. I know some say that would be an unfair way to determine a winner, and it's true the baseball season would be a lot shorter, as would the basketball and hockey playoffs, but I prefer the one-and-done system to the series system. Regardless of what some may say, that's the way life is. We only get one chance to get it right—not the best of seven, or eighty, or a million. You either get it right this time or you don't, and the only way to get it right is to put our lives in the hands of Jesus Christ. He's the only One that can make a life right, who can help us win with this one chance we have. Some see that as narrow-minded and unfair. I say that's missing the point. I say the fact we even have a chance to get life right through Jesus Christ with the one shot we have is very good news.

November 30
Why You Do that Thing You Do
"If you love me, you will obey what I command"
(John 14:15).

'M A LUCKY MAN. I have a wife who has learned to like things that I like to do. For instance, she has learned to like videogames and she enjoys playing them with me. Also, she has learned to like football. Not only does she watch games with me, she's even picked out her own team to root for and during the football season we have lively discussions about how well our teams are doing. And yes, I've learned to do some of the things she enjoys doing, like going to the Tea Room (a little restaurant that's like something out of a Jane Austin novel). I bring this up because I want to point out that when you love someone, you want to do things that please that person. When people ask me why I do some of the things I do as a Christian, the simple answer is I love Jesus and therefore I want to do the things that make Him happy. I don't obey some outdated morality code out of an irrelevant sense of ancient obligation. I obey because of a relationship filled with love and admiration that's alive and growing every day. I obey because I want to please the One I love, Jesus Christ. It's just what you do when you love someone. You do the things they like whether it's videogames and tea or the Ten Commandments and evangelism.

December

"Come now, and let us reason together,"
Says the Lord, "Though your sins are
like scarlet, They shall be as white as
snow; Though they are red like
crimson, They shall be as wool.

Isaiah 1:18

December 1

Getting the Morning Started Right

*"Let the morning bring me word of your unfailing love,
for I have put my trust in you. Show me the way I should go,
for to you I lift up my soul"*
(Psalm 143:8).

DON'T KNOW ABOUT YOU, but I'm not really a morning person. I have a hard time getting started in the morning, and when it's cold outside, well, that just makes it that much tougher for me to want to get out of bed. We all have our little routines to help us get started in the morning. For some that involves coffee; for the less sophisticated, such as myself, it might involve Cocoa Puffs and a little hot cocoa. (I've heard apples are actually a healthier and better way to wake up in the morning, but they're not made of chocolate . . .) One good morning routine I try to stick to is reading my Bible. Now before you think I'm saying this to impress you, let me just say that as a non-morning person I'm not that coherent in the morning when I read my Bible. Sometimes I can't even get my eyes to focus properly. Other times my eyes may be open but my brain is asleep, and I wouldn't be able to tell what I just read. So why do I do it? Why read when I won't comprehend what I'm reading because I'm barely awake? Well, I have a theory: you can't go wrong with getting your morning started with a little good news. So whatever your morning wake-up routine may be, I hope you'll consider including a little Scripture with it.

December 2

Getting What You Don't Deserve

"He saved us, not because of righteous things we had done, but because of his mercy"
(Titus 3:5).

A MAN IN NEW JERSEY got in big trouble for accepting paychecks from a company he never worked for. Apparently the man did apply for a job at the company, but after he was accepted for the position, he changed his mind. However, his name was never deleted from the computer and as a result he was paid almost $500,000 over the course of the next five years. Five years, and no one noticed that someone who never showed up was getting paid. Well, since this guy never told anyone he was being paid, he eventually faced charges of theft and time in prison. That's an example of getting something you didn't earn being a bad thing, but there is one instance where it's a good thing: God's grace. We didn't earn God's forgiveness, nor could we ever earn it. We have done nothing to deserve His grace and favor, and yet because of His love for us Jesus Christ died on the Cross and rose from the dead in order that we might be free from sin and have eternal life. God just *gives* us eternity in His Kingdom, access to all His power and wealth, and all He wants in return is our love. That's far better than getting a paycheck you didn't work for. That's the best deal I've ever heard—and it's definitely good news.

December 3
Frosty Mornings

*"But your iniquities have separated you from your God;
your sins have hidden his face from you, so that he will not hear"*
(Isaiah 59:2).

HATE SCRAPING FROST from my car windshield. I hate it because it makes a cold morning even colder. Of course, if I skip scraping the ice and just get into my car and try and stay warm, I won't be able to see where I'm going. And if I can't see where I'm going I might crash and die, which wouldn't make for very happy news for my family. So I get up in the cold morning and scrape ice from my car windshield and endure the cold in order that I might see well enough to get safely to work. We need to do something similar with sin. We need to scrape sin from our lives through repentance and the righteousness of Christ in order that we might see God more clearly and therefore be able to pursue Him more persistently. Even those little sins that we think don't hurt anyone can obscure our view of God. If we let enough of them build up, we won't be able to see Him at all and life will crash down around us as a result. It may not be pleasant to scrape sin from our lives—it might even make us uncomfortable and it will require us to be humble and honest—but I don't think any of us want to risk trying to get through life with sin blocking our view of God. That's why it's such good news that through Christ we can scrape it away, even if we have to do it every single morning.

December 4
Fixing the Red Lights of Death
"I call on the Lord in my distress, and he answers me"
(Psalm 120:1).

REALLY ENJOYED owning an Xbox 360, except for the fact that it kept breaking. In fact, I believe there was (if I kept track correctly) four times where my Xbox 360 flashed the three red lights of death. Now what do you suppose I did all those times when my Xbox stopped working? Did I call Nintendo and ask them to fix it? Did I call up Sony and complain about how my Xbox 360 kept breaking? Of course not, I called Microsoft, the maker and creator of the Xbox. You see, there's a very valuable lesson in all of this. When our life is broken, when things aren't working the way they're supposed to, where do we turn? Do we turn to ourselves and rely on our ability to fix things? Do we look for help and answers in the world, which by the way is usually the cause of our problems? Of course not. When we're broken, when we hurt, when our life isn't working quite the way it should, we need to go to the One who made us. Only the creator of the Xbox can fix an Xbox (or at least that's the theory), and only your Creator can truly fix your life and put you back together. Just as it sounds silly to ask Nintendo to fix an Xbox, it's silly to ask anybody else to help people when they're broken. Only our Creator can do that, but the good news is that He loves us so much that when we ask Him for help, He's always there to give us the help we need.

December 5

How to Sin Less

"'Come now, let us reason together,' says the Lord, 'Though your sins are like scarlet, they shall be white as snow; though they are red as crimson, they shall be like wool'"
(Isaiah 1:18).

IN ORDER TO AVOID GOING TO JAIL, a Pennsylvania woman and her adult daughter stood outside of the courthouse for over four hours holding a sign that said, "I stole from a nine-year-old-girl on her birthday. Don't steal or this could happen to you." That got me thinking about my own sin. How would I feel if I had to carry around a sign that told everyone what my sins are? I think two things would happen: one, people would look at me differently, and two, I'd probably think twice about committing those sins again. Isn't it strange that we're more concerned about people finding out about our sins than God? Shouldn't we be tripping over ourselves in gratitude that even though God sees all of our sins, He forgives us and loves us as His own children? God loves us so much He doesn't make us pay for our sins, He doesn't make us carry the burden of our sins, and He doesn't display them for all to see. He takes them away through Jesus Christ. We don't have to carry around sign, serve probation, or go to hell as punishment for our sin because of Jesus' death on the Cross and His Resurrection from the grave. That's definitely good news—good news that motivates me to do my best to keep sin out of my life.

December 6
Getting What We Deserve
"For the wages of sin is death, but the gift of God is eternal life in Christ Jesus our Lord"
(Romans 6:23).

RECENTLY I'VE STRUGGLED with our society's sense of entitlement. I don't know if you've noticed, but there's a general attitude in our culture today that suggests we should be treated well, everything should be fair for us, and we certainly shouldn't be deprived of anything we want. After all, we deserve it. Kids naturally have this sort of attitude, but what's disturbing to me is we don't seem to be growing out of it any more. Well, let me share with you a little dose of reality. If you really want to know what you deserve, if you really want to know what you're entitled to, here it is: hell. The only thing we're truly deserving of is an eternity of suffering and grief in the flames of hell. That's what sin entitles us to. That's what's fair. That's what we deserve. I know, it's not a pleasant thought, and some may argue that isn't what they deserve, but I'm just telling you what the Bible says. That's why I'm so thankful for grace. That's why I'm glad God didn't pander to my sense of entitlement, that He didn't do what was fair and that He didn't give me what I deserved. But rather through the death and Resurrection of Jesus Christ He saved me from hell, He gave me the gift of new life and forgiveness, and He gave me far more than I ever deserved. In light of the truth about what we're truly entitled to, I think it's really good news that we don't get what we deserve.

December 7
The World Will End . . . Eventually
"Therefore keep watch,
because you do not know the day or the hour"
(Matthew 25:13).

THE WORLD WAS SUPPOSED TO END on December 21, 2012, or, at least it was in the movie *2012*. That movie was based on the idea that the ancient Mayan calendar predicted the world's end on that date. For some reason, people really latched on to the idea and for a time were obsessed with the world ending that day. Of course it didn't, but the movie was a shallow, albeit sort of fun, special effects extravaganza. One of the tag lines from the film was simply: "We were warned." That's actually a pretty good tag line; one I think could also be put on the cover of the Bible. The fact is the world *is* going to end, we just don't know when. The other fact is if you don't have Jesus Christ in your life, there won't be any escaping the end of the world. The final fact is we *have* been warned. The Bible tells us exactly what to expect when the world ends and how to avoid the judgments that will come as a part of that end. The good news is we can be saved; the question is, are we willing to listen to the warnings of the Bible? Or, if we already have, how desperate are we to get others to listen. I promise you one thing. Watching the world end for real won't be nearly as fun as it is in the movies.

December 8

Math Ain't so Easy

"Now what I am commanding you today is not too difficult for you or beyond your reach . . . No, the word is very near you; it is in your mouth and in your heart so you may obey it" (Deuteronomy 30:11,14).

I'M GOING TO LET YOU IN on a little secret. The reason I became a writer isn't because I'm good with words; it's because I'm bad with numbers. All through school I had a hard time with any sort of math, so when I got to college, I majored in whatever I could find that had the least amount of math involved, which just so happened to be writing. Math just isn't in me, I don't get it, and I can't do it. One thing I can do, however, is obey God. Now I know that's something a lot of people say is too hard or just plain pointless, but I don't think that's true. The good news is God has done most of the hard work for us. God's Law was kept perfectly through Jesus Christ and God then allowed us to have Christ represent us. In essence, His hard work and His perfection becomes our own when Christ is in our lives. Math may not be in me, but Jesus is, and I'm so glad that through Him, obeying God is not only possible, it's made easy. Now if He could just help me out with that math stuff.

December 9
Get a Name Audit

" . . . I will also give him a white stone with a new name written on it, known only to him who receives it"
(Revelation 2:17).

PEOPLE LIKE UNUSUAL NAMES, but they don't always know what they mean, especially in other languages. Take Tom Cruise's daughter Suri. That name means, "pickpocket" in Japanese, "turned sour" in French, and "horse mackerels" in Italian. In order to help people, and especially celebrities, avoid some of the pitfalls of choosing a name, a London company will do a name audit for you for a small fee, about $1,500. I suppose it is worth it if you don't want your child named "pickpocket." They'll do all the research for you to make sure the name you're choosing doesn't mean something weird in Africa, just in case your kid ever travels there and has to be introduced. There is one name, however, that doesn't need an audit: the name Jesus Christ gives us. Someday when we get to Heaven, Jesus will give us a new name, a secret name that only we'll know. Isn't that cool? Jesus will give you a name known only to you and Him; like you two are a part of some secret club. I'm excited to find out what my name is going to be. One thing's for sure; it won't be name that means anything like "horse mackerels." And the fact that I won't have to spend fifteen hundred bucks to make sure it doesn't mean anything weird is definitely good news.

December 10
The Twilight Bible Story

**"The LORD appeared to us in the past, saying:
'I have loved you with an everlasting love;
I have drawn you with loving-kindness'"**
(Jeremiah 31:3).

AUDIENCES HAVE SWOONED for the *Twilight* movie series, to the tune of well over two billion dollars. It seems to me that if people find the romance of *Twilight* so exhilarating, they should try opening their Bibles because that book contains a rather compelling romance as well. In the Bible's story, a being with supernatural powers is in love with a mere mortal—you—but is separated from the one He loves by another, jealous, malicious foe. Longing for the one He loves, this powerful being realizes the only way He can truly be together with His loved one is by giving up His life. And so He allows himself to be beaten, humiliated, and killed all for the sake of love. Then, in a moment of great victory, this powerful being overcame death and returned to the one He loved. Sadly, though, that loved one didn't always return His love, and sometimes flat out rejected this amazing being who had given everything, including His own life, to demonstrate His love. You see, what I'm saying? Vampires and werewolves have nothing on romance when compared to the Bible. And the good news is not only is this story true, but you can be a part of it and experience its happy ending.

December 11
Friends Who Will Do Anything
"Greater love has no one than this,
that he lay down his life for his friends"
(John 15:13).

THE DISNEY COMEDY *Old Dogs* starring John Travolta and Robin Williams is a story about two guys who have been friends their entire lives and how that friendship helps them through some tough times. These are friends who would truly do anything to help each other out. Now when I think about true friendship, I think about what Jesus said, that true love in friendship means being willing to give your life for your friend. I started thinking about that and I wondered: How many real friends do I have? How many friends do I have I would do anything for? How many do I have I would give my life for? How many friends do I have that if they did something worthy of death and I knew for sure they were guilty, I would still be willing to sacrifice my life to save theirs? As I pondered these thoughts, I realized I could learn a lot about friendship from being a friend of Jesus Christ. I also realized it's really good news that Jesus wants to be my friend and that He was willing to give His life for my own.

December 12
Holiday Lighting

"In him was life, and that life was the light of men.
The light shines in the darkness,
but the darkness has not understood it"
(John 1:4-5).

ONE OF MY FAVORITE holiday activities is putting the Christmas lights on our house. I love putting up lights at Christmastime. I like the way they make a house look different, how they make the house look festive. They transform the appearance from something dark and cold during this month of December to something warm and inviting. Best of all, they physically represent what this season is all about: light. Jesus came into this world to be its light when He was born in Bethlehem, but not everyone welcomed that light. The Christmas lights we put up each year aren't just pretty, they're reminders that in a world full of darkness and despair God sent us His Son to bring light and hope. The lights are a visual reminder of the truth that everyone passing by our house can see. Just as you and I should be reminders of that truth by the way we shine the light of Christ in our lives. Sometimes I think it would be easier to be a light in the world by wearing Christmas lights, but seeing as how that's not practical, I guess I'll just have to do my best to let the light of the good news shine through me this Christmas season and throughout the rest of the year.

December 13

It's Not About Stuff

"Then he said to them, 'Watch out! Be on your guard against all kinds of greed; a man's life does not consist in the abundance of his possessions'"
(Luke 12:15).

LOVE the *Raving Rabbids* series of video games from Ubisoft. In one of them, called "Rabbids Go Home," you play those crazy, zany rabbids who now happen to believe their home is on the moon. In order to reach the moon, you and your fellow rabbids start collecting a bunch of "stuff" in order to make a pile of junk that's tall enough to reach the moon. Silly, I know, but it's also kind of fun. My point, however, is this game is focused on collecting stuff, and it got me thinking about what our focus is on during the Christmas season. There are always lots of reports about how much stuff is sold on Black Friday, Cyber Monday, and during all the epic holiday sales. We also hear about all the discounts on stuff and how much money we can save on stuff . . .but the stuff of Christmas shouldn't be our focus. After all, God's gift to us wasn't more stuff, but rather life: the life of the baby Jesus, the life of the grown Jesus sacrificed on the Cross, the life of the resurrected Jesus that's promised to all who believe in Him. Now I'm not saying that getting a bunch of stuff at Christmas is bad, I look forward to as much as the next guy, but let's not forget that Christmas wasn't about stuff, but rather about the gift of life. A gift God gives to each one of us. And it's a gift we can share with others when we share the good news.

December 14
Tiger Isn't Perfect

"But because of his great love for us, God, who is rich in mercy, made us alive with Christ even when we were dead in transgressions—it is by grace you have been saved"
(Ephesians 2:4-5).

WHEN TIGER WOODS got busted a few years ago for his many marital transgressions, he made a rather interesting statement about the whole situation. He said he was sorry for his transgressions, but he wasn't perfect. Now, I read two things into a statement like that. 1), he realized he had sinned, but 2), there wasn't anything he could do about those sins. His lack of perfection meant he was bound to sin. Well, he was right; there isn't anything that Tiger or any of the rest of us can do about our sin. Sin is a part of who we are, but the good news is it doesn't have to stay that way. We may not be able to do anything about sin, but God can and did. Jesus Christ's death and Resurrection is the only way known to man to completely wipe away our sins and transgressions, it's the only way to be forgiven for them, and the only way to be free from them. So, Tiger Woods was right—he isn't perfect. But Christ is. In Christ's perfection and His sacrifice we can find the solution to sin. That's good news someone needs to share with Tiger, and good news we need to share with everyone we can.

December 15

Curiosity Kills

"... and do not give the devil a foothold"
(Ephesians 4:27).

THE ORIGIN OF THE PHRASE "Curiosity killed the cat" can be traced all the way back to 1598, and the play *Every Man in His Humour*, which contains a line that says "Helter skelter, hang sorrow, care'll kill a Cat, up-tails all, and a Louse for the Hangman." The term *care* in "care'll kill a Cat" means worries and sorrows, and this phrase eventually led to the more common expression of curiosity killing the cat. Wherever it came from, I find the expression very apt when it comes to sin. Have you ever been curious about sin? Have you ever been curious to see what it would be like to do the things everyone else is doing? I must confess I have, and recently I gave into that curiosity. Praise God for His conviction. Thank God for His grace and forgiveness. The truth is, no matter how alluring sin may appear, no matter how curious you may be about it, you can be sure it will only lead to death and destruction. It's always more trouble than it's worth. The good news is that through Jesus Christ and the help of the Holy Spirit, we can resist the lure of sin; we can set aside our curiosity, and instead enjoy life in the presence of God. Curiosity may kill the cat, but sin will kill the soul and it just isn't worth the risk.

December 16
Spooky Morning, Comforting God
**"His lightning lights up the world;
the earth sees and trembles"
(Psalm 97:4).**

IT WAS ABOUT THIS TIME last year when I needed to be at work a little earlier than usual, and let me just say, even the studios of a Christian radio station can seem a little creepy at five in the morning. That's especially true when it's windy and dark and rainy and snowy. Then to top things off, the lightning and thunder that particular morning was enough to make me want to hide under the covers. Only I was at work so there weren't any covers to hide under. For some reason, I think lightning is spookier when there's snow falling. (It's a good thing that's a rarity.) After all of that happening in the wee hours, I found it more than a little curious this verse in Psalms happened to be the passage I read that morning for my quiet time. It did remind me of two important things. One, our God is a mighty God; He's powerful and holy and infinite and it's easy to see how the Earth might tremble in the flashing lighting of His presence. And two, those of us in Christ need not fear when the lightning flashes, for that same God is also our heavenly Father, and we can dive into the comfort of His arms any time. Which is far cozier than merely hiding under bed covers. I consider that good news—especially on spooky mornings when I'm all alone and the lightning is flashing.

December 17

The Danger of a Fake

"Many will say to me on that day, 'Lord, Lord, did we not prophesy in your name, and in your name drive out demons and perform many miracles?' Then I will tell them plainly, 'I never knew you. Away from me, you evildoers!'" (Matthew 7:22-23).

DON'T KNOW WHY anyone would want a surplus fire hydrant, but there was a person in Houston who actually bought one and set it outside his house. The problem was the city thought it was a real fire hydrant and they repainted it and added a serial number to it. Thinking a fake fire hydrant might be a bad thing to confuse with the genuine article during a real fire (good thought), the owner called the city and explained the situation. Another situation where it would be a bad idea to try and pass off a fake as the real thing is when Jesus returns. The truth is we can paint ourselves up with all the good deeds, Christian-ese, and church attendance we like, but that won't hide the fact we haven't really given our lives to Christ. Only a real fire hydrant does any good in a fire, and only someone who's truly given their life over to Jesus will escape the fire in the end. So which are you—the real deal or a painted fake?

December 18
Who Decorated That Cookie?

"I praise you because I am fearfully and wonderfully made; your works are wonderful, I know that full well"
(Psalm 139:14).

ONE OF MY FAVORITE holiday traditions is making and decorating sugar cookies. I love cutting out the shapes of candy canes, snowmen, and gingerbread men, and then decorating them with frosting and candy. (Although sometimes I eat the frosting before it ever gets onto the cookie, and sometimes I eat the cookie before I can frost it.) You know, the interesting thing about cookies is they don't really draw attention to themselves. You don't really hear anyone say "What a good job that cookie did of decorating itself." Instead the person who decorated the cookie is the one who gets the recognition and the praise. Sometimes I think we forget that we can't make or decorate ourselves into anything worthwhile apart from God. We can try, but we'll have about as much success as cookie trying to frost itself. However, when we let God mold, shape, bake, and decorate us, we become a reflection of His splendor and glory and talent. People will look at us and say "What a good job God did with that person's life. I wonder if he could do the same with me?" I'd say that is pretty good news . . . but all this talk of cookies is making me hungry.

December 19
A Season of Discontent?

"But godliness with contentment is great gain. For we brought nothing into the world, and we can take nothing out of it. But if we have food and clothing, we will be content with that" **(1 Timothy 6:6-8).**

I'VE DEDUCED ONE THING from Christmas advertising: Christmas is supposed to make me happy only if I get a car. I've also learned that if you get the right TV it'll change your life, for the better I presume. And finally I've learned that the joy of the season is getting all the right presents. It seems like every year Christmas advertisements are focused on telling people this can be a Merry Christmas despite hard times, but only if we buy the right stuff. I have a feeling that's going to generate a lot of discontentment and thereby generate more problems than can be solved. Contentment is not something we generally have in our nation, and Christmas ads seem like they are out to destroy it all together. That's why it's so important for us as Christians to show that true contentment can be found not in the right gift, but in the gift of Jesus Christ. We need to demonstrate the joy of Christmas is not because of what's under the tree, but because of who was in the manger. Stuff is nice, don't get me wrong, but I think Paul was directly addressing Christmas advertising when he said, *"Godliness with contentment is great gain."* That's good news that doesn't come in a box.

December 20

Winners Are Remembered Forever

"Then one of the elders said to me, 'Do not weep! See, the Lion of the tribe of Judah, the Root of David, has triumphed . . .'" (Revelation 5:5).

ONE OF THE BEST Super Bowl sermons I ever heard was from my dad. In that sermon, he pointed out that with a few rare exceptions (such as the perfect, yet losing, New England Patriots), when the Super Bowl is over the winner goes on to glory and fame and the loser fades into obscurity and anonymity. Generally, people don't remember much about the loser. So it is with us. When this life is over we will either go on to glory in great victory, or we will soon be forgotten in destruction. It's such a simple yet powerful illustration of what's at stake in eternity. If you think the Super Bowl is big, this is a thousand times bigger. The winner of the Super Bowl just has to come back and do it again next year, and the loser will get another chance to be a winner. We, on the other hand, will get no such chance. If we lose, we lose for eternity. If we win, that victory will never be taken away from us. Time is growing short, my friend. We are in the fourth quarter, and when life is over, we won't get overtime. So we must, with all our strength and dedication, make sure this world knows which team is the winning team, and what the cost of losing—eternity in hell—really means. The fact that Jesus Christ gives us the victory in the most important contest in the cosmos is the best and greatest good news we'll ever know. And it's time to start sharing it before it's too late.

December 21
Fake or Real?

"But from everlasting to everlasting the Lord's love is with those who fear him . . . "
(Psalm 103:17).

DURING THE CHRISTMAS SEASON there's often controversy over whether or not a "religious symbol" like the Christmas tree should be displayed on public or government property; a controversy that seems to crop up somewhere just about every year. I don't have a very strong opinion about it; I just think it's ironic that people argue over the Christmas tree as a "religious symbol" when originally it was a part of pagan tradition. The other controversy, when it comes to Christmas trees, is whether or not you should have a real or a fake one. Here I have a very strong opinion. Although fake trees today do look very nice, I say there's nothing that can ever replace having a good, old-fashioned, real Christmas tree in your home. There are lots of reasons for that, but for me personally one of the most important reasons is it reminds me of the good news. The fir tree and the evergreen to me are symbols of God's everlasting love. Just as a fir tree is always green in winter, fall, spring, and summer, so God's love for us is everlasting in every season of life. In fact, He put that love on display when Jesus was born in a manger. When we go get our Christmas tree each year, I get very excited because it's yet one more reminder on display in our house what Christmas is really all about: the love and the gift of God that lasts forever.

December 22
A Thought on the Virgin Birth

"How will this be," Mary asked the angel, "since I am a virgin?" The angel answered, "The Holy Spirit will come upon you, and the power of the Most High will overshadow you. So the holy one to be born will be called the son of God"
(Luke 1:34-35).

AS I WAS LISTENING to a sermon about the Virgin Birth of Christ, something was pointed out to me I've never considered before. Did you notice how the child came to be in Mary? It was through the Holy Spirit. New life was birthed in Mary through the Holy Spirit. You may be thinking, "So? We all know that part of the Christmas story." True, but have you considered the implications, because I know I haven't. Think of it this way: what happens when we become Christians? Isn't new life birthed in us through the Holy Spirit? Ah, now you see where I'm going with this. Most of us are familiar that the Bible says the same power that raised Christ from the dead dwells within us, but have you ever thought about the fact that the same Spirit that birthed new life, the life of our Savior, into the womb of a virgin has also given new life to us? It's the same Holy Spirit doing the same thing; giving new life. Isn't that exciting? Isn't that amazing? Isn't that good news?

December 23
A New Christmas Greeting

"The angel went to her and said, 'Greetings, you who are highly favored! The Lord is with you.' Mary was greatly troubled at his words and wondered what kind of greeting this might be"
(Luke 1:28-29).

EVERY YEAR ABOUT THIS TIME, people get all riled up over the annual controversy over whether or not it's more appropriate to say "Happy Holidays" or "Merry Christmas." Some feel that "Happy Holidays" is too generic and doesn't carry with it the true meaning of the season. Others feel that "Merry Christmas" excludes those who don't celebrate Christmas as a Christian holiday. In one poll, 21 percent of Americans felt more comfortable saying "Happy Holidays" while 77 percent preferred "Merry Christmas." No matter what your preferred holiday greeting may be, try to imagine how Mary must have felt at the angel's greeting to her. In fact, how would any of us feel if an angel appeared and called us *highly favored*? Well, as Christmas is so close, let's keep in mind that no matter how we greet people, the fact is what the angel had to say is really a Christmas greeting for us all. We are highly favored because God loved us so much that He sent His Son into our world to live, to die, and to live again. Better yet, the Lord is with us because of Jesus' death and Resurrection. So perhaps we should use the angel's greeting instead of those others that everyone loves to argue about. Then when people wonder what manner of greeting that is, we can share the good news with them.

December 24
The Baby Who Changed Everything

"She will give birth to a son, and you are to give him the name Jesus, because he will save his people from their sins" (Matthew 1:21).

A BABY CHANGES EVERYTHING. That's what you're told when you're young and just married. Being the naïve Mr.-Know-It-All that I was when I first got married, I'd often chuckle and say, "Sure, everything." Then we had a baby, and guess what? Everything changed. Some things for the better, some things . . . well, let's just say it's debatable if they were improved. Still, it's kind of strange. Considering that babies can't really do much—they can't talk, they can't walk, they can't feed themselves or change themselves or do anything at all really—they sure do have a huge impact on everything and everyone around them. The world shifts each time a baby is born. Never was that more true than when Jesus was born. Now, on Christmas Eve, I often reflect on how Jesus was a baby who truly did change everything. He changed how we date our calendar. He changed the lives of wise men from the East. He changed the reign of a king. He changed the lives of two young people engaged to be married. And He changed my life forever. Babies do change everything, but no baby has changed things more than Jesus Christ. And you know what, that's good news.

December 25
The Date Doesn't Matter

*"While they were there, the time came for the baby to be born,
and she gave birth to her firstborn, a son.
She wrapped him in cloths and placed him in a manger,
because there was no room for them in the inn"*
(Luke 2:6-7).

THERE'S OFTEN A LOT OF DEBATE this time of year whether or not we should really celebrate Jesus' birthday in late December. In all likelihood, He wasn't born anywhere near December 25th, but probably in the spring or summer or some other time of winter depending on which theory you adhere to. That's all fine and good, but it really misses the point. You see the good news isn't that Jesus Christ was born on December 25th, or April 14th, or June 22nd, or whatever date you happen to choose. No, the good news is the fact that Jesus Christ was *born*. You could arbitrarily choose to celebrate my birthday any day of the year you wish, but that wouldn't change the fact that I was born. The same is true for Christ. December 25th most likely isn't His birthday, but what we're celebrating is the fact that He was born at all; that God loved us so much that He would send His Son as a baby to bring light and redemption to humanity. That's good news worth celebrating any time of year, so why not on December 25th? Merry Christmas everyone, and happy birthday Jesus!

December 26

Good News for Everyone

"Do not be afraid. I bring you good news of great joy that will be for all the people. Today in the town of David a Savior has been born to you; he is Christ the Lord"
(Luke 2:10-11).

I'VE ALWAYS FOUND IT INTERESTING that when God stepped into history as the baby Jesus, He didn't announce this momentous event to heads of state or the rich and influential. No, the first announcement of His arrival was to shepherds. Now, shepherds weren't exactly at the pinnacle of society; in fact they were considered pretty lowly by most. But that was exactly the point, wasn't it? The angels announced they had good news for all people. *All* people. Whether we admit it or not, whether we realize it or not, sin makes us all exactly the same. Because of sin no matter what our position is in this world, we are all going to end up in the same place: hell. God, however, gave us a wonderful gift in Jesus Christ. He gave us the gift of forgiveness from sin and the promise of eternal life, a gift that is available to all of us. When the angels came to announce this good news to the shepherds, I think it was God demonstrating He said what He meant and meant what He said. It is good news, for all people, for unto us, all of us, a Child is born, and He is Christ the Lord.

December 27

Achieving Something Worthwhile

For no one can lay any foundation other than the one already laid, which is Jesus Christ. If any man builds on this foundation using gold, silver, costly stones, wood, hay or straw, his work will be shown for what it is, because the Day will bring it to light. It will be revealed with fire, and the fire will test the quality of each man's work.
(1 Corinthians 3:11-13)

THE WORLD'S TALLEST BUILDING, the Khalifa Tower, that reaches a half-mile into the sky, is located in the small little nation of Dubai. The building cost over a billion dollars to construct. This is ironic considering that at the time it was built, Dubai was around twenty-five billion dollars in debt. Now I'm not saying this is the next tower of Babel. But I do find it interesting that something that was supposed to trumpet human achievement was most noted for costing too much, being completely impractical, and otherwise not the greatest achievement in the world—aside from being the tallest building on Earth, for whatever that's worth. For me, it's just one more reminder that nothing we ever do, accomplish, or succeed in will ever measure up in light of eternity. No matter what we build here we can't take it with us. The good news, however, is we can invest in something that lasts. It's not the tallest, or the biggest, or even the most expensive, but it is the most valuable: an eternal soul. When we share the good news with people we can save a life from the pits of hell. I think I'd rather be known for that than for building the tallest building in the world.

December 28

Good or Bad First?

"Surely he will never be shaken; a righteous man will be remembered forever. He will have no fear of bad news; his heart is steadfast, trusting in the Lord"
(Psalm 112:6-7).

DO YOU WANT the good news first or the bad news first? I'm never quite sure how to answer that question. If I get the bad news first I may be so depressed or anxious I won't even hear the good news. Then again, maybe the good news will make the bad news seem not so bad. However, if I get the good news first, the bad news may make the good news not seem all that great after all. It's a quandary, and one that usually makes me want to walk out of the room instead of trying to figure it out. However, I was encouraged when I came across this verse. It makes the whole good news or bad news dilemma moot. When we trust in the Lord, bad news is never all that bad because we know God make something good out of it. So I have resolved not to worry or fear bad news, and to answer the question of "Good news or bad news first?" with, "It doesn't matter because when you trust God, it's all good."

December 29
Quote Me

**"Do not let this Book of the Law depart from your mouth;
meditate on it day and night, so that you may be careful
to do everything written in it.
Then you will be prosperous and successful"
(Joshua 1:8).**

*T*HE WALL STREET JOURNAL once quoted a few words from one of my movie reviews. Needless to say, I was pretty excited about that. It's not every day *The Wall Street Journal* quotes you . . . at least it isn't for me. I went around sharing and showing the article to everyone I knew. That got me thinking about memorizing and quoting the Bible. For some reason, I got this picture in my head of God getting excited every time we quote His words. I had a picture of Him pulling aside the angels and saying, "Check this out; Yo quoted me. Isn't that cool?" You're probably wondering why God would ever be excited about us quoting His words, but I think He'd be pleased by the fact that we know His words and that we're willing to share His words. The sad truth is that just as *The Wall Street Journal* doesn't quote me every day, I'd have to say the same is true for how often I quote God. But considering all the good news He's shared in His Word, I think that's something I should change.

December 30
The Year of the Batman

"Let us hold unswervingly to the hope we profess, for he who promised is faithful. And let us consider how we may spur one another on toward love and good deeds"
(Hebrews 10:23-24).

A S WE NEAR THE END of another year and as we approach the dawn of a new one, I have to be honest with you: I feel discouraged, I feel worn out, beat down, and in other ways like just giving up. This past year was full of challenges, travails, and unwanted surprises. Next year holds the promise of even more challenges and difficulties. In the midst of my broodings and discouragement, however, I received inspiration from one of my favorite heroes: the Batman. In a story I got for Christmas, I was reminded that one of the defining characteristics of the Batman is that he never gives up, he never gives in, and he never goes down. He will carry on his crusade against evil and injustice till the day he dies. That should be true of us as Christians, too. We may face an enemy who wants to destroy us, a world that hates us, and a life filled with tragedy, challenges, and difficulties, but in Christ we can find the strength and joy to carry on. He endured the Cross, He conquered death, and He offers that strength and the joy of that victory to each and every one of us. I may leave this past year's battle worn and weary, but I did not go down. Next year may have even more battles and challenges and tragedies for me to face, but I will not give up. I will carry on in Christ and continue to share the good news however I can. No one ever said it would be easy, but nothing worth doing ever is. So this coming year is the year of the Batman for me; the year when I will stand fast no matter what, the year when I will be defined by the fact I will never give up, give in, or go down. What about you?

December 31
Getting Ready for a New Year
"O Lord, you are my God; I will exalt and praise your name, for in perfect faithfulness you have done marvelous things, things planned long ago"
(Isaiah 25:1).

WHAT WILL YOU REMEMBER about this past year? Will you remember it as a good year or a tough year? What made this past year memorable to you? What events will stick out in your mind as you look back on this year that's about to end? There are a lot of things, events, circumstances, and even people who can help define a year for us. As for me, I'll remember it as a year of growth, challenges, stretching, conflict, reinvigoration, and change. And to be honest, I expect more of the same in the next year. No matter how you look at the old year or look forward to the new one, I hope you'll be encouraged by the good news found in today's verse. No matter what the years may bring, we can know two things; first, that God is our God, He loves us and made us His children so we could know Him personally, and therefore truly can say He is our

God. Second, we can know this loving God of ours has planned marvelous things for us, things He planned for us long before we were ever born. We have a purpose, and we have meaning in our lives because of that. So as this year ends and the next one begins, I hope that's good news that will truly make it a Happy New Year for you.